THEOLOGIES IN CONFLICT

the Challenge
of Juan Luis Segundo

Alfred T. Hennelly

Theologies in Conflict

THEOLOGIES IN CONFLICT

THE CHALLENGE OF JUAN LUIS SEGUNDO

Alfred T. Hennelly

ORBIS BOOKS

Maryknoll, New York 10545

The Catholic Foreign Mission Society of America (Maryknoll) recruits and trains people for overseas missionary service. Through Orbis Books Maryknoll aims to foster the international dialogue that is essential to mission. The books published, however, reflect the opinions of their authors and are not meant to represent the official position of the society.

Library of Congress Cataloging in Publication Data

Hennelly, Alfred T
  Theologies in conflict.

  Bibliography: p.
  1. Segundo, Juan Luis. 2. Liberation theology. I. Title.
BT83.57.S449H46   230' .2'0924   79-11760
ISBN 0-88344-287-6

In memory of my father, Paurick Joseph Hennelly—
in his youth a warrior for the liberation of Ireland,
a man of profound peace in the Americas

The Spirit of the Lord is upon me,
because he has chosen me
to preach the Good News to the poor.
He has sent me to proclaim liberty to the captives,
and recovery of sight to the blind;
to set free the oppressed,
and announce the year when the Lord will save his people.
—Luke 4:18–19

Our being Christians today will be limited to two things: prayer and right-eous action among men. All Christian thinking, speaking, and organizing must be born anew out of this prayer and action. . . . It is not for us to prophesy the day (though the day will come) when men will once more be called on to utter the word of God that the world will be changed and renewed by it. It will be a new language, perhaps quite nonreligious, but liberating and redeeming—as was Jesus' language; it will shock people and yet overcome them by its power; it will be the language of a new righteous-ness and truth, proclaiming God's peace with men and the coming of his kingdom.

—Dietrich Bonhoeffer, *Letters and Papers From Prison*

CONTENTS

CHAPTER NINE
THE CHALLENGE OF MARXISM   157

EPILOGUE
APPRENTICES IN FREEDOM   176

BIBLIOGRAPHIES   187

PREFACE

I suppose it is normal for the first reaction of an author confronted with a book about his own work to be a certain amount of curiosity. And it must be said that in this case at least the curiosity has not been disappointed. To my surprise I was able to discover many things that had been left behind or forgotten in the recesses of memory over the course of many years of work. Indeed I must go further and say that this impression turns to delight when one proceeds to discover on every page a great sensitivity in one's interlocutor, much convergence of ideas, and a sympathy that would turn into friendship with the mere act of reading, if it did not exist from the start.

This first sensation of curiosity, however, is joined by a second reaction that is intermingled with an aftertaste of sadness; and I myself would like to figure out exactly why that is so. I suppose that this second reaction must also be normal and almost inevitable. While writing all the things that are studied in this book—be they great or small, important or unimportant—I had the feeling of thinking in the midst of a living dialogue with people and groups that were equally alive. Indeed, going back over my memories, I could almost inscribe a person's name, a place, an event, or a face on every page, and sometimes on a particular phrase or sentence. Of course it would be illusory to expect that this would be noticed in a line of thought that has been turned into a "book." The point is that this present "book about books" reveals to you that a line of thought that was once living and vital has already been turned into a book without your even noticing the fact.

As my friend Hennelly points out, and as he has adeptly managed to carry through in practice, there is certainly no question here of feeling that you have been classified, boxed, and turned into "subject matter." In other words, there is no question of feeling that you are already dead when you are still full of questions, projects, and tentative groping. No, the problem is rather that you cannot help feeling and knowing that for the first time you have inevitably become an object of study; that without willing it, you have placed one more book, good as it may be, in the library of a theologian or a student of theology.

In all honesty I must say that this inevitable impression dimmed or disappeared as I read the concluding pages of each chapter. For in them I

Translated by John Drury.

immediately encountered another person, Hennelly himself, dialoguing with me and with others and posing his own problems. He does it sympathetically, but he also puts the proper and necessary distance between himself, me, and others. He establishes the distance that all authors, and everyone who is talking with another, would like to see in their interlocutors if there is a real interest in dialogue. Here one finds understanding, to be sure, but also otherness, an awareness of the author's own situation, and new problems.

I don't think I am minimizing Hennelly's work or treating it unfairly if I say that I was more interested in his observations about North American theology and its challenges than in his examination of my own thinking. After all, what would be more natural? For in the last analysis it is this that represents the new step forward; and my own thought, however well understood and expounded it may be here, cannot take that step on its own.

Now it is precisely at this juncture that I would like to move away from the things that relate to me personally and introduce a more general theme into the conversation. The only problem, of course, is that in the very act of doing this I realize that this theme, too, relates to me personally. It may well be one chapter more in the book, disguised under the deceptive title of Preface.

But what else can I do? Hennelly is to blame for the fact that still another book has slipped out through my fingers even though it was not my idea. So it is he who has made me realize, perhaps a bit too late, how important and necessary it is today, and even more so tomorrow, to put on the brakes if theology is to continue to be theology; if it is to dovetail with the act of theologizing; if it is not to become theological consumption or, to use an expression in vogue in other fields, "consumer theology."

I recall the time in Buenos Aires when I first proposed the idea of my five-volume series to my publisher and friend, Carlos Lohlé. I left it up to him to choose an overall title for the series, and he came up with *Teología abierta para el laico adulto* ("an open theology for the adult lay person"). When I first saw it, I must confess that I did not like it, though I did not say anything. After all, he was my friend and he was risking his money in the maddest venture to be found in today's world: publishing theology. But then, as time went on, I began to realize that there was profound wisdom in his title. Perhaps, after all, those books were successfully managing to avoid being consumer theology precisely insofar as they were addressed to lay people rather than to theologians; insofar as they were trying to open up paths rather than provide systematic solutions; insofar as they offered a method more than a body of content; insofar as they did not prompt people to stop theologizing because in them people could find valid answers to presumably general problems.

And this brings me to a related problem that is becoming more and more deeply entrenched in the whole problem-complex of my own life. The assumption is that theology, like philosophy for example, is a science whose trackless wastes can be explored by scientific approaches; that there should be professors of theology just as there are professors of Sanskrit—so that worthwhile elements of culture will not be lost, if for no other reason. This confusion becomes fatal when future clergy or pastoral agents are given training similar to, if more limited than, that of theology professors. The circle is almost fatal because the teachers are professors, professors talk about what they know, and thus they transmit the species even without meaning to do so.

But the clergy or pastoral agents need a different kind of theology, a different kind of theologizing. When theology is made the required discipline for professionals—be they called clergy or not—the obvious assumption is that in their lives theology is to be the main tool for solving the problems presented to them.

But in such a case the situation is similar to what would happen in medicine or engineering. For all such "data-bank" type of theological information is the very negation of the goal intended: i.e., to inculcate the serious and original exercise of an "art" in the face of real problems with the aim of solving them.

And the problem is even more serious in theology because the world, the modern world at least, does not generally seem to pose theological problems. For every time that a question will come up as to how they are to understand the faith and the gospel vis-à-vis a real-life human being, there will be countless times when the real-life problems presented to the clergy will have to do with organizing and maintaining parochial services, or creating a group with its own inner dynamism, or finding the psychological means to help or console a human being in crisis! So the clergy become second-hand psychologists, social workers without degrees, doctors or judges without credentials. And all the while they are waiting for someone or other to get the idea of posing problems for which they learned the correct answers.

As I see it, then, there is an urgent need to reconsider what types of training might be necessary and adequate for that particular theological task, a task viewed as central, ongoing, and aimed at the adult. And I say "aimed at the adult" in line with the logic of Bonhoeffer's thinking. For the adult in full possession of his or her faculties, the adult who does not need us for anything else, is the criterion for knowing whether our theological responses are relevant and interesting in themselves, whether they can be real solutions to equally real problems.

By way of example, let us assume with Tillich that the specifically theological domain, the domain of understanding the faith, is situated in the realm of those things that have to do most deeply and profoundly with the meaning of our existence. Wouldn't the logical consequence be that "practical theologians" (quite different from theology professors in universities)

JUAN LUIS SEGUNDO, S.J.

have to learn the difficult analytical method: (1) of discovering these ultimate concerns in the people they ordinarily meet in life, even though these concerns are seldom mentioned directly and explicitly; and (2) of relating the data so uncovered to the content of faith? Wouldn't it be suicide to leave that to the intuitive capacities of individual candidates?

Now this diving into the uttermost depths of existence is never performed in the solitude of the individual. It is effected within the coordinates, and with the elements, of a specific society. So how can we properly prepare practical theologians without giving them, through a serious and studied process of training, a practical and intensive knowledge of the social components involved in human beings' reflection on themselves—ranging from everyday problems to the most profound and ultimate ones?

Moreover, what if we accept the idea that seems to have become a commonly shared notion in the West since Mannheim, whatever one's political stance may be. I refer to the notion that culture is never neutral, that consciously or unconsciously it is guided by the interests of the human groups that go to make it up. Must we not then draw a conclusion that will be of the utmost importance for the training of the "practitioners of theology" about whom we are speaking? The conclusion is that in their work it will be absolutely necessary for them to have a set of analytical instruments of suspicion; and these will be designed to discard, insofar as possible, the commonplaces, the tranquillizing escapisms, the false explanations, and the false problems that are presented to them in all good faith.

And so we come to our first conclusion: Instead of providing practitioners of theology with all sorts of theological information, we must devote a considerable portion of their training, perhaps half of it, to what we might call the equivalent of medical pathology in the training of a doctor: i.e., diagnosis. In other words, we must develop in them the ability—partly reasoning and partly practice exercised until it becomes instinct—to *interpret* human problems and situations within a culture that has been to a large extent bent out of shape.

Without such training, what is the point of learning the solutions proposed by other theologians to problems which, at best, the practitioners will not find consciously formulated by their interlocutors and which, at worst, they will find to be ideological traps laid by their culture to make sure that human beings do not face up to the real problems and thereby endanger more or less conscious interests?

And what is to stop our maliciousness from going further and suspecting that the whole present way of training clergy or pastoral agents is merely a way for society to protect itself right from the start from theologians by replacing their ability to analyze and criticize with endless, erudite bibliographies?

Consider, for example, the problem that Blondel treated in *The Essence of Christianity*. Today we can find works on the same topic that offer such interminable bibliographies in each chapter that readers, naive as they may be, cannot help but ask certain questions: e.g., Did the author read these works? The obvious answer seems to be no, if one totes up the basic hours available for work and reading. But the really more important point is that if the author did read those books, that itself would explain the shallowness of the chapter; for the author simply had no time to think. Coming fifty years after Blondel, the work of the present-day author is a step backward compared to his work.

Very well, let us adopt a different supposition. By some miracle of intellectual bilocation, author number one was able to read the huge list of books and articles, and author number two was able to analyze the topic right down to its core. What does the huge bibliography mean for readers? Even if it was read—and it could only have been read cursorily, or thumbed, as the expression goes—our author could not possibly guarantee the overall or specific quality of this enormous amount of material. Besides, anything that can be read so cursorily must necessarily be superficial. Otherwise it would demand reflection, exploration, and criticism of the thought contained therein.

What, then, does the bibliographical listing mean? Does it mean that these authors found nothing interesting or profound in the books or articles that would oblige them to linger over one item or another? Does it mean that they are offering the lists to us simply to prove that they are not unaware of anything important dealing with their subject? In that case I would believe them even if they offered no bibliography, so long as I saw a profound analysis of the subject in the content of their chapters.

Does it mean that any student of the subject who wants to master this particular topic must read those books *plus* the author's work? And so on and so on with every new book about the subject, with correspondingly less and less time to think about the topic itself.

Or will we get into a situation where today's theologians will have scribes at their disposal (or vice-versa) to read and summarize for them the books published on a certain topic; that the books themselves will be fished out by computers, which are increasingly being linked up with good libraries around the world; and that all this will facilitate the task of staying on top of all that is being written about a given subject? But if I did not trust the cursory reading of the author, how will I be able to trust the reading of the scribe? What will happen if one of the books to be summarized by the scribe turns out to be a book like *Sein und Zeit?*

It is a matter of urgent necessity that erudition be replaced by analysis. This must be done in the training of theological practitioners. It must be done if we are to have the needed cultural criticism. It must be done if we are to escape the trap of a consumer theology. Slowly, intensely, and doggedly we must teach the practitioners of theology to analyze.

But since it is also necessary to teach them to think *theologically,* another equivalent part of their training will have to be aimed in that direction. That is not easy either, nor can it be considered free from the temptation described above. In other words, even though this portion of the training is restricted by the portion described above, it cannot be limited to providing the students with the habitual type of theological information.

If the "practitioners of theology" must be taught how to theologize, then they will have to handle and use the tools of their trade on their own. Just as we must avoid every sort of fundamentalism here, so must we also avoid something else that often leads to the same thing: i.e., the excessive, overly detailed consumption of information. Instead we must gear the necessary information toward a critical use of the Bible and of the history of church dogmas; and this use, set in its proper context, must not be naive in its applications. Later on there will always be some time and some way to amplify the necessary information, to find out what other theologians of the past and present did with these tools in the face of other problems, and to find inspiration in them for solving one's own problems. But here again the important thing is to handle the Bible oneself, not to absorb ready-made information about biblical theology, to give just one example.

My feeling is that offering these cursory and somewhat autobiographical reflections in this Preface is the best and most authentic testimony I can offer to vouch for Hennelly's work. I approached it with a little alarm at the start. But having probed more deeply into this book, which is largely devoted to my own thinking, I think I have every right to expect that it will not join the ranks of the consumer theology that now overwhelms us even more than we may think.

There is the further fact that Hennelly's thinking is directed toward other horizons and other problems that are even more his own. This is the best guarantee that the reader will be able to dissociate this book from myself. Not because of any lack of fidelity to my thinking, but rather precisely because Hennelly has understood it, his book offers the reader a store of inspiration which goes far beyond me and ultimately lies in the thinking of Hennelly himself.

Juan Luis Segundo, S.J.

PROLOGUE

THE BLOOD-STAINED FACE
OF HISTORY

This book reflects the initial stages of a personal dialogue with Latin American authors in the movement called liberation theology. While writing it and constantly confronting a vast and varied mass of materials, I was often encouraged by recalling the old French proverb: "It is the first step that counts." The book then is very decidedly a "first step," although I am hopeful that a number of subsequent steps along the same path will continue throughout my lifetime.

It is, moreover, a work of theological reflection, although certainly not systematic theology in the classical sense. The attempt to force liberation theology into a finished systematic framework would be doomed from the start, since that would entail throttling what is most original and creative in its approach. An initial working description of the approach I have adopted is an "open theology of dialogue." This concept will be refined further in subsequent chapters.

In this prologue I would like to review briefly some of the influences and experiences that led me to engage in such a dialogue with Latin American theologians. The latter authors assign great emphasis to the "partiality" of the theologian, and insist that a posture of absolute neutrality in the discipline of theology is impossible. They also stress the need to recognize the "interest" of theologians, that is, to ask for whom they are writing and from whose perspective, and what they hope the impact of their work will be on both church and society. I am in agreement with these emphases and thus will try to state as clearly as possible the genesis and present state of my own partiality and interest. It is hoped that this will be seen not as a personal intrusion but as essential background to facilitate still another stage of dialogue, that is, with the reader of this book.

A first major influence on the genesis of my own approach resulted from the experience of studying and teaching for six years as a Jesuit scholastic in the Philippine Islands. Although the differences there from the Latin American situation are many, significant parallels also exist. Both regions experienced centuries of colonization under Spain and the United States, although the control of the United States was political in the Philippines and economic in Latin America. Today both regions represent the only examples of nations that are both predominantly Catholic and at the same time former colonies.

The influences of those six years are many and varied, but for the sake of brevity I will focus on one central problematic that arose there: the question of the "Americanization" of the Philippines. During those years a number of Filipino critics objected strenuously to the wholesale import not only of United States culture and values (summarized in the phrase "Coca-colonization") but also of American religious practices, attitudes, and theology. Like many Americans, I thought at the time that the criticisms were somewhat exaggerated; however, in subsequent years I changed this view and came to the conclusion that they were substantially correct not only with regard to the Philippines but also to other areas of the third world. As a consequence, when I first came into contact with the Latin American theology of liberation, I was immediately struck by its unswerving emphasis on theologizing from the standpoint of its own historical and geographical "reality" or situation. In brief, it appeared to me to represent a possible model of reflection that was urgently needed in the third world and that could have enormous consequences for the future of the universal church.

Another major influence occurred as a result of my doctoral studies during and after the Second Vatican Council. These studies were heavily influenced by various strains of personalist thought and by a creative incorporation into theology of the latest liturgical research. Both influences appeared as a much needed advance over the lifeless abstractions of pre-Vatican II scholastic theology, and for myself and many other students constituted a genuine liberation.

During the same period, however, the wider society of the United States was experiencing two major convulsions that were unparalleled in its history. These involved the issues of racism, as dramatized in the civil-rights struggle, and of war, as exemplified in the passionate divisions and agonies of conscience that arose as a result of the conflict in Vietnam. While acknowledging the values of a personalist and liturgically oriented theology, I did not find it helpful in reflecting on the praxis of myself and others involved in those central issues of the society at large. In fact, it appeared at times to offer a religiously based evasion of any responsibility for commitment in these areas.

During that decade, moreover, official Catholic teaching itself was also undergoing a momentous evolution. Beginning with Pope John XXIII's *Christianity and Social Progress (Mater et Magistra)* in 1961, a steadily increasing stress was brought to bear on the Christian's responsibility in society, a stress that climaxed in Vatican II with one of the most extraordinary documents in the history of ecumenical councils, the *Pastoral Constitution on the Church in the Modern World.* Clearly, in this and a number of subsequent magisterial documents, a genuinely political and cultural as well as social theology had expanded enormously within a relatively brief span of history.

Again, this development surged far beyond the boundaries of a purely personalist theology, and posed a sharp challenge regarding the integration of its insights into theological reflection and Christian practice. At the time I found valuable contributions for the task of integration in the work of such theologians as Dietrich Bonhoeffer, Pierre Teilhard de Chardin, J. B. Metz, Jürgen Moltmann, and on the American scene, Martin Luther King, Jr. Nevertheless, an initial reading of Latin American theologians convinced me that they were articulating with still greater depth, range, and seriousness a theology that would be responsive to the magnitude of the challenge. Once again, it appeared to me that they had a contribution to make that would be of significant value to the entire contemporary church in its search for a synthesis of Christian faith and the struggle for justice.

A third factor leading to my interest in Latin American theology consists not so much in an influence as in a similarity of theological tasks. A teacher in a liberal arts college does not usually enjoy the luxury of specialization that is common in universities, but is generally obligated to teach courses in Scripture, systematic, historical, and moral theology, or various combinations of these disciplines. Moreover, his students are not graduate students professionally interested in theology but simply young adults, Christian or not.

The majority of the writings of Latin American theologians appears to me to fall into this same multidisciplinary approach, resulting in an integration of the various branches of theology. Most of these authors, moreover, are not primarily university professors, and their reflections are not usually based on issues that have resulted from debate within the academy itself. Rather their theology has resulted from actual contact with issues that deeply affect their nations, and has tried to provide interpretations of these issues as well as projected directions for the future. This does not imply that much of their work is not scholarly, but rather that the scholarship is integrated in a more holistic fashion and is constantly tested in the light of praxis. In brief, I have found this approach to be in harmony with my own interests and to be the source of many valuable insights for my own task as a theologian.

Perhaps all of the above statements may be synthesized by stating that my interest in the dialogue with Latin American theology has stemmed from a personal reading of the signs of the times in church and society. For the moment, this idea will not be developed, since I will comment on it in the first chapter of this book.

To return to the questions of partiality and interest mentioned at the beginning, I will now state my present thinking on those issues. My partiality is to that majority of the human race, in my own nation and abroad, that are not only poor but are daily victims of massive human suffering. The assembled bishops of my own church referred to this situation in 1965 as "the scandal of humanity," and I wholeheartedly concur. The theology that best responds to such a scandal at the present time is, in my judgment, liberation theology. And so I enter into dialogue with it in the hope of contributing not merely to a change in attitudes but also to a change in practice that will lead to more vigorous attempts toward the transformation of this situation of suffering.

Also, in presenting and commenting on the views of authors whose works are often not available in English, my interest is frankly to effect a change in theology. The urgency of the need for social, economic, and political transformation in terms of human lives is not always evident in western theology, in its choice of priorities, its emphases, and its methodologies. Whether the dialogue presented here will actually effect some change I do not know; at the very least it has already profoundly changed my own thinking and practice. The Catholic church has clearly one of the most unique and effective communications networks of any community on this planet; but the obverse side of the coin is the awesome responsibility before God of what that network says and what actions it encourages vis-à-vis the present crisis of humanity.

At this point, I would like to acknowledge my indebtedness to some of the many persons who aided me in various ways in the writing of this book. In the first place, I wish to thank Fr. César Jérez, S.J., now Jesuit provincial of Central America. During an international conference held at Le Moyne College in August 1972, Fr. Jérez presented a dynamic and incisive exposition of liberation theology as well as distributing extensive mimeographed notes and a bibliography. This first personal encounter with someone not only doing but living liberation theology has left a permanent imprint on my own life and reflections.

I also wish to express my gratitude to numerous members of the Society of Jesus and their associates working on the island of Jamaica. In the summer of 1973, they provided both hospitality and enormous expertise for myself and five students who were engaged in an interdisciplinary third-world project on that beautiful and troubled island. My special thanks are due to Frs. Richard Ho Lung and Daniel Mulvey as well as to the Jamaicans of the tiny and impoverished farming village of Avocat, who accepted us as friends and co-workers in their fields for three weeks that remain in my memory as a profound joy and an even deeper sorrow.

In addition, I am indebted to the Jesuit community at Le Moyne College and to the New York province for financing a seven-week stay in Peru in the summer of 1974, on the "Horizons for Justice" program of the United States Jesuit Conference. The many friends, Peruvian and North American, lay and religious, who provided us with both companionship and a profound understanding of *la realidad peruana* on that voyage are beyond numbering. But I would like to acknowledge my special thanks for the extraordinary labors on our behalf of Frs. Harold Bradley, Robert Dolan, and Edward Schmidt and of Mr. Louis Fischer.

A number of persons were of great help in commenting on various drafts of this book, including Frs. William Ryan, Peter Henriot, Thomas Clarke, and John Baldovin as well as Dr. William Barnett, Joe Holland, and Lee Cormie. Fr. Sergio Torres, director of the "Theology in the Americas" project, rendered invaluable service both by his own reflections and by his invitation to me to attend the conference with Latin American theologians that was held in Detroit in August 1975. But my greatest debt in this area is to Juan Luis Segundo, who read my manuscript and made a number of valuable suggestions which have been incorporated into the final draft.

I am also indebted to Fr. William Reilly, S.J., and to Le Moyne College for the academic sabbatical during the year 1975–76 that enabled me to advance my research and to begin to write this book. And an award of some sort should be given to my brothers in the Society of Jesus at Carroll House in Washington, D.C., who supported and bore patiently with me during that taxing year.

Finally, I wish to acknowledge my indebtedness, both from personal contacts and from written works, to all my colleagues in the southern half of the Americas. Perhaps the best way of summarizing what I have learned in this conversation is to say that they have shown me a way of answering the words of Albert Camus that have haunted me for a considerable number of years:

What the world expects of Christians is that they should speak out loud and clear, and they should voice their condemnation in such a way that never a doubt, never the slightest doubt, could rise in the heart of the simplest man, that they should get away from abstraction and confront the bloodstained face history has taken on today. The grouping we need is a grouping of men resolved to speak out clearly and pay up personally.

Alfred T. Hennelly, S.J.
Syracuse, New York

CHAPTER ONE

FAITH, JUSTICE, AND LIBERATION

A growing awareness is rising to the surface throughout all the Christian churches today that Christianity has arrived at a great turning point, a watershed with immeasurable consequences for the future. A very knowledgeable observer of world missions, Walbert Bühlmann, has referred to the phenomenon as "the coming of the third church,"[1] a church of the nations of the third world, located primarily in the southern hemisphere. After considering the statistical evidence, Bühlmann concludes that the "migration of the Church toward the southern hemisphere is . . . an indisputable fact, an important event in Church history and, at the same time (this the most important consideration), an *outstanding opportunity*."[2]

If Bühlmann is correct, this momentous shift cannot fail to have enormous repercussions for those of us who live in the first world. The entrance of third-world peoples as actors on the stage of history forces us to look with new eyes at the world and at the church's role in the world.

In my view, a holistic picture of that world is now beginning to emerge in human consciousness, much as the details of a photograph gradually emerge in the process of development. Amid the welter of differing political, economic, and social systems, the picture reveals a world structured in such a way that roughly a fifth of its inhabitants utilize four-fifths of its limited resources for their sustenance and pursuit of happiness, while the remaining four-fifths of the population struggle—and often fail—to survive with the aid of a meager 20 percent of the goods of the earth. And the inequity does not involve mere gradations on a ladder of relatively decent existence (as might be the case in a typical North American suburb), but a shocking contrast, on the one hand, between levels of overconsumption and waste and, on the other hand, levels of almost total deprivation of the absolute essentials of life—food, clothing, housing, and medical care—as well as a lack of literacy, work, security, and the barest minimum of human culture.

Moreover, the privileged one-fifth in the photograph appears (with the exception of Japan) as overwhelmingly white. And in it are included most of the members of the historic Christian churches, those who have accepted the call to follow the Servant Jesus in announcing the kingdom of God to the world, a "kingdom . . . of justice, love, and peace."[3]

It is also apparent that the whole process of inequity has not yet completed its full cycle. The birthrate of the white, Christian minority is declining while its share of the world's resources continues to increase. At the same time, the marginal four-fifths, largely nonwhite and non-Christian, are prodigiously expanding in population while every indicator points to the conclusion that they will have to struggle to survive on even less of the world's resources in the foreseeable future.

In short, the developed photograph confronts the Christian churches with a very radical challenge: how to proclaim and to practice the Good News of Jesus Christ, when the vast majority of humankind is trapped in structures that speak to them eloquently and unambiguously of very bad news indeed. It is understandably difficult for the latter to accept a gospel of love from Christians in the developed world who appear determined at any cost to maintain the system that causes the suffering of the poor.[4] As the Spanish theologian Juan Alfaro has phrased it, "We cannot continue in our indifference to the fate of the marginalized and oppressed. If the love of man is the great Commandment of Christ, selfishness and injustices are the great sin of the world, *the very negation of Christ.*"[5]

Official Church Teaching

On the level of Christian practice, an astonishing number and variety of responses to this situation have taken place all over the world. Numerous examples of this can be found throughout the book of Bühlmann cited previously.

In this introductory chapter, however, I would like first to mention briefly the response to the challenge posed above in official Catholic teaching and then to present my own survey of promising developments in theology and theological method. In the theological area I have tried to be as ecumenical as possible. However, as regards official teaching, I have confined myself to the Catholic church, since there appear to be many better qualified to interpret such conferences as Geneva, Uppsala, and Nairobi from within the Protestant tradition.

As regards official Catholic teaching, one of the most significant doctrinal and pastoral developments in its entire history has taken place over the brief span of the past two decades. The eruption began with the astonishing charismatic initiative of Pope John XXIII in his encyclical *Christianity and Social Progress (Mater et Magistra,* 1961) and in his letter to the whole world *Peace on Earth (Pacem in Terris,* 1963).[6] This opening was vigorously forwarded by the Second Vatican Council when that assembly published its *Pastoral Constitution on the Church in the Modern World (Gaudium et Spes,* 1965), a bold entry into the political and cultural arena unprecedented in the history of the church's ecumenical councils. Indeed, one recent commentator has referred to the constitution as "perhaps the strongest public document ever made expressing faith in Christ, the transformer of culture."[7]

Pope Paul VI continued to pursue this new direction in a number of documents, the most significant being his encyclical *On the Development of Peoples (Populorum Progressio,* 1967) and his apostolic letter *The Eightieth Anniversary of "Rerum Novarum" (Octogesima Adveniens,* 1971). At the same time, through the new collegial structures created by Vatican II, the bishops of the world contributed their own perspectives in *Justice in the World* (1971) and *Evangelization of the Modern World* (1974). A crystallization of the bishops' approach may be found in the unambiguous and epoch-making statement that "action on behalf of justice and participation in the transformation of the world fully appear to us as a constitutive dimension of the preaching of the gospel, or, in other words, of the Church's mission for the redemption of the human race and its liberation from every oppressive situation."[8]

In summary, the Roman Catholic church over the past two decades has been led to a profound re-evaluation of its mission in the world and even of its very understanding of the Christian message that it proclaims. What had come to be known since Pope Leo XIII's *Rerum Novarum* (1891) as the "social teaching" of the church had thus expanded enormously into what must now be termed the political, economic, and cultural teaching as well.

Excellent analyses of all these documents have been produced, and I do not wish to review that material here. I would stress, however, that even a cursory reading of this material will show that there has been a constant *development* of ideas and that this process continues at the present time. Joseph Gremillion has carefully traced the development and analyzed key issues for the future in the introductory essays to his collection of the documents.[9] With this in mind, we will now turn to recent developments within theology itself, for it seems safe to assume that they will provide material for official church teaching in the future.

New Frontiers in Theology

In this regard I would suggest that five central *areas of emphasis* have emerged during the past fifteen years, all of which help illumine the problematic of Christian faith and the struggle for justice. These areas are: personalization, secularization, history and orthopraxis, eschatology and hope, and sociopolitics. Some highlights of the five trends will now be briefly indicated.

1. *Personalization.* Of primary importance in this area was Rudolf Bultmann's demythologizing project or "existentialist theology"[10] as well as many important contributions from the field of phenomenology, such as

the important work of Paul Ricoeur. Meanwhile, in the Catholic sphere, the insights of Maurice Blondel, Emmanuel Mounier, and Gabriel Marcel continued to be studied and integrated into theological reflection.

This whole development led to a profound deepening in Catholic spirituality, for example, in understanding the role of personal freedom in the act of faith; for it was becoming everywhere apparent that the cultural milieu no longer encouraged belief but rather militated against it in a massive way. The movement also served to deepen the understanding and practice of interpersonal relations, again in a world where the demands of technology had induced a growing depersonalization, with its consequent feelings of alienation and isolation in many members of "the lonely crowd."

At the same time a serious deficiency in this approach became apparent, namely, its overly individualistic perspective, or what J. B. Metz has referred to as its "privatizing tendency."[11] Still, some recent attacks from this direction appear to me to be guilty of overkill. For surely any genuine social change, even in the poorest nation, should contribute to fuller personalization and more authentic personal relations; thus what is needed is not an abandonment of hard-won personalist insights, but an incorporation of them in a broader synthesis. In my view many of the following areas offer abundant material for just such a dialectic.

2. *Secularization.* It is important, first, to note that by secularization I do not mean "secularism," that is, an ideology that bases its affirmation of the secular on the rejection of religion. Rather secularization is here understood as a more neutral reality: the historical process by which human institutions progressively free themselves from the hegemony of sacral or ecclesiastical direction. It is a process, moreover, that is increasingly affecting all religions in all parts of the world.[12]

During recent years, this theme exploded in the popular consciousness through Harvey Cox's best-seller, *The Secular City,*[13] although it was already familiar to theologians through the writings of Dietrich Bonhoeffer and Pierre Teilhard de Chardin, among others. On a more profound level, Arend Th. van Leeuwen produced a penetrating analysis of secularization in his *Christianity and World History,* while it recurs as a central theme in much of the recent writings of Edward Schillebeeckx and Karl Rahner.[14]

The phenomenon appears to me to confront the church with a truly fateful decision. On the one hand, it can continue to interpret the neutral development of secularization as an antireligious trend, and consequently devote its limited resources to a struggle against it. This would seem to be an updated version of King Canute's posture before the massive and inexorable tide of history.

On the other hand, from the perspective of justice in the world, the church could recognize the profound ambiguities—the potential for both good and evil—that are entailed in the process of secularization. Its limited energies could then be dedicated to informed, prophetic discernment of those secularizing trends that appear truly humanizing, along with the development of practical strategies to assist them; at the same time, it could discern, and attempt in practice to negate, those trends which foster dehumanization.[15] Obviously, this is an enormous and complex task, but it appears to be faithful to the vision of Vatican II, which emphasized that the "Church believes she can contribute greatly toward making the family of man and its history more human."[16]

3. *History and Orthopraxis.* Both of these developments have profound importance for the creation of a theology of faith and justice. The new emphasis on history is perhaps best expressed by one of the most crucial texts of Vatican II: "Mankind has passed from a rather static concept of reality to a more dynamic, evolutionary one."[17] The council's central emphasis, moreover, on the importance of the Bible—the record of God's mighty acts in history—provided a strong reinforcement for this tendency.

This area found more developed expression, on the Catholic side, in Leslie Dewart's *The Future of Belief,* which called for a movement beyond demythologizing to the "de-Hellenization of dogma."[18] Although Dewart's tentative proposals for de-Hellenization were not generally accepted, his book remains a brilliant statement of the tension between modern humanity's historical sensibility and the static categories of traditional articulations of belief.

Meanwhile, in the Protestant sphere, Gerhard von Rad's seminal work, *Old Testament Theology,*[19] influenced both Jürgen Moltmann and Wolfhart Pannenberg toward a renewed emphasis on the radically historical nature of Christianity. An early work of Pannenberg and his school, entitled *Revelation as History,*[20] provoked a dialogue that continues to develop and to increase in vitality up to the present moment. One of Pannenberg's recent commentators, E. Frank Tupper, has described his approach quite succinctly: "Instead of securing faith in the fortress of subjectivity, Pannenberg restores the crucial significance of history for the integrity of Christian faith and the definition of the church's theology."[21] Also it seems clear that both Catholic and Protestant developments in "process theology" have further advanced the emphasis on historical consciousness.

Closely linked with the renewed accent on history has been the realization of the need for transforming action within history, which has been termed "orthopraxis," or, in the recent phrase of Gerald O'Collins, "Christopraxy."[22] In this regard, Edward Schillebeeckx has noted bluntly that for centuries "the church focused on orthodoxy and left orthopraxis in the hands of nonmembers and nonbelievers,"[23] at the same time calling for a reversal of emphasis in these priorities.

Although Vatican II insisted that "the force which the church can inject into the modern society of man consists in . . . faith and charity *put into vital practice,*"[24] taking this seriously would clearly entail a profound *metanoia* or conversion. Mere assent to doctrinal formulations would no longer take precedence over the need for transformed and transforming Christian practice that would be truly efficacious in history. From this viewpoint, versions of Catholicism that accentuate the "two planes" of sacred and secular realms, or of Protestantism that stress a "two-kingdoms" dichotomy, would be seen as alienating, a convenient mask for individual egotism, or, on the social level, for comfortable acquiescence in the status quo.[25] Rather the church would be understood not as a separate in-group of the saved but as a community with a special responsibility to embody and proclaim, actively and creatively, God's saving presence within the one integral history of humanity.

4. *Eschatology and Hope.* The renewed attention to these two areas was of crucial significance for social thought and action. For the orthopraxis in history mentioned above risked the danger of confining itself within the status quo of the present; however, the retrieval of an eschatological perspective and the flourishing theology of hope have dynamically opened it up to change and to the future. The two trends were nourished not only by the recapturing of fundamental biblical insights but also by the dialogue with Marxism, especially in the person of Ernst Bloch.[26] Again a key figure in the dialogue was Jürgen Moltmann, whose *Theology of Hope* appeared in 1967, to be followed in 1974 by a complementary work, *The Crucified God.*[27] On the Catholic side, Karl Rahner has furnished a strong impetus to both trends through his continuing articulation of the notion of Christianity as "the religion of the absolute future."

Inevitably, too, both eschatology and hope have led to a more positive evaluation of utopian thought. Once a synonym for unrealistic dreaming, a utopian perspective is now understood by many as an essential precondition of the imagination in order to effect change in society. Its necessity has been succinctly expressed by the Brazilian Rubem Alves who describes utopia as "not a belief in a perfect society, but rather the belief in the nonnecessity of *this* imperfect order."[28]

A few examples will suffice to illustrate the impact of these movements on Catholic social thought. One of the problems in the latter's early development lay in a very strong emphasis on stability and order; thus it was redolent of a rather static quality vis-à-vis a world that was not only in the process of rapid change but also in dire need of yet more fundamental changes. For instance, Pope John XXIII's *Peace on Earth* in 1963 gave only brief mention to persons who, unwilling to tolerate injustice, "feel enkindled with the desire to change the state of things, as if they wished to have recourse to something like a revolution."[29] He then proceeds to warn that "to proceed gradually is the law of life in all its expressions" and that, as regards institutions, "it is not possible to renovate for the better except by working from within them."[30] This, of course, is generally true in the context of Europe, but elsewhere the experience of numerous former colonies (including the United States) provides abundant historical exceptions.

Moreover, less than a decade later, there is evidence of a significant shift in Pope Paul VI's *Octogesima Adveniens*. After noting that utopian thought can constitute an escape from reality, he proceeds to strike a more positive note:

. . . it must clearly be recognized that this kind of criticism of existing society often provokes the forward-looking imagination both to perceive in the present the disregarded possibility hidden within it, and to direct itself towards a fresh future; it thus sustains social dynamism by the confidence that it gives to the inventive powers of the human mind and heart.[31]

Clearly, the emphasis has changed here from stability to a concentration on humanity's utopian hopes for a better future.

5. *Sociopolitics.* In my opinion, this last area is the most important of all those mentioned—and certainly one of the most hotly debated. The word "sociopolitics" is used here to denote a broad understanding of the political order that would include all the social institutions, policies, structures, etc., through which a given community expresses its own form of corporate existence.[32]

During the past decade, a number of movements strove to come to grips with Christianity's role vis-à-vis the political process thus conceived. For a brief period, intense discussion flared up concerning a theology of revolution, an excellent analysis of which may be found in José Comblin's book *Théologie de la révolution*.[33] However, perhaps because the ominous consequences of such reflections became more apparent, this movement declined in influence.

A theology of development also flourished for a time, spurred on in the Catholic church by Pope Paul VI's famous question in *The Progress of Peoples:* "If the new name for peace is development, who would not wish to labor for it with all his powers?"[34] A penetrating analysis of the ethics of development was provided by Denis Goulet, among others, especially in his book *The Cruel Choice*.[35] However, this movement, too, suffered a decline, since many underdeveloped nations viewed it as concealing a first-world perspective that could only eventuate in their continued domination and dependence. Also, because of their divergent historical and economic circumstances, development according to the model of the first world appeared to many of them to be neither possible nor even desirable.[36]

The term "political theology" was introduced into the debate by J. B. Metz's *Theology of the World*, which called for the "deprivatizing" of Christianity as the major task of contemporary theology.[37] Dorothee Soelle published a number of works along similar lines, including one entitled *Political Theology*. And Jürgen Moltmann devoted considerable attention to this area in many of his writings, especially in the last chapter of *The Crucified God*.[38] An illustration of the impact of all this on Catholic thought may be found again in *Octogesima Adveniens;* there Pope Paul VI refers to the need "to pass from economics to politics," inasmuch as "each man feels that in the social and economic fields, both national and international, the ultimate decision rests with political power."[39]

In the past five years, however, a serious challenge to even the most progressive European theologians has been mounted by the Latin American theology of liberation, which can be considered as basically an indigenous political theology.[40] Again, the investigation of their objections and the possible contributions of Latin American thought to a theology of faith and justice will occupy the major portion of this book. At this point, however, I would like to turn from the consideration of areas of emphasis in theology and move to an even more fundamental problematic, that is, to the question of theological methodology. As in the above section, a brief survey of significant contributions regarding this question would appear to provide a helpful backdrop for further discussion. In this review, the focus of attention will be on methodologies that illuminate the relation of the church to a world scarred by massive human suffering.

Theological Method

First of all, in his influential *Method in Theology,*[41] Bernard Lonergan divides the activity of theologians into eight specialties, which he carefully analyzes throughout the book. The last of these (which Lonergan considers to be the fruition of the first seven disciplines) is designated "communications," and deals with theology "in its external relations," that is, "with the effective communication of Christ's message."[42] The message is described as "cognitive" and "constitutive" of Christian community, but also "it is effective inasmuch as it directs Christian service to human society to bring about the kingdom of God."[43]

Lonergan believes that the specialty of communications is urgently needed, since we live "in a time of ever-increasing change due to an ever-increasing expansion of knowledge." Consequently, the church must be engaged in continual renewal, which "will bring theologians into close contact with experts in very many different fields. It will bring scientists and scholars into close contact with policy makers and planners, and through them with clerical and lay workers engaged in applying solutions to the problems and finding ways to meet the needs both of Christians and of all mankind."[44] Aside from the stress on interdisciplinary work and adaptation to diverse communications media, it must finally be admitted that Lonergan's description of this specialty remains on a very general plane as compared with his analysis of the other seven disciplines.

Karl Rahner has also published reflections on the same general area in a series of articles in his *Theological Investigations.* In an earlier study he discusses the discipline he terms "practical theology," and proceeds to define it as "that theological discipline which is concerned with the church's self-actualization here and now," that is, "which attempts to be of service in continually overcoming the church's given deficient self-realization and transcending it in the next new form to which the church is being called."[45] While insisting on the originality and significance of this discipline in its own right, he also emphasizes that "it will continue to make other disciplines aware that their tasks are not to be fulfilled in the unhistorical and sterile realm of eternally valid truths, but in the historical situation which is ours at any one particular time."[46]

In another article Rahner returns to this line of inquiry. As a starting point he alludes to the "astonishing" fact that so little attention was devoted in Vatican II to the very nature and rationale of a new type of teaching, that is, a "pastoral constitution," such as *Gaudium et Spes*.[47] The basic difficulty that surfaced in this document, he believes, consists in the fact that, while concrete decisions and actions belong to the intrinsic nature of the church, they cannot be deduced with certainty from the principles of revelation. This leads to the very significant consequence that "the Church has need of a non-revelatory kind of knowledge, a knowledge which does not belong to the *depositum fidei* (deposit of faith), in order to be herself and to be able to act."[48] Thus, the church embarked rather unreflectively on a new course in the pastoral constitution *Gaudium et Spes,* and Rahner concludes by describing this new kind of document as "charismatic instructions formulated with the assistance of the Spirit in the Church."[49]

Finally, Rahner approaches the problem once again in an article that is concerned with the phenomenon of secularization. Recognizing that the church no longer directs or controls society on a doctrinal or juridical level, he affirms that it has embarked on a new course, which may be termed "prophetic."[50] He then offers a sketch of this enormous task, which he feels has scarcely been begun in the church:

A "political theology" of a fundamental kind would have to be developed. That is, theology (considered as content) and ecclesiology in particular would have to be developed in their significance for social politics and the shaping of history, and thereby the exaggeratedly narrow and individualist view of revelation as pertaining to the salvation of the individual in isolation would have to be overcome.[51]

Rahner next proposes the creation of still another discipline within the scope of "practical theology," to which he assigns the rather ponderous title of a "practical ecclesiastical cosmology."[52] Its approach, he notes, cannot be that of systematic theology, for its task is constantly changed by the changes that take place in the society into which the church is inserted. Again, the note of "prophetic decision" is stressed, going beyond mere analysis of the church and the contemporary situation. Finally, Rahner admits that "today the task which awaits a 'cosmology' of this kind is an almost immeasurable one"; at the same time, however, it "is in fact far from being recognized sufficiently clearly in its urgency or in its importance."[53] All in all, it appears to me that there is still a great need in Rahner's thought for further theoretical explication of the characteristics of the new discipline.

Another theologian who has analyzed this methodological problem is David Tracy, especially in his recent book *Blessed Rage for Order*.[54] In this work Tracy articulates five basic models in contemporary theology: orthodox, liberal, neo-orthodox, radical, and revisionist. Since the first four of these are deemed inadequate for the task of contemporary theology, Tracy's entire book is a sustained and erudite argument for the revisionist model which, in his own terms, involves "the dramatic confrontation, the mutual illuminations and corrections, the possible basic reconciliation between the principal values, cognitive claims, and existential faiths of both a reinterpreted post-modern consciousness and a reinterpreted Christianity."[55]

After an application of the revisionist model to fundamental, systematic, and historical theology, Tracy in a final chapter focuses it on "practical theology," which is also referred to as a "theology of *praxis*," and whose most representative members are said to include Jürgen Moltmann, J. B. Metz, Carl Braaten, Rubem Alves, Richard Shaull, Juan Luis Segundo, Gustavo Gutiérrez, and Dorothee Soelle.[56] The author first notes the positive values of this approach in transcending individualism in favor of a model of social humanity; in opening up the possibilities of the future disclosed by a Christian eschatology; and in enriching Christian thought with "the enduring Marxian insights into the centrality of *praxis*."[57]

However, from his revisionist perspective, Tracy also finds fault with these theologians for not being faithful to the full demands of praxis, and suggests that the reason for this failure lies in their "seeming refusal to challenge the neo-orthodox model of their immediate theological predecessors."[58] This criticism is admitted to be tentative with regard to Latin American theologians other than Gutiérrez; in fact, Tracy does not offer much evidence of having read these other authors. In his most recent work Gustavo Gutiérrez has replied by offering some comments on Tracy's book. Gutiérrez's major objection is that the latter's theological models are lacking in social context and in "concrete insertion" in history.[59]

The Canadian theologian Gregory Baum has also directed his attention to the problem of method in his book *Religion and Alienation*.[60] There Baum argues for an approach that he refers to as "critical theology," which is variously defined as "the sustained dialogue with the critical thought of the Late Enlightenment" and again as "the critical application of the various theories of alienation to the self-understanding in faith of the Christian Church."[61]

Futhermore, Baum's entire book provides a graphic illustration of the method of critical theology. Its fundamental theme appears to be the recognition of the permanent ambiguity of religion, that is, its capacity for generating either alienation or creativity; many illuminating analyses of this thesis are presented with regard to the personal and social dimensions of religion, both of which are considered essential by Baum. For present purposes, however, we may allude merely to the relation he sees between his method and that of liberation theology.

First of all, Baum believes that both approaches are structurally identical. This identity is grounded in the fact that "they are reflections on faith conversion, they are grounded in social commitment in favor of the oppressed, they raise consciousness, lead to social involvement, and regard themselves as the reflective or contemplative component of the liberating human action, in which God is redemptively present to the sinful world."[62] On the other hand, despite the structural similarity, there are important differences. The major one involves the "combination of factors in the analysis of social evil," for example, racist and sexist as well as class factors, but other differences include the diverse forms in which commitment will be embodied in North and South America as well as the diverse symbols that are drawn from varied historical experiences.[63] At present, I do not believe that Baum has been able to convince the Latin Americans that his "interstructured" social analysis is really a better heuristic model than their "holistic" one based on economic and class analysis;[64] at any rate, it is clear from this book that Baum will continue to be a key figure in any dialogue in the Americas.

Despite some differences and a number of generalities that lead to vagueness, we can still perceive a common agreement in this survey of different theologians: the urgent need to refine theological methods so that they may come to bear in an effective way on the social problems that afflict humanity. It is my own conviction that much greater sophistication and profundity in such an endeavor can be realized by an authentic dialogue with liberation theology; however, the proofs for this assertion must be postponed until that theology is analyzed in detail in subsequent chapters of this work.

An Approach to Liberation Theology

At this point then it would appear most helpful to clarify my own approach to what I believe is a very significant dialogue. First of all, my principal objective in this book will be to establish a "first moment" of dialogue, that is, the attempt to hear as accurately as possible what the other partner in the conversation is actually saying. And it must be forthrightly acknowledged that this is no easy task.

For in order to hear the other in this "first moment," one must try to suspend or bracket the ordinary categories, the accustomed mental screens, by means of which one interprets the world and articulates a Christian perspective on it. The difficulty of achieving this in everyday conversation is patent to all, but the problem is compounded for theologians, who are burdened with a far larger freight of philosophical and theological baggage. Although these constructs are essential to their task, they can also function as a procrustean bed, lopping off the heads and limbs of different perceptions of reality before they are adequately understood.[65] A major effort of this book, then, will be to bracket these North American mental screens in order to articulate as accurately as possible what our neighbors to the south are actually saying.

One immediate advantage of this approach is related to the present state of the world dialogue in theology. For in this our accustomed partners up to now have almost always been Europeans; we simply did not look south of the border for theological enlightenment, nor was a knowledge of Spanish considered a necessary tool for theological reflection. As a result, even the libraries of large Catholic universities in North America have largely ignored the proliferation of works in Spanish, not to mention Portuguese, that have been produced in the past decade; if a similar situation existed, for example, with regard to German theological thought, it would be looked upon as intolerable. Consequently, since it is extremely difficult even to locate basic Latin American sources, I believe it is a useful service in itself merely to make their thought more available to English speakers and readers.

The "second moment" in the dialogue will require more extended discussion. As has already been mentioned, the Latin Americans place great emphasis on praxis in a dialectical relation with reflection as a source of theological understanding. In this "second moment," therefore, I will make some exploratory applications of Latin American insights to the area of Christian praxis in North America. These suggestions will not be fully developed in the present work since, as will be pointed out later on, it appears that there will be abundant time in the future for such elaboration.[66]

Also, a most important characteristic of my approach in this "second moment" is that it will be consciously *positive* in its orientation. Thus I will be asking questions with regard to what possible value, what new perception, what fundamental contribution liberation theology might have to offer to theological thought and praxis in North America.

The importance of this decision is highlighted if we glance at just a few of the studies of Latin American theology that have appeared recently. For instance, Bonaventure Kloppenburg has published a booklet with the title *Temptations for the Theology of Liberation;* although the author states his intention "not to slight its positive side," his treatment is on the whole negative, and he rather naively does not advert to the serious "temptations" involved in competing theologies or current operative theologies.[67] The Dominican H. Lepargneur has also written a long article on the topic in an issue of the *Nouvelle Revue Théologique*.[68] Again, after a brief introduction, the vast bulk of the article is devoted to a discussion of the numerous "ambiguities," "exaggerations," and "confusions or false options" the author finds in the movement; moreover, Lepargneur somewhat ingenuously admits that this long catalogue of charges is based "on the least possible exegesis of texts" and therefore on his "personal experience."[69]

But perhaps the best example may be found in a recent series of articles written by a long-time foe of liberation theology, the Belgian Jesuit Roger Vekemans.[70] This author begins with the quite candid acknowledgment that he is "systematically" presenting the most negative possible aspect of the movement, whether this be termed a "risk, temptation, danger, or deviation pure and simple." However, Vekemans does go on to admit that "a more positive projection would be equally legitimate" and, in fact, necessary for an objective discernment of liberation theology.[71] It is, therefore, precisely that positive stance that I will be adopting in this study.

In this regard I would also advance my view here that there will be ample time for both positive and negative evaluations of the theology of liberation in the years ahead. For unlike the numerous theological fads that waxed and waned in Europe and the United States in the past decade, I make my Pascalian wager that this movement will continue and develop throughout the last quarter of the twentieth century and beyond.[72] My basic reason for this assertion is that it is not founded on fashionable philosophies that may happen to be in vogue in the West but rather on the configuration or moral geography of the real world itself. As long as that world remains split, as it is now, into segments of overconsumption and desperation, the liberation dialogue will continue also. And as regards the differing evaluations of the authors just mentioned and myself, the solution will no doubt be found in what has been called the "Gamaliel test": "For if this plan or this undertaking is of men, it will fail; but if it is of God, you will not be able to overthrow them. You might even be found opposing God! " (Acts 5:38–39).

Also, as a corollary to this positive approach in the "second moment" of dialogue, I will include references to European and North American theologians whose works I have found to be significant or useful in a deeper understanding of the subjects under discussion. These do not pretend to encompass a complete survey of the available literature; indeed, such a task would be literally impossible. For Latin American authors simply do not abide by the rules we have established in North America and Europe for the careful demarcation of the areas of theological work; that is, one person concentrates on fundamental theology, another on systematic, and so on through historical, pastoral, and moral theology, as well as the many modalities of scriptural exegesis. Rather they use elements from all these disciplines in order to create a new form of theology, a liberating theology, that they believe will respond to the urgent needs of their own continent at this moment in history. In selecting references from so many areas, therefore, one can only act like the householder in the parable of Matthew "who brings out of his treasure what is new and what is old" (Matt. 12:52).

It should, however, be strongly emphasized that throughout this book the references to European and North American theologians reflect my own judgment on possible points of dialogue and not the judgment of the Latin Americans themselves, who generally stress the substantial divergences between their work and that of their western counterparts. It is especially important to keep this in mind with regard to the writings of Juan Luis Segundo.

Dangers and Concluding Reflections

It must be admitted, too, that certain dangers exist regarding both moments of the dialogue we have been discussing. In my view the most serious danger is that of the cooptation of liberation theology; in other words, there is the possibility—perhaps the probability—that a North American will take the hard sayings and basic challenges issuing from the south, smooth off the rough edges of challenge and conflict, and present liberation theology as an interesting and exotic new product, calculated to relieve any tedium that may have developed in the western theological marketplace. Thus, once its conflictive nature is blunted and its challenge muted, the movement may be fitted into the extant paradigms of the West and soon thereafter forgotten.

This, as I said, is a real danger. What encourages me to risk it is the fact that even if this or other studies turn out to be coopting, the Latin Americans are simply not going to allow themselves to be coopted, nor will they tailor their product, if you will, to suit western markets. One of their number expresses this very forcefully when he notes that "they will refuse to be subject to the academic theology of the West as a sort of *norma normans* to which all theology is accountable."[73]

For from personal contacts as well as from reading, I am convinced of one thing: these are *serious* theologians. Their operative goals are not to secure promotion, to win the kudos of colleagues, to sell books, or to become internationally known as intellectuals; rather their basic goal is to create a theology that will aid in the transformation of the situation of utter misery in which millions of their compatriots are trapped. They are serious, too, because doing theology in such a situation involves the risk—often the actuality—of imprisonment, torture, exile, and death.[74] Such threats, of course, are very similar to those experienced by the theologians who originally created the Old and New Testaments. As a consequence, misapprehensions or bad reviews from the north can be regarded as unfortunate but of little lasting importance.

Another danger, which is articulated with some frequency on the North American theological scene, is that we must be wary of facile imports from Latin America, since such imports are foreign to our own historical experience as a people. If we are just beginning to turn away from European imports, the objection goes, let us not now turn to Latin America but rather work with our own North American resources. There is an obvious element of truth to this objection, as was previously noted in the observations of Gregory Baum. At the same time, however, there are a number of reasons why I believe the Latin Americans can furnish aid in the task of articulating a North American theology.

First of all, they help us realize that in the past European imports were relatively easy to accept and to absorb because the "doing of theology" was confined to persons within the same basically prosperous ambit of the North Atlantic nations. However, a theology articulated from outside that milieu would provide a kind of "antienvironment," that is, a distanced perspective from which to survey the western theological task and the role of the theologian in society. Just as one learns to view one's own culture more objectively after having lived in a foreign country, so one can reevaluate one's "thought-world" with greater clarity after having entered into a different world of discourse. Thus, for example, the question could be raised as to what interests are served by the necessary choice of priorities in theological research in the West; do these choices in fact buttress the status quo of the privileged and the powerful or do they speak to the needs of the marginalized and the powerless? Or, more commonly, is there tacit agreement that such questions are not germane to the "impartial" science of theology? The latter position, of course, becomes increasingly tenuous as the sociology of knowledge continues to advance; my position is that liberation theology can be of considerable help to us in answering the very pointed questions raised by that discipline.[75]

A second response would emphasize that far from being an exotic import, Latin American theology is, in fact, profoundly "relational."[76] That is to say, it reminds us that the historical experience of the United States is not something that has developed in splendid isolation but rather in a close interrelationship with the history of other nations, including especially the nations of Latin America. From their perspective, our nation's prodigious "development" was achieved at the expense of the "underdevelopment" of Latin America and other parts of the world as well as of various minority groups within this country itself. Again from their view, the political, economic, and cultural structures that led to our developmental breakthrough continue to function, constituting in effect a gigantic social machine that appears, at least, to offer little hope of change for the masses of their continent. Considering that the outlook for the present, and especially for the future, projects an even broader and deeper complex of relationships, it follows that the recognition of this situation must play a key role in any articulation of an indigenous North American theology.

A last response to the alleged danger of a Latin American "import" would consist in drawing attention to a reality that is often overlooked: in point of fact, there already exists, within the borders of the United States, a substantial Latin American "nation." An increasingly articulate spokesperson for this community, Virgilio Elizondo, has estimated that there are 17 or 18 million Spanish speakers in the United States, which is more than the entire population of Central America.[77] Moreover, when birth rates are considered, these Spanish-Americans, who are overwhelmingly Catholic, will continue to constitute an ever-growing proportion—perhaps in time a majority—of the American Catholic church. And it is a fact that Elizondo and others in this community have welcomed liberation theology as an invaluable aid in articulating their North American historical experience. The influence can perhaps be detected in the message which Elizondo recently brought from the Spanish-American community to the members of the Catholic Theological Society of America:

Become one with the little ones of today's society. Join us in our sufferings, our struggles, and our *movimientos* so that, having become one with those of us at the bottom, you may exercise your ministry by unveiling and denouncing the demonic powers which are present and at work in the invisible structures which are oppressing people in today's world. . . . We need you to help us announce the kingdom as it is gradually and painfully coming into being through the creation of new structures which hopefully will be ever more human and humanizing.[78]

With regard to the *content* of Latin American theology to be considered in this dialogue, I was confronted with an embarrassment of riches, that is, such an enormous mass of material that it was difficult to select those areas that were essential and those that were peripheral. Conversely, there was also great difficulty—sometimes failure—in locating important texts, since theological libraries in this country have not been assiduous in acquiring works written in Latin America. However, I was able to obtain the major works and most of the minor works of the Uruguayan Jesuit Juan Luis Segundo. It became clear, moreover, that he has a substantial corpus of writing, since he has been publishing theological works since 1962.

Consequently, I decided to devote the second chapter of this book to a general overview of Latin American theology, utilizing whatever sources were available in this country. It was clearly recognized that a number of authors and ideas treated summarily in this chapter would deserve and repay more careful study in the future. The remaining chapters in the book are devoted to an analysis of key ideas in Segundo's work, especially those which appear to clarify and deepen an understanding of the relationship between Christian faith and justice. In doing this, I have concentrated on works in Spanish, since translated works are already accessible to English-speaking readers.

This chapter may be concluded with a few speculations, from an outsider's point of view, regarding the reasons for the efflorescence of liberation theology in a continent previously undistinguished for its contributions to Christian thought and practice. Beyond historical events like Vatican II and the Medellín Conference, which will be discussed in the next chapter, one could perhaps point to the very *Sitz-im-Leben* or concrete situation of their reflections. For Latin America has not been as successful as we have been in the north in segregating the victims of misery and isolating them from public consciousness, in ghettos, reservations, camps for migrant workers, and so forth. The swarming *barriadas, favelas, mocambos* and slums by other names—far worse than any slum we know of—encircle their great cities in massive, Dantesque rings of deprivation that simply cannot be ignored. The impact of this squalor has been graphically depicted in George H. Dunne's narrative of the thousands of families that live, suffer, and die literally on garbage heaps in Recife, Brazil, a sight which Dunne aptly entitles "A Look Into Hell."[79] We might say that here what Jürgen Moltmann has referred to as "circles of death"[80] are translated from the realm of mental constructs into the realm of terrifying reality. Thus the challenge to the Christian conscience presented by such a situation is utterly impossible to avoid.

Another answer may be found in the historical, perhaps providential, destiny of the Latin American church. For this is the only continent which has been both a colony and Christian since its conquest by Spain and Portugal. Furthermore, even the most superficial attention to world events and proliferating world conferences should suffice to show that the end of colonialism and the struggle by countries of the third world to overcome economic domination comprise some of the most dramatic events of the past several decades. In this historic evolution, Latin America with its rich religious heritage has been confronted with the task of being the Christian voice of the poor in today's global village. We might well reflect deeply on the terse description of this situation recently articulated in the context of Central America: "The full and integral salvation of the Third World, the world of the poor, is a great historical challenge. Responding to this challenge should be regarded as the fundamental charism of the Latin American Church."[81]

NOTES

1. Walbert Bühlmann, *The Coming of the Third Church: An Analysis of the Present and Future of the Church* (Maryknoll, N.Y.: Orbis Books, 1977).

2. Ibid., p. 22. Italics are the author's.

3. The quotation is from the preface for the feast of Christ the King in the Roman Catholic liturgy.

4. In his book *Christ Sein* (Munich: R. Piper, 1975), Hans Küng makes a similar observation when he notes that in Latin America "theology faces the problem of how one should speak of God and his love for men in an inhuman world, not only to non-Christians, as elsewhere, but to non-persons or sub-persons" (p. 555); Eng. trans.: *On Being a Christian* (New York: Doubleday, 1976).

5. Juan Alfaro, *Theology of Justice in the World* (Vatican City: Pontifical Commission on Justice and Peace, 1973), p. 41; italics mine. For a developed and thoroughly documented exposition of Alfaro's views, see *Esperanza cristiana y liberación del hombre* (Barcelona: Herder, 1972), especially the chapter on "La esperanza cristiana en su compromiso por la liberación del hombre," pp. 199–227. Other important works of the author include: *Hacia una teología del progreso humano* (Barcelona: Herder, 1969) and *Cristología y antropología* (Madrid: Cristiandad, 1973).

6. For a collection of documents cited here and other related ones, see the recent work of Joseph Gremillion, *The Gospel of Peace and Justice: Catholic Social Teaching since Pope John* (Maryknoll, N.Y.: Orbis Books, 1976).

7. Gregory Baum, *Religion and Alienation: A Theological Reading of Sociology* (New York: Paulist Press, 1975), p. 181.

8. *Justice in the World*, no. 6; Gremillion, *Gospel of Peace and Justice*, p. 514.

9. Ibid., pp. 1–138. For an excellent Protestant perspective on both Catholic documents and those of the World Council of Churches, cf. Robert McAfee Brown, *Theology in a New Key: Responding to Liberation Themes* (Philadelphia: Westminster Press, 1978), pp. 19–49.

10. A veritable library exists on the work of Bultmann; I have found the most helpful works to be his own *Theology of the New Testament*, 2 vols. (New York: Charles Scribner's Sons, 1951), and John MacQuarrie's excellent study, *An Existentialist Theology: A Comparison of Heidegger and Bultmann* (London: SCM, 1955). A brief survey of the five areas of emphasis was published in my " 'Church and World' and Theological Developments," *America* (28 February 1976): 153–56.

11. J. B. Metz, *Theology of the World* (New York: Herder and Herder, 1969). Typical of Metz's approach is his statement that "the deprivatizing of theology is the primary critical task of political theology" (ibid., p. 110). Another vigorous challenge to existentialist theology has been mounted by Dorothee Soelle, especially in her book, *Political Theology* (Philadelphia: Fortress Press, 1974); the essence of Soelle's argument can be found in her statement that "ideological criticism takes the place of demythologization for us" (ibid., p. 61).

12. For an excellent survey of this process in four major world religions, see Donald Eugene Smith, *Religion and Political Development* (Boston: Little Brown, 1970), especially chapter 4, "The Secularization of Politics" (pp. 85–123), and chapter 7, "The Religious Legitimation of Change" (pp. 201–45).

13. Harvey Cox, *The Secular City: Secularization and Urbanization in Theological Perspective* (New York: Macmillan, 1965). Cox later acknowledged a certain one-sidedness in this work which he strove to remedy in his subsequent books, *The Feast of Fools* (New York: Perennial Library, 1972) and *The Seduction of the Spirit: The Use and Misuse of People's Religion* (New York: Simon and Schuster, 1973).

14. Arend Th. van Leeuwen, *Christianity and World History* (New York: Charles Scribner's Sons, 1964); Edward Schillebeeckx, *God the Future of Man* (New York: Sheed and Ward, 1968) and *God and Man* (New York: Sheed and Ward, 1969). An example of Rahner's approach may be found in "Theological

Reflections on the Problem of Secularization," *Theological Investigations X* (New York: Herder and Herder, 1973), pp. 318–48.

15. In this regard, the similar positions of van Leeuwen and Rahner may be noted. Van Leeuwen insists that "the relation of the Christian Church to the advancing history of secularization is in any event a positive one; it carries responsibility for it and is intimately concerned and involved with what that process brings in its train, with all that it so richly promises and with its appalling threats and dangers" (Van Leeuwen, *Christianity and World History*, p. 334). In his article Rahner presupposes "the idea that the dynamism inherent in Christianity itself gives rise to a justifiable process slowly working itself out in history by which the world becomes worldly, even though in the concrete the representatives of Christianity and the Churches have often been so misled in their understanding of the world, due to their ideas being ossified at particular epochs, that they have actually sought to hold back this process" (Rahner, "Theological Reflections on the Problem of Secularization" p. 321).

16. *Gaudium et Spes*, no. 40, in Gremillion, *Gospel of Peace and Justice*, p. 275.

17. Ibid., no. 5, p. 247.

18. Leslie Dewart, *The Future of Belief: Theism in a World Come of Age* (New York: Herder, 1966), p. 49.

19. Gerhard von Rad, *Old Testament Theology*, 2 vols. (New York: Harper and Row, 1963–65). The influence of von Rad on both authors is carefully traced by M. Douglas Meeks in his *Origins of the Theology of Hope* (Philadelphia: Fortress Press, 1974). Meeks concludes that "if we were to designate a *primum movens* of the new eschatological thought, first in the person of Pannenberg and then Moltmann, it would be the new understanding of the biblical views of revelation and history arrived at by Gerhard von Rad" (ibid., p. 68).

20. Wolfhart Pannenberg et al., *Revelation as History* (New York: Macmillan, 1968). Cf. also Pannenberg's *Basic Questions in Theology*, vol. 1 (Philadelphia: Fortress Press, 1970), where he notes that "Israel not only discovered history as a particular sphere of reality; it finally drew the whole of creation into history" (p. 21) and "the theology of history now appears in principle at least as the legitimate heir of the biblical understanding of reality" (p. 31).

21. E. Frank Tupper, *The Theology of Wolfhart Pannenberg* (Philadelphia: Westminster Press, 1973), p. 291.

22. Gerald O'Collins, *The Case Against Dogma* (New York: Paulist Press, 1975). In this work, O'Collins raises the question "Has dogma a future?" and answers that "it did not have a past" (p. 97). For the future, he suggests the attitude that " 'Christopraxy' serves to identify genuinely orthodox Christianity" (p. 99).

23. This is quoted by Gustavo Gutiérrez in *A Theology of Liberation* (Maryknoll, N.Y.: Orbis Books, 1973), p. 10.

24. *Gaudium et Spes*, no. 42, in Gremillion, *Gospel of Peace and Justice*, p. 277; italics mine.

25. For a Protestant view, see Carl Braaten's "A Critique of the Two-Kingdom Doctrine," in *The Future of God: The Revolutionary Dynamics of Hope* (New York: Harper and Row, 1969), pp. 145–52. Braaten develops these ideas further within the framework of mission in *The Flaming Center: A Theology of the Christian Mission* (Philadelphia: Fortress Press, 1977), especially in "The Kingdom of God in History," pp. 39–63.

26. Bloch's *Gesamtausgabe* now numbers fifteen volumes (Frankfurt am Main: Suhrkamp, 1969–75); his most cited work is *Das Prinzip Hoffnung*, 3 vols. (Frankfurt am Main: Suhrkamp, 1959). Works available in English include: *Man on His Own* (New York: Herder and Herder, 1970); *A Philosophy of the Future* (New York: Herder and Herder, 1970); *On Karl Marx* (New York: Herder and Herder,

1971); and *Atheism in Christianity* (New York: Herder and Herder, 1971).

27. Jürgen Moltmann, *Theology of Hope* (New York: Harper and Row, 1967) and *The Crucified God: The Cross of Christ as the Foundation and Criticism of Christian Theology* (New York: Harper and Row, 1974). Some of Moltmann's lectures while on a trip through the United States in 1967–68 are included in *Religion, Revolution and the Future* (New York: Charles Scribner's Sons, 1969), while his "Theology as Eschatology" and "Towards the Next Step in the Dialogue" are included in Frederick Herzog, ed. *The Future of Hope: Theology as Eschatology* (New York: Herder and Herder, 1970), pp. 1–50 and 154–64. Most recently Moltmann has applied the dialectic of cross and resurrection developed in earlier works to ecclesiology in *The Church in the Power of the Spirit: A Contribution to Messianic Ecclesiology* (New York: Harper and Row, 1977).

28. Rubem Alves, "Christian Realism: Ideology of the Establishment," *Christianity and Crisis* (17 September 1973): 175. See also the recent statement of Frederick Herzog: "Opening up new dimensions for the imagination is the foremost challenge of systematic theology as liberation theology in North America" ("Liberation and Imagination," *Interpretation* [July 1978]:228).

29. *Pacem in Terris*, no. 161, in Gremillion, *Gospel of Peace and Justice*, p. 236.

30. Ibid., no. 162, pp. 236–37.

31. *Octogesima Adveniens*, no. 37, in Gremillion, *Gospel of Peace and Justice*, p. 502. The section is entitled "Rebirth of Utopias."

32. This definition is adapted from one suggested by Pedro Arrupe as "the highest and best meaning as well as the original meaning of 'politics,' " in his *A Planet to Heal: Reflections and Forecasts* (Rome: Ignatian Center of Spirituality, 1975), p. 68.

33. José Comblin, *Théologie de la révolution* (Paris: Editions Universitaires, 1970). Comblin believes that "the revolution of tomorrow obliges us to go beyond the narrowness of the theologies inspired by Rahner or Metz, while at the same time it prevents us from looking for consolation in archaism" (p. 14).

34. *Populorum Progressio*, no. 87, in Gremillion, *Gospel of Peace and Justice*, p. 413.

35. Denis Goulet, *The Cruel Choice: A New Concept in the Theory of Development* (New York: Atheneum Publishers, 1971). Cf. also Goulet's later work, *A New Moral Order: Studies in Development Ethics and Liberation Theology* (Maryknoll, N.Y.: Orbis Books, 1974).

36. For a brilliant analysis of the reasons for this statement, see George H. Dunne, *The Right to Development* (New York: Paulist Press, 1974), or his briefer treatment in "Development—A Christian Concern?" *America* (2 December 1972):466–69.

37. See n. 11. The reference to Dorothee Soelle's book is also included there.

38. Jürgen Moltmann, "Ways Toward the Political Liberation of Mankind," in *The Crucified God*, pp. 317–40.

39. *Octogesima Adveniens*, no. 46, in Gremillion, *Gospel of Peace and Justice*, p. 507.

40. This is the view of the Spanish theologian Alfredo Fierro in his *The Militant Gospel: A Critical Introduction to Political Theologies* (Maryknoll, N.Y.: Orbis Books, 1977). In part 2 of his book (pp. 129–301), he presents a lengthy synthesis of the common features of different forms of political theology.

41. Bernard Lonergan, *Method in Theology* (New York: Herder and Herder, 1972).

42. Ibid., pp. 132 and 361.

43. Ibid., p. 361.

44. Ibid., p. 367.

45. Karl Rahner, "Practical Theology within the Totality of Theological Disciplines," *Theological Investigations IX* (New York: Herder and Herder, 1972), pp. 102 and 104.

46. Ibid., pp. 106–07.

47. "On the Theological Problems Entailed in a Pastoral Constitution," *Theological Investigations X* (New York: Herder and Herder, 1973), pp. 293–317.

48. Ibid., p. 308.

49. Ibid., p. 306.

50. "Theological Reflections on the Problem of Secularization," *Theological Investigations X* (New York: Herder and Herder, 1973), pp. 318–48.

51. Ibid., p. 336.

52. Ibid., p. 337.

53. Ibid., pp. 338–39.

54. David Tracy, *Blessed Rage for Order: The New Pluralism in Theology* (New York: Seabury Press, 1975).

55. Ibid., p. 32.

56. Ibid., p. 242.

57. Ibid., p. 244.

58. Ibid.

59. Gustavo Gutiérrez, *Teología desde el reverso de la historia* (Lima: CEP, 1977), p. 57. See the recent excellent article on method by Matthew Lamb, "The Theory-Praxis Relationship in Contemporary Christian Theologies," *Catholic Theological Society of America: Proceedings of the Thirty-First Annual Convention* (New York: Manhattan College, 1976), pp. 149–78. Lamb sees Tracy's method as a critical theoretic correlation (p. 170), while the Latin Americans are understood as employing a critical praxis correlation (pp. 171ff.).

60. See n. 7.

61. Ibid., p. 194.

62. Ibid., p. 220.

63. Ibid.

64. This suggestion is made on the basis of conversations with the Latin American theologians who dialogued with Baum at the 1975 "Theology in the Americas" conference in Detroit. Further references to this conference will be given in chapter 2.

65. In my opinion an excellent sample of such procrustean dissection is the review of Juan Luis Segundo's *Theology for Artisans of a New Humanity* series by Richard Neuhaus, "A Theology for Artisans of a New Christendom," *Commonweal* (24 July 1975):243–46.

66. One example of the fuller development needed for the future is the article by John Coleman, "Vision and Praxis in American Theology," *Theological Studies* (March 1976):3–40.

67. Bonaventure Kloppenburg, *Temptations for the Theology of Liberation* (Chicago: Franciscan Herald Press, 1974).

68. H. Lepargneur, "Théologies de la libération et théologie tout court," *Nouvelle Revue Théologique* (February 1976):126–69.

69. Ibid., p. 129. Lepargneur's discussion of ambiguities extends from pp. 135–46; the exaggerations occupy pp. 147–58; and the confusions and false options are treated in pp. 159–69.

70. Roger Vekemans, "Panorámica actual de la teología de la liberación en América Latina: Evaluación crítica," *Tierra Nueva* (April 1976):5–33, and ibid. (July 1976):72–78.

71. Ibid., pp. 5–6.

72. I developed my rationale for this view in "Today's New Task: Geotheol-

ogy," *America* (18 January 1975): 27–29.

73. José Míguez Bonino, *Doing Theology in a Revolutionary Situation* (Philadelphia: Fortress Press, 1975), p. 86.

74. Enrique Dussel has been prominent in speaking of the "martyrs of the Church in Latin America," for example, in "Sobre la historia de la teología en América Latina," *Liberación y cautiverio: Debates en torno al método de la teología en América Latina* (Mexico City: Comité Organizador, 1975), pp. 61ff.

75. On this issue see the article of Gregory Baum, "The Impact of Sociology on Catholic Theology," *Catholic Theological Society of America: Proceedings of the Thirtieth Annual Convention* (New York: Manhattan College, 1975):1–29. The main tenor of Baum's presentation is that "theologians can no longer stand back from the ideological critique of the Christian religion, to which the sociologists have led them" (p. 23).

76. John C. Bennett places great stress on this point in his *The Radical Imperative: From Theology to Social Ethics* (Philadelphia: Westminster Press, 1975), p. 134: ". . . this theology has a direct message to the United States and especially to Christians here because of the effect of the power of the United States on the people of Latin America."

77. See Virgilio Elizondo, "Reflexión teológica de los Latinoamericanos en los Estados Unidos," *Liberación y cautiverio* (n. 74), pp. 319–21, and "A Challenge to Theology: The Situation of Hispanic Americans," *Catholic Theological Society of America: Proceedings of the Thirtieth Annual Convention*, pp. 163–76.

78. Elizondo, *Proceedings of the Thirtieth Annual Convention*, p. 175.

79. George H. Dunne, *The Right to Development*, pp. 15–24.

80. Jürgen Moltmann, *The Crucified God*, pp. 329ff.

81. Ignacio Ellacuría, *Freedom Made Flesh: The Mission of Christ and His Church* (Maryknoll, N.Y.: Orbis Books, 1976), p. 148.

CHAPTER TWO

THEOLOGY THROUGH THE OPTIC OF THE POOR

Thirty years ago, Fr. Gustave Weigel wrote an article on theology in South America, which reflected his long labors and abundant experience in that area of the world as well as his conviction that "to most theologians in North America and Europe, South America is as well known as the heart of Africa."[1] When one reads Weigel's views today, they appear somewhat ambivalent. He points out the critical deficiencies in libraries and the lack of theological publications while noting also that "most of the theologians are engulfed in a profusion of external activity, which makes quiet and constant study impossible."[2] In concluding, Weigel asserts that although theologians there have hopes for the future of South American theology, in his own view "we have no right to expect that it will flower overnight in published studies that will rock the world."[3]

It can only be surmised that Weigel would be vastly surprised but at the same time delighted if he were alive today. For an extraordinary abundance of theological work has indeed flourished beneath the Southern Cross and, ironically, the "profusion of external activity" that Weigel envisioned as a major obstacle has become the central core of its originality and creativity. And finally, at least in my own judgment, it does seem destined to rock the world.

In this chapter I will undertake a review of the history and major themes of this theology, although the attempt must be prefaced by several caveats. First of all, liberation theology propounds what has been called an "open theology," one of constant flux, self-criticism, and development according to the results of praxis. Thus the present sketch is merely provisional; in my view the major contributions of the movement are still to be written. Also I have had to make what I hope is not an arbitrary selection from an immense body of literature; again, I believe this will continue to increase, rivaling if not surpassing the huge library that developed around Rudolf Bultmann's demythologizing project in the past few decades.

It should be noted, too, that the very name "theology of liberation" has presented difficulties for some pioneers in the movement. José Míguez Bonino has expressed his anxiety that the term may lead to the cooptation of the approach as just another "consumer-good" in the European-North American marketplace. He even states flatly that "to the extent that the theology of liberation is—and is made into—a new 'school,' a set of self-contained theological tenets or positions, it will have its day and be gone."[4] A European author has also adverted to the reservations some have concerning the seriousness of outsiders who utilize the term and even about the latter's basic ability to understand what the Latins are talking about.[5] Despite these difficulties, however, the name has been accepted by the major figures in the movement, apparently for purposes of unity, and it is now firmly established as its designation in other areas of the world.

History of the Movement

Enrique Dussel, an Argentine who is a prolific historian, has observed that "existing histories of the 'universal' church are really histories of the European church for the most part. Little or nothing is said in them about Latin America."[6] Dussel is firmly committed to remedying this situation, and in a recent article has provided a useful framework for understanding the growth of Latin American theology.[7]

In the evolution of this theology, Dussel perceives six distinct periods, which can be presented here in only the most summary form. A "prophetic theology" existed from 1511 A.D. until the era of conquest and evangelization (1553). In November of 1511, the Dominican Antonio de Montesinos preached a sermon which embodied the first "criticoprophetic outcry" in the Americas. One of his listeners, Bartolomé de las Casas, was eventually converted by these words to the cause of justice and became one of the most eloquent and prolific defenders of the rights of the Indians.[8]

This was followed by a theology of "colonial Christendom" (1553–1808), which tended to mask injustices, both in the old world and the new, although there were prophetic exceptions, such as the work of the Jesuit José de Acosta in Peru and the construction of the Reductions in Paraguay. A theology centering on practical and political emancipation before independence appeared next (1808–1831), to be succeeded by a conservative, defensive neo-colonial trend (1831–1930).[9]

A "New-Christendom" mentality characterized the next period (1930–1962). Along with the rapid expansion throughout the continent of Catholic Action, this included such promising developments as the creation of a number of theological faculties and periodicals, the emergence of centers for social studies such as the Centro Belarmino in Santiago, the formation of the Latin American Bishops' Conference (CELAM) in 1955, and a widespread renewal of biblical studies. Nevertheless, Dussel believes that the basic thrust in this period was imitative of European models and lacking in a real historical understanding of the Latin American situation.[10]

Finally, the period of liberation theology is located by the author in the years 1962 until the present. And even within this brief span, he delineates three clearly discernible movements. The first extends from the beginning of Vatican II until the conference of bishops in Medellín, Colombia, in 1968; this is understood as a preparatory phase, still characterized by a developmentalist outlook. A second moment—1968–72—marks the formulation of liberation theology proper. Lastly, the period extending to the present has been dominated by reaction and persecution as well as by a profound maturation in understanding the breadth of the task of liberation. All this has resulted in the characterization of the latter period as a time of "captivity" and "exile."[11]

In the entire process it is clear that the application of the insights of Vatican II to the Latin American continent that took place at Medellín has great historical importance. The documents endorsed by the bishops at the latter assembly bear ample witness to a strong emphasis on a new understanding of salvation that includes liberation and the construction of the world. In their final statement, for example, the bishops refer to a new epoch in their history, insisting that "it appears to be a time of zeal for full emancipation, of liberation from every form of servitude, of personal maturity and of collective integration."[12] At the very outset of the meeting, the Cardinal Archbishop of Lima, Juan Landázuri Ricketts, had stressed a similar theme: "In Latin America, salvation, which is the realization of the kingdom of God, involves the liberation of all men, the progress of each and all from a less human condition to one more human."[13]

Although some of the bishops who attended the Medellín conference displayed diminishing enthusiasm for its message upon returning to their home dioceses, a number of other factors contributed to an acceleration of the momentum of the movement. Hugo Assmann has noted that "1970 was the first year in which conferences and symposia on the theme of 'theology of liberation' became commonplace throughout Latin America."[14] He goes on to describe an international symposium on the topic held in Bogotá, Colombia, on March 2–7 of that year; a meeting of biblical scholars on the theme of "Exodus and Liberation" was convened in Buenos Aires, Argentina, in July; an ecumenical seminar in Buenos Aires was held August 3–6; and finally, in Ciudad Juárez, Mexico, on October 16–18, there was another international gathering, which was attended by Harvey Cox and other widely recognized scholars.[15]

Of central importance also was the appearance of the book *A Theology of Liberation,* written by a Peruvian priest, Gustavo Gutiérrez, and first published in 1971; it was soon translated into a number of languages, providing non-Latin Americans with their first scholarly and comprehensive description of the new approach.[16] Furthermore, a meeting of "Christians for Socialism" was convened in April of 1972 in Santiago, Chile, under the direction of Gonzalo Arroyo, and appeared to move many people to more radical positions, both politically and theologically. The final document of this meeting declared unambiguously that "revolutionary praxis comes to be recognized as the matrix that will generate a new theological creativity," and that "thus theological thinking is transformed into critical reflection in and on liberation praxis—in a context of permanent confrontation with the exigencies of the gospel."[17]

Also in 1972, an important meeting was held with European theologians at El Escorial in Spain, with papers centering on the topic of "Christian Faith and Social Change in Latin America."[18] In August of 1975, the movement moved northward to Mexico City; the increasingly brutal repression experienced in Chile and elsewhere on the continent was reflected in the theme adopted there: "Liberation *and Captivity.*"[19] This was followed immediately by a week-long conference with North American theologians and activists in Detroit, which was entitled "Theology in the Americas: 1975" and organized by an exiled Chilean priest, Sergio Torres. The remarkable ecumenical openness of the latter meeting is clearly evident in a number of accounts written soon after it.[20] Furthermore, no fewer than eight projects or affinity groups have sprung up as a result of the conference, utilizing the liberation methodology in doing theology from different backgrounds throughout the United States and Canada. These projects include blacks, Hispanics, women, native Americans, Asian Americans, a task force of professional theologians, a labor-church dialogue, and a group seeking liberation in the white churches.

Theology in the Americas, moreover, has developed a related but separate international dimension, which uses the liberation methodology to articulate distinctively African and Asian theologies. This, too, is in full operation, with an ecumenical planning conference for all three continents already held in Dar es Salaam, Tanzania, in 1976 and an ecumenical pan-African meeting conducted at Accra, Ghana, in December of 1977. At this writing, arrangements are being made for an Asian conference in 1978, a Latin American meeting in 1979, and a final synthesizing world conference in 1980. An Ecumenical Association of Third World Theologians has also been formed to coordinate these meetings, with an Asian as president and an African as vice-president.[21]

Gutiérrez as Pioneer

But how can we describe this new approach that has by now reached every corner of the world? To answer this, I will examine in more detail Gutiérrez's book, the Magna Carta of liberation theology, and afterwards outline some other major developments in theology that have followed its publication. It should be noted that many of the ideas in the book were developed by Gutiérrez in dialogue and discussion with a number of other theologians (including Juan Luis Segundo) during the decade that preceded its publication. The author's major achievement, therefore, was to bring all these ideas together into a well-organized synthesis; this was especially helpful for theologians working outside the ambit of the theological discussions occurring within the Latin American continent.

Gutiérrez begins *A Theology of Liberation* appropriately enough with a clarification of the meaning of the two nouns in the title. In discussing "theology," he briefly traces its historical evolution into what can be categorized as "spiritual wisdom" and, at a later date, "ordered rational knowledge." Without abandoning these methodologies but rather subsuming them dialectically, Gutiérrez places great emphasis on a new characteristic: the privileged position as a theological source of Christian praxis, that is, of the actual Christian experience of commitment in a given historical situation, under the guidance of the Spirit.[22]

But there is an essential second "moment" in the approach, inasmuch as, by its clarification of the present and future, theological reflection on praxis strives to make a contribution to ongoing praxis; in other words, it "does not stop with reflecting on the world, but rather tries to be part of the process by which the world is transformed." Of crucial importance, therefore, for understanding his theology is the author's assertion that "the theology of liberation offers not so much a new theme for reflection as a *new way* to do theology."[23] Lastly, various currents of thought that prepared the way for the new method are mentioned: Maurice Blondel and his masterwork *L'Action;* the thought of Karl Marx, especially as condensed in his thesis against Feuerbach ("The philosophers have only *interpreted* the world, in various ways; the point, however, is to *change* it"); the evolution in Christian spirituality from an attitude of contempt for and withdrawal from the world to one of active presence in and on behalf of the world; and lastly the documents of Vatican II, seen not as a definitive program but as a springboard for continuing theological development.[24]

Gutiérrez then moves on to the second term, "liberation," and establishes the reasons why it is a much more fruitful and efficacious term for Latin Americans than the notion of "development," which had held a privileged place for several decades. For some today, he asserts, development has become synonymous with economic growth, while others view it as a total process, which includes social, political, and cultural aspects in addition to the economic ones. In rejecting both of these concepts, Gutiérrez advances three basic arguments for his preference for the notion of "liberation": (1) it highlights the *conflictive nature* of present reality, that is, the conflict of the poor classes with regard to the wealthy; (2) it implies a *new* consciousness, which leads human beings to assume conscious responsibility for the determination of their own destinies, and thus "leads to the creation of a new man and a qualitatively different society";

and (3) it manifests a more profound correspondence with the biblical sources and with the liberating life and death of Christ. Conversely, the deficiencies of the notion of "development" with regard to each of these three critical areas are carefully pointed out.[25]

Gutiérrez is well aware that such an emphasis on liberation leads inexorably to the question of the church's role in liberation, that is, to the question of the very meaning of Christianity and its function in the world. In seeking to answer these questions, he first rejects the model of "Christendom," wherein "the Church is regarded substantially as the exclusive depository of salvation,"[26] since such a concept is now obsolete and basically reactionary. The model of the "New Christendom" (as elaborated by Jacques Maritain), which stressed the autonomy of the temporal sphere with regard to the church, is also considered. Again this position is rejected, since it often masked a tacit alliance of the church with oppressive regimes and also appeared to be a totally inadequate response to the enormous misery and injustice everywhere evident in Latin America. In place of either model, Gutiérrez argues for a stress on humankind's "single vocation to salvation," a position which "gives religious value in a completely new way to the action of man in history, Christian and non-Christian alike."[27] Following from this, a basic orientation of the new approach lies in the recognition that "the building of a just society has worth in terms of the Kingdom or, in more current phraseology, to participate in the process of liberation is already, in a certain sense, a salvific work."

The third major part of Gutiérrez's book involves an effort to develop further a positive model of the church by utilizing the theological method described earlier; that is, he bases his reflections on praxis, on the actual experience of committed Christians in the recent history of Latin America. After the obvious failure of such strategies as the Alliance for Progress and the Decade of Development, he observes, Latin Americans arrived at several crucial discoveries. First of all, it became evident that their real situation was characterized, not only by underdevelopment, but by *systemic dependence;* in other words, "the underdevelopment of poor countries, as an overall social fact, appears in its true light: as the historical by-product of the development of other countries."[28] Conversely, it also became clear that the remedy for this situation was not development but liberation, inasmuch as "the Latin American peoples will not emerge from their present status except by means of a profound transformation, a *social revolution,* which will radically and qualitatively change the conditions in which they now live."[29]

Within this overall framework, a considerable number of documents, containing the reflections of lay and clerical groups engaged in some form of praxis, is examined in detail. Although their experiences are often diverse, certain common features appear to have emerged: they all stress the need for a prophetic denunciation of injustice; for an evangelization that places stress on conscientization; for a return to solidarity with the poor through voluntary poverty; for radical changes in the structures and lifestyles of the church; and for concrete commitment to the revolutionary process now so urgently demanded on their continent.[30]

In the last part of his book, Gutiérrez initiates a fresh and more profound reflection on the Christian sources in an attempt to answer some fundamental questions raised by the praxis just discussed. A first basic question is: what is the meaning of this struggle for liberation in the light of the gospel? He replies with an analysis of various facets of "salvation" as an absolutely central concept of Christianity, and with an understanding of Christ as the "complete" liberator for all humankind. This leads him to conclude that "salvation embraces all men and the whole man; the liberating action of Christ—made man in this history and not in a history marginal to the real life of man—is at the heart of the historical current of humanity; the struggle for a just society is in its own right very much a part of salvation history."[31]

Another question is phrased as follows: what does the option for liberation mean for human beings? Gutiérrez's answers focus on the analysis of the concept of all humanity as God's true temple and on the need for conversion to the neighbor through justice and efficacious love. He ends by sketching the lineaments of a "spirituality of liberation" based on these attitudes, which would entail a profound revision in some traditional understandings of spirituality.[32]

A last question raises the issue: how does the option for liberation relate to the future? In his reply Gutiérrez emphasizes the importance of utopian thinking and also of eschatology, which is seen as the "driving force of a future-oriented history."[33] Moreover, he includes a detailed study of the political dimensions of the life of Jesus, concluding that "his testimony and his message acquire this political dimension precisely because of the radicalness of their salvific character: to preach the universal love of the Father is inevitably to go against all injustice, privilege, oppression, or narrow nationalism."[34]

Gutiérrez concludes his book with a call to the church to abandon its ecclesiocentric concerns and to become what it truly is, a "sacrament of salvation" for all humankind. Clearly, in Latin America, this means being "the visible sign of the presence of the Lord within the aspiration for liberation and the struggle for a more just and human society."[35] Gutiérrez believes that only a poor church can be credible as such a sign today; thus he returns at the end to renewed emphasis on the centrality of poverty, a virtue which necessarily involves a creative tension between "solidarity with the poor" and at the same time a "protest against poverty."[36]

Although he has not produced another work of such scope as *A Theology of Liberation*, Gutiérrez continues to develop his reflections, especially in the area of pastoral practice. This can be clearly seen in a work published in

1973, entitled *Christianity and the Third World*.[37] The first part of this book presents an explanation and theological analysis of four possible pastoral approaches in Latin America. Rejecting the approaches of "Christendom," "New Christendom," and "maturity in the faith," he himself opts for a "prophetic" pastoral orientation.[38] In the latter section of the book, he synthesizes the expectations and desires of the young people who comprise the vast majority of the population in the third world and presents his views on a pastoral strategy that will correspond to their aspirations.[39]

In 1974, another book was published, *The Praxis of Liberation and Christian Faith*, which was also presented in condensed form at the conference at El Escorial mentioned earlier.[40] In this work Gutiérrez develops themes already sketched in *A Theology of Liberation*, but he also places new emphasis on the need for a "church of the people."[41] In this connection he announced at the Detroit conference on "Theology in the Americas" that he was founding an institute at Lima for intensive work with Latin American Indians. The institute was named after Fray Bartolomé de Las Casas, the Dominican champion of Indian rights in the sixteenth century.

A Theology of Liberation was never intended by Gutiérrez to be a complete *summa* of liberation theology, but rather a comprehensive outline of its basic features. I will now survey some of the work that has been done by other authors to extend and deepen those features.

A Liberating Spirituality

The articulation of a *spirituality* that would be harmonious with active social commitment has become the special interest of a Chilean priest, Segundo Galilea. He expresses the need for a synthesis well in a *Concilium* article: "The commitment to liberation in the Christian must be a place of encounter with God, and therefore a source of inspiration to his theological life and his contemplative life."[42]

Galilea's early writings surveyed the whole range of pastoral practice and its problems.[43] Later, a more specific focus on spirituality led to the publication in 1972 of *Contemplation and the Apostolate*.[44] In that work he clearly points out the dialectical process involved in this area, for he notes that "in the future one will not be able to be a Christian without being a contemplative," while on the other hand, "one cannot be a contemplative without having an experience of Christ and of his reign in history."[45]

However, the best survey of Galilea's thought may be found in the book *A Spirituality of Liberation*,[46] published in 1973. In it he explains that because the Christian message concerns the liberation of human beings, it "is called to create persons evangelically free, and to transform the world into a 'new heaven and new earth' ";[47] thus, *any* living out of the Christian message, that is to say, any authentic spirituality, is by its very nature liberating. Galilea then delineates five "fundamental intuitions" which form the basic structure for such a spirituality, and which he believes would be applicable in any area of Latin America.

First of all, he stresses that a conversion to God and a commitment to Christ can take place only through a conversion to our neighbor and through a commitment to those who suffer oppression. A second intuition insists that there exists a profound relationship between "salvation history" and the genuine liberation of the poor in Latin America so that "to commit oneself to the latter is to work together with Christ the Redeemer and to enter into his saving work." Third, liberating tasks must be seen as an anticipation and advancement of the kingdom of God, a kingdom which is marked by justice, equality, fraternity, and solidarity. The fourth basic intuition envisions liberating praxis, that is, the activity that transforms society on behalf of the oppressed, as one of the most important exercises of Christian charity, since Christian love has to be incarnated and made efficacious in reality. Lastly, he emphasizes the value of poverty, which is not only a sharing in the plight of the poor but also a sharing in their struggle for justice, and which implies accepting persecution as a form of poverty and of true identification with Christ.[48]

Galilea goes on to reject a "Greek-oriental" view of contemplation as a flight from the world, a view which has infiltrated Christian spirituality; rather he insists that "contemplation is to have an experience of God, real but obscure, in all the dimensions of human life."[49] Moreover, he sees contemplation as characterized by a double encounter, a personal encounter with Christ and a personal encounter with our neighbor, and insists that these are inseparable, for "the first stresses that Christianity is transcendent, the second that it is incarnate."[50] In this "mysticism of commitment" a central reality is participation in the Passover of Christ; this results in a "paschal dialectic," that is, progressive deaths and resurrections that form the underpinning for a spirituality of change and even revolution.[51] In the remainder of the book (and in many subsequent articles), Galilea has continued to elaborate and expand what is basically a synthesis of the Christian militant-contemplative.[52]

A Christology of Liberation

Hugo Assmann, in an early work, had pointed out the lack of an authentic *Christology* in Latin America and saw the development of a Christology from within the Latin American experience as an urgent contemporary need.[53] At the present time, however, a powerful and comprehensive effort to overcome this lacuna has been made by the Brazilian Franciscan, Leonardo Boff, especially in his best-known work, *Jesus Christ Liberator*.[54] Boff is thoroughly familiar with the best of European and North

American scholarship; at the same time, as he pointed out in his address at the Mexico City conference, he has adopted the basic methodology of a liberating theology as sketched by Gutiérrez above. His book is thus a synthesis that combines an analysis of contemporary Christology with many original insights from the perspective of Latin America. The work deserves serious attention from scholars in the field; what follows are merely a few selections that illustrate his approach.

In his first two chapters Boff reviews the contemporary research concerning the "historical Jesus" and also concerning hermeneutics or the interpretation of scriptural texts. After a careful analysis of three modern hermeneutical approaches (historicocritical, existential, and salvation-history models), he delineates what he considers to be the characteristics of a distinctively Latin American approach to Christology. It should be noted that he considers this to be an extremely important task since "the future of the Catholic church, considering the population decline in Europe, is undeniably in Latin America."[55]

First of all, Boff stresses the primacy of the anthropological element over the ecclesiological; in other words, the Latins are interested "not so much in the church as in the person whom the church must aid, must create, and must humanize."[56] Next, his approach gives priority to utopian perspectives over factual ones, for "the determining element . . . is not the past (for our past is European and one of colonization) but the future."[57] With regard to the future, utopian thought does not become an illusion or flight from reality; rather basing itself on the "hope-principle," it contributes to maintaining the social process in a permanent opening to transformation and thus "constructs and slowly anticipates the definitive world that was promised and shown to be possible by Jesus Christ."[58]

A third characteristic consists in an emphasis on the critical element over the dogmatic. A critical stance is seen as an absolute prerequisite for permanent openness to the future, for ecclesiastical institutions and traditions "often become obsolete, anachronistic, and centers of conservatism, which impedes the dialogue between faith and the world, between the Church and society."[59] The primacy of the social over the personal is the next characteristic, which is made necessary by the marginalization of immense masses of people throughout Latin America. Thus the church "after the manner of Jesus should pay attention in a special way to those without names and without voices," so that the coming kingdom will be "not for a few of the privileged, but for all."[60]

The fifth and last emphasis Boff enumerates is that of orthopraxis over orthodoxy. He observes that the fundamental theme of the synoptic gospels consists in "the following of Jesus"; for Christ and for the early church, he insists, "the essential thing was not to reduce the message of Christ to systematic categories for intellectual understanding, but to create new ways of acting and living in the world."[61] In the remaining eleven chapters of the book, Boff incorporates these five priorities into many Christological themes with a profundity that I will not attempt to summarize at this point.

Although barely forty years old, Boff has written a number of other books; moreover, he is editor of the influential *Revista Eclesiástica Brasileira* and contributes numerous articles to this and other Brazilian journals.[62] Thus there is every indication that he will emerge as one of the most influential theologians on the international scene in the next quarter of a century.

The Centrality of Method

A number of references have already been made in this chapter and the previous one to the question of *methodology;* the subject is obviously of paramount importance for liberation theology since, as it constantly emphasizes, it presents not so much a new content as a "new way of doing theology," or as Boff terms it, "a true methodological revolution."[63] The urgent need of further clarification and analysis of method is demonstrated by the fact that methodology was chosen as the central theme of the 1975 meeting in Mexico City. According to published reports, one of the most enlivened debates at that meeting erupted concerning the validity of the Latin method vis-à-vis the ideas proposed by Bernard Lonergan in his *Method in Theology.*[64]

A number of other studies have also concentrated on this problem, including a detailed essay of Ignacio Ellacuría[65] and a book by the Mexican priest Raúl Vidales, entitled *Questions with Regard to the Method of the Theology of Liberation.*[66] Vidales begins the latter work with the statement: "No one can overlook the fact that Latin American theology faces, with ever clearer urgency, the problem of its method."[67] Recently, a Basque Jesuit working in Central America, Jon Sobrino, has presented an analysis of the difference between Latin American and European methods which is extraordinary for its lucidity and profundity. Entitled "Theological Understanding in the Theology of Europe and Latin America,"[68] the article in its entirety deserves a much wider audience in the international theological dialogue; at this point, some of the major ideas may serve to indicate the general thrust of his thought.

In general, Sobrino believes that European theologians are basically responding to the "first moment" of the Enlightenment; this is symbolized above all in Kant, who liberated reason from all authoritarianism and established its autonomy. On the other hand, the Latin Americans, or at least those in the liberation school, are responding to the challenge of the "second moment" of the Enlightenment, whose central symbol is Marx. This, too, involves a liberation, but "it aims directly at liberation from the suffering of reality, which demands not only a new way of thinking, now autonomously, but also a new way of acting.''[69] In very general terms the interest that moves the Europeans to do theology (an absolutely fundamental question for Sobrino) is *rationality;* the interest that moves liberation theologians to the same pursuit is *transformation.*

Such a bifurcation of interests, Sobrino continues, has important repercussions. For European theology tends to harmonize the reality of generalized misery, for example, with the demands of reason in order to demonstrate that it is meaningful to believe in God in a world of misery. But that approach can have an alienating function, for often "it leaves the reality untouched and in that sense justified or justifiable.''[70] On the other hand, the Latin Americans focus rather on the need to transform the sinful situation and thus "they 'confront reality' in a manner that is as real and free of ideology as possible.''[71] Or to put it in a slightly different way, "the first viewpoint can lead to seeking the reconciliation of meaninglessness only within the subject himself or herself; the second viewpoint sees reconciliation as possible only in the solution of the crisis of reality itself, or at least in the attempt at a solution.''[72] The diversity of perspectives explains also why the Latin Americans seek aid for these solutions not first of all from philosophy but from the social sciences, since these "analyze the concrete misery of reality, the mechanisms of that misery, and the possible concrete models of liberation from that misery.''[73]

Sobrino devotes the second part of his essay to the problematic implied above of the relation between theory and praxis. European theology is seen as primarily interested in transmitting a body of truths or meanings, that is, it is fundamentally "theory or a history of theory," even in the act of reflecting on the relationship of theory and praxis. However, the Latin Americans stress the need first for a contact with reality before reflecting on the theology implied in that contact. Furthermore, for them "it is not a question of thinking beginning with experience, but of thinking beginning with a determined experience, beginning with a praxis that not only is influenced by the misery of the world . . . but which starts with the transformation of that misery.''[74]

As regards theological method, therefore, from the Latin perspective it is conceived fundamentally as a "way" (*camino*), so that the actual "following" of Jesus is seen as the epistemological place for truly "knowing" him; or, in other words, Christ is "truth" only insofar as he is "way." For them then theological method consists in going over again the path of Jesus, and not in merely thinking about it.

The last section of Sobrino's analysis is concerned with what he refers to as the "epistemological break" in theological understanding. Its meaning is clarified when he affirms that Scripture presents this break in two forms: "insofar as it affirms the transcendence of God as futurity, theological understanding has to be *distinct* from natural understanding; insofar as it affirms the transcendence of a crucified God, theological understanding has to be *contrary* to natural understanding."[75] The author then presents a very nuanced analysis of how various contemporary theologies either embody or do not embody this break as well as many insights from his own understanding of it, which can not be treated here. We can, however, mention his fundamental assertion that "the crucified God marks the dividing line between a theology which is authentically Christian and any religion, philosophy, or ideology because it is the most radical expression of God's assumption of history."[76]

In concluding, Sobrino acknowledges the accomplishments of European theology (such as those that led to Vatican II), but faults it for its lack of self-criticism, both historically and geographically. The geographical lack consists in its failure to perceive that it was doing theology from the center, and not the periphery, of the world; thus it remained unaware that the world is not merely the center, but rather a totality of center and periphery in tension, and that from a Christian perspective it is the periphery that is the privileged place for theological understanding.

In summary, he asserts that Latin American theology claims to have overcome not only a number of theological dualisms but the most radical dualism of all, the one between the believing subject and history, or between theory and praxis. In this way it has recovered the profound biblical sense of what it means to know theologically: "To know the truth is to do the truth, to know Jesus is to follow Jesus, to know sin is to take on the burden of sin, to know suffering is to free the world from suffering, to know God is to go to God in justice."[77]

Other Developments

In addition to the areas of spirituality, Christology, and method, the development of liberation theology has proceeded apace in a number of other specialties, which can merely be referred to at this point. In biblical studies the translation into English of José Porfirio Miranda's book *Marx and the Bible* brought his work to the attention of scholars in Europe and North America although, predictably, it did not always win their approbation.[78] J. Severino Croatto has also contributed a book and regular articles from a liberation perspective in *Revista Bíblica*,[79] while Alfonso Castillo's work combines exegesis with the clarification of hermeneutical method.[80] Also, Jon Sobrino's recent work has accented the importance for Christology of a consideration of the historical Jesus as well as the risen Christ, especially for the biblical understanding of Christian discipleship.[81]

As regards historical studies, it was noted earlier that Enrique Dussel has been extraordinarily productive in his project of reinterpreting Latin American history and reinserting it within the perspective of world history.[82] Dussel's prodigious output has also extended to the field of ethics.[83] In this area, too, José Míguez Bonino was an early contributor, having published in 1972 a work that was subtitled *Toward an Ethic of the New Man.*[84]

But perhaps Míguez Bonino's major importance lies in the fact that, as a Methodist pastor, he is the major Protestant figure within the liberation movement in theology, which, all agree, has a profound ecumenical thrust. During the 1972 meeting at El Escorial in Spain, he utilized the rather meager data available to sketch a history and interpretative evaluation of Protestantism in Latin America.[85] Although its historical evolution manifests significant differences from that of Catholicism, Protestantism at the present time is depicted as confronting analogous challenges and dilemmas in its praxis. One could thus speculate that whatever ecumenical reunion occurs in Latin America will flow from some general agreement on common praxis vis-à-vis these challenges rather than from mere assent to commonly accepted doctrine.

Another important Protestant writer is the Brazilian Rubem Alves. In his works that have appeared in English, Alves appears to be speaking out of a more European and North American context than any of the writers previously mentioned. Thus *A Theology of Human Hope* is centered around the importance of language, although it is informed throughout by a vision of theology as a "language of freedom."[86] On the other hand, *Tomorrow's Child* basically comprises a critique of western culture and its suppression of the imagination, with the result that currently "the politician and the sergeant major, the banker and the lawyer, are stronger than the poet and the philosopher, the prophet and the saint."[87] But Alves has also demonstrated that he is able to speak very convincingly from a Latin American perspective, as in his trenchant reply to North American "realists" in the article, "Christian Realism: Ideology of the Establishment."[88] Since he is a thinker of great range and profundity, it can be safely predicted that he will have much to contribute to the future development of Latin American theology.

All these divergencies in approach between western and Latin American theologians have been graphically summarized in an anecdote related by Hugo Assmann. A colleague of his once depicted the writings of the socially progressive theologians of the rich world as "prologues in search of courage," while the approach of the Latin Americans was characterized as that of "courage with primitive weapons."[89] If the survey above has any value, it should serve to indicate that courage is still extant in abundance; the once primitive intellectual weapons, however, are now being refined and improved in combat all over the continent.

Dialogue with Europe

In the remainder of this chapter, attention will be given to the dialogue that liberation theology has been able to establish with the Christian churches in other sectors of the world. On the European scene there already exists a huge body of literature that appears to be, in the phrase of Richard McCormick, "out of control."[90] However, I believe it is possible to achieve an accurate focus on the debate by examining in detail the exchange of views published by Míguez Bonino and the distinguished German theologian Jürgen Moltmann, for this certainly appears to be at the cutting edge of the Latin American–European debate.

The Argentinean's objections to Moltmann are directed specifically against his "theology of the cross," as elaborated in *The Crucified God*.[91] It should be stressed at the outset that this is not some kind of vindictive attack, for Míguez Bonino acknowledges his own indebtedness to the theology of Moltmann but, despite this, asserts that Molmann's "coherent and brilliant argument seems . . . to fail to grasp the basic challenge of Latin American theology and to remain, therefore, within the circle of European political theology."[92] It appears to me that the main lines of his disagreement with Moltmann can be reduced to the following propositions: (1) Moltmann's treatment of the "demonic circles of death" (to be explained below) as they exist in the contemporary world remains on too general and abstract a level; (2) he provides no concrete content for the important task of "identification with the oppressed"; and (3) his conception of the "critical function" of the theologian needs to be thoroughly "de-ideologized." These assertions will now be examined in greater detail.

Moltmann explains the meaning of "demonic" or "vicious" circles of death in the last chapter of his book, entitled "Ways Towards the Political Liberation of Man." There he asserts that "just as there are psychological pattern formations which make men ill, so too there are hopeless economic, social and political formations which drive men towards death." One consequence of this is that talking about a "theology of liberation" in the singular does not make sense, for "it is necessary to speak of 'liberations' in the plural and to advance the processes of liberation in several dimensions of oppression at the same time."[93] The five demonic circles that drive men toward death are then identified as poverty, violence, racial and cultural alienation, the industrial destruction of nature, and meaninglessness or godforsakenness.

Míguez Bonino's quarrel with this analysis is expressed quite bluntly. He asks if it is possible to be satisfied with such a general description of the circles, without attempting to explain their roots and dynamics through a coherent socioanalytic treatment; and his conclusion is that "if theology is to take history seriously, it must incorporate—with all necessary caveats —a coherent and all-embracing method of sociopolitical analysis. Moltmann does not seem to be conscious of this need."[94]

The second objection, failure to identify concretely with the oppressed, is viewed by Míguez Bonino as an even more serious weakness. He quotes Moltmann to the effect that "the crucified God is really a God without country and without class. But he is not an apolitical God; he is the God of the poor, of the oppressed, of the humiliated.'' The Argentinean's response to these statements is quite sharp: ''But the poor, the oppressed, the humiliated *are a class* and *live in countries.* Is it really theologically responsible to leave these two sentences hanging without trying to work out their relation? Are we really for the poor and the oppressed if we fail to see them as a class, as members of oppressed societies?''[95] It may be noted that the questions are directed not only to Moltmann but to even the most history-conscious among other European and North American theologians, who ''want to remain at some neutral or intermediate level in which there is no need to opt for this or that political praxis, i.e., to assume a particular analysis and a particular ideological projection.'' Míguez Bonino himself adopts the opposite position, while admitting a certain risk involved, ''for nobody will claim, in fact, that his analysis of social, political, and economic reality is more than a rational exercise, open to revision, correction or rejection.''[96]

Míguez Bonino's final objection is related to the first two, but focuses on the concepts of the ''critical function of the theologian'' and the ''critical freedom of the gospel.'' The adoption of such an approach, according to the Argentinean, allows Moltmann and most European theologians ''to remain above right and left, ideologically neutral, independent of a structural analysis of reality,'' because they wish to avoid sacralizing a particular ideology or power structure. But he believes that this attitude itself must be desacralized, for it conceals the *de facto* ideology of Moltmann and progressive European theologians, which is a ''liberal social-democratic project.'' He then concludes by demanding that this ''should not be camouflaged as 'the critical freedom of the gospel' but analytically and ideologically justified in human political terms in the same way as our own option for socialism and a Marxist analysis.''[97]

Such forthright criticism has drawn a response from Moltmann in the form of an open letter.[98] In the course of this publication, he flatly denies the charges mentioned by Míguez Bonino, but he also moves to the attack by enumerating the elements he finds dissatisfying in the writings of Míguez Bonino and other Latin Americans. In the first place, he objects, their work does not give evidence of being a genuine Latin American theology at all, but rather a ''re-import'' of progressive European theology. After severely criticizing the Europeans, the Latin Americans end up advancing their own positions as novelties while in fact these positions can be found in Bonhoeffer, Barth, Gollwitzer, and Metz as well as in the writings of Moltmann himself. After suggesting that there may be an Oedipal relationship or vestiges of unconscious colonialism involved in the process, the German theologian suggests that a more positive relationship for the future would be ''to work in concert at a new construction of theology rather than in a rivalry to pass each other by on the 'left' or the 'right' or in the 'middle' and in the process step on each other's toes."[99]

A second exemplification of the Latin Americans' lack of an indigenous perspective is seen in their unoriginal reliance on "seminar-Marxism," for obviously Marx and Lenin are Europeans and, in fact, Germans. Moltmann insists that, in contradistinction to China, for example, which found its own way to socialism through Mao, "there are still scarcely any beginnings of a peculiarly Latin American way to socialism." Once again, he advances a positive suggestion, namely, that the major task of both European political theologians and Latin American liberation theologians still lies ahead of them, and that it involves "a radical turn toward the people."[100]

Lastly, the most decisive difference between the two groups, Moltmann believes, is to be found in their different assessments of the present historical situations. All would agree on the need for speedy and radical transformations in socioeconomic systems but, he asks, "what use is the best revolutionary theory when the historical subject of the revolution is not at hand or is not ready?" The subject is, of course, the people themselves, with whom the various elites have lost contact. Speaking out of his own European context, Moltmann believes that the most realistic and promising movement at present is democratic socialism, since "in the European countries—and here we include also the United States—one cannot develop socialism at the cost of democracy." He marshals a number of convincing arguments to explain the people's rejection of the "state socialism" of Russia and the East European countries while admitting that the applicability of his views to the Latin American context will have to be judged by the Latins themselves.[101]

In concluding, the German theologian amplifies a remark made at the beginning of his letter with regard to the need for overcoming provincialism and creating a "common world-theology." This is seen as absolutely necessary, for the common goal of all "lies in a world society in which human beings no longer live against but with each other."[102] It is highly probable that the debate over a world-theology will be sharpened still further, as the Latin Americans reply with equal candor to Moltmann's incisive remarks. Moreover, the debate promises to have immense consequences for all Protestant churches, since Moltmann is one of the most influential Protestant theologians on the European scene while in November of 1975 Míguez Bonino was elected as one of the six presidents of the World Council of Churches.

Dialogue with Other Continents

Some developments in the dialogue in other parts of the world will now be surveyed rather briefly. Within the Western Hemisphere the important 1975 conference in Mexico City has already been mentioned. In the Caribbean area an excellent example of Latin American influence may be seen in the work of Michael McCormick, entitled "Liberation or Development: The Role of the Church in the New Caribbean."[103] McCormick forthrightly states his thesis in the following terms: "The basic problem facing the Caribbean today is not under-development, but dependency, the solution to which is not development but liberation."[104] In the same area, an influence is apparent in the vigorous speech that Michael Manley, Prime Minister of Jamaica, delivered at the World Council of Churches assembly in Nairobi; in his address, entitled "From the Shackles of Domination and Oppression," Manley even quotes verbatim from the Medellín documents of 1968.[105]

If we move to North America, we find that the dialogue does not appear to have reached as yet the level of systematic analysis achieved in Europe. In my view the Canadian Gregory Baum has advanced furthest in this regard, as evidenced by his long article on the Detroit conference[106] and by his responses to Latin American views in his book *Religion and Alienation*.[107] Robert McAfee Brown has also turned his attention to liberation theology in his writings of the last several years;[108] unlike Baum's more analytic approach, however, his emphasis has been on the changes that the Latin American movement calls for in North American lifestyles, noting that "if we take liberation theology seriously, we will have to reexamine our jobs. . . . We will have to become uneasy with our affluent standard of living. . . . We will have to question the whole fabric of our culture."[109]

The Detroit meeting of 1975, moreover, marked an important contact of liberation theologians with leading representatives of black theology, such as James Cone and J. Deotis Roberts, of women's theology, including Sheila Collins and Beverly Harrison, and with members of other minority groups within the United States. Although the exchanges there were at times rather sharp because of divergent perspectives, the contacts that were made promise very fruitful developments in the future. In this area, too, Frederick Herzog has published significant interpretations on both the black and Latin American liberation movements from a white, Protestant perspective.[110] A Mexican-American priest, Virgilo Elizondo, director of the Mexican-American Cultural Center in San Antonio has also been quite sympathetic to liberation theology, and this will undoubtedly influence him in his key role of interpreting the Chicano experience and its future directions in this country.[111] Some other Americans who have contributed important studies in explicit contact with liberation theology include Francis Fiorenza, John Coleman, Rosemary Ruether, Phillip Berryman, Monika Hellwig, and Glenn R. Bucher.[112]

If we turn to Asia and Africa, it is readily apparent that the religious and cultural situations encountered there differ greatly from those found in Latin America. However, these two continents do share a fundamental third-world outlook from their position on the periphery of the centers of political and economic power. Thus, the powerful voices emanating from Latin America have been carefully listened to, and the possibilities are already being explored as to whether these voices may be helpful in articulating and directing distinctively Asian and African paths for the future.

Greater clarity concerning this dialogue will certainly be achieved as the results of the international conferences already mentioned are published. At any rate, it is patently obvious that the world-theology proposed by Moltmann is already in the process of creation in every corner of the global village. Whether the prophecy of Robert McAfee Brown will be fulfilled, namely, that "leadership in the future, theological or otherwise, is not going to come from Europeans and North Americans, but from Asians, Africans and Latin Americans"[113] must be left for the time being to the verdict of history.

NOTES

1. Gustave Weigel, "Theology in South America," *Theological Studies* 9 (1948): 561–66. The citation is from p. 561.

2. Ibid., p. 565.

3. Ibid., p. 566.

4. José Míguez Bonino, *Doing Theology in a Revolutionary Situation* (Philadelphia: Fortress Press, 1975), p. xix. Hugo Assmann also observes in *Opresión-liberación: Desafío a los cristianos* (Montevideo: Tierra Nueva, 1971) that "the verbal expression 'Theology of Liberation' has an importance that is very relative" (p. 82).

5. Georges Casalis, "Libération et conscientization en Amérique Latine," in *Idéologies de libération et message du salut*, ed. René Metz and Jean Schlick (Strasbourg: Cerdic, 1973), p. 167.

6. Enrique Dussel, *History and the Theology of Liberation* (Maryknoll, N.Y.: Orbis Books, 1976), p. 33. Dussel's views are included here because he is the author who has written most extensively on the history of Latin American theology. However, I will stress strongly in the opening paragraphs of Chapter Three that some aspects of his analysis are oversimplified. Perhaps a better guide for understanding the history of liberation theology has been published recently by Roberto Oliveros Maqueo, *Liberación y teología: Génesis y crecimiento de una reflexión, 1966–76* (Mexico City: CRT, 1977). Unfortunately, I received the book too late for inclusion in this survey.

7. Enrique Dussel, "Sobre la historia de la teología en America Latina," in *Liberación y cautiverio: Debates en torno al método de la teología en América Latina* (Mexico City: Comité Organizador, 1975), pp. 19–68. A very helpful chronological outline is found on pp. 67–68. This book contains the papers presented at a conference of Latin American theologians at Mexico City in August 1975 and will henceforth be referred to as *Liberación y cautiverio*. Pablo Richard has published a similar historical review in *LADOC* (July/August 1977):31–41. His statement that it "is impossible to understand the Theology of Liberation apart from its historical context" (p. 31) is in accord with the purpose of this chapter. I

have published briefer surveys, utilizing some of the materials in this chapter, in "Apprentices in Freedom: Theology Since Medellín," *America* (27 May 1978): 418–21, and "Courage with Primitive Weapons," *Cross Currents* (Spring 1978):8–19.

8. *Liberación y cautiverio*, pp. 33–38.

9. Ibid., pp. 38–46.

10. Ibid., pp. 47–49.

11. Ibid., pp. 49–62. It may be noted that Dussel provides an extensive bibliography both of secular and church history in *History and the Theology of Liberation*, pp. 183–89. Some have suggested that, because of increased repression in recent years (under the banner of "national security"), Latin American theology should be referred to as a "theology of captivity." In rejecting this, I have been persuaded by the recent argument of Pablo Richard: "To set aside the theme of liberation in favor of that of captivity increases the risk of encouraging . . . hopeless defeatism and this would be the worst political service we could render to the oppressed people. The greater the captivity and repression, the more we affirm our hope and strengthen the desire for liberation" ("Liberation Theology and Current Politics," *LADOC* [July/August 1977]: 44).

12. *The Church in the Present-Day Transformation of Latin America in the Light of the Council II: Conclusions* (Washington, D.C.: Division for Latin America—USCC, 1973), p. 35.

13. *The Church in the Present-Day Transformation of Latin America in the Light of the Council I: Position Papers* (Washington, D.C.: Division for Latin America—USCC, 1973), p. 23. Note that a meeting of theologians held prior to Medellín focused precisely on this issue; cf. G. Gutiérrez, J.L. Segundo, S. Croatto, B. Catão, and J. Comblin, *Salvación y construcción del mundo* (Santiago: Nova Terra, 1968).

14. Hugo Assmann, *Theology for a Nomad Church* (Maryknoll, N.Y.: Orbis Books, 1976), p. 52. This book is a translation of the first part of Assmann's *Teología desde la praxis de la liberación: Ensayo teológico desde la América dependiente* (Salamanca: Sígueme, 1973). The British edition is entitled *Practical Theology of Liberation* (London: Search, 1975).

15. Ibid., pp. 52–53.

16. Gustavo Gutiérrez, *Teología de la liberación: Perspectivas* (Lima: CEP, 1971). The English translation is entitled *A Theology of Liberation: History, Politics and Salvation* (Maryknoll, N.Y.: Orbis Books, 1973).

17. *Christians and Socialism: Documentation of the Christians for Socialism Movement in Latin America*, ed. John Eagleson (Maryknoll, N.Y.: Orbis Books, 1975), p. 174.

18. *Fe cristiana y cambio social en América Latina: Encuentro de El Escorial, 1972* (Salamanca: Sígueme, 1973).

19. See n. 7 above; italics are mine. For a very lively and colorful account of the Mexico City conference, see Vicente Leñero, "Teología de la liberación," *Christus* (October 1975):62–70.

20. See Alfred T. Hennelly, "Who Does Theology in the Americas?," *America* (20 September 1975): 137–39; Beverly Wildung Harrison, "Challenging the Western Paradigm: The 'Theology in the Americas' Conference," *Christianity and Crisis* (27 October 1975): 251–54; Alice Hageman, "Liberating Theology Through Action," *Christian Century* (1 October 1975): 850–53; Robert McAfee Brown, "Reflections on Detroit," *Christianity and Crisis* (27 October 1975): 255–56; and Sheila Collins, "Liberation Theology: A Challenge to American Christians," *JSAC Grapevine* (September 1975), no pagination. The longest and most thorough account and analysis of the meeting was published by Gregory Baum in *Ecumenist*

(September–October 1975):81–100, and entitled "The Christian Left at Detroit."
More recently, a full account of the meeting, together with position papers and
pertinent articles, was published as Sergio Torres and John Eagleson, eds.,
Theology in the Americas (Maryknoll, N.Y.: Orbis, 1976).

21. The proceedings of the Dar es Salaam meeting were published in Sergio
Torres and Virginia Fabella, eds., *The Emergent Gospel: Theology from the Underside of History* (Maryknoll, N.Y.: Orbis Books, 1978). The results of the
conference in Ghana may be found in *African Theology En Route*, Kofi Appiah-
Kubi and Sergio Torres, eds. (Maryknoll, N.Y. Orbis Books, 1979). An excellent
account of the Ghana meeting has been published by Gayraud Wilmore in
"Theological Ferment in the Third World," *Christian Century* (15 February 1978):
164–68. The address of Theology in the Americas is 475 Riverside Drive, Room
1268, New York, N.Y. 10027; the address of the Ecumenical Association of Third
World Theologians is: 475 Riverside Drive, 16th floor, New York, N.Y. 10027.

22. Gustavo Gutiérrez, *Theology of Liberation*, pp. 3–15. Gutiérrez does not
provide an explicit definition of praxis but speaks in general terms, e.g., when he
notes that his "intention is to recognize the work and importance of concrete
behavior, of deeds, of action, of praxis in the Christian life" (p. 10). An excellent
analysis of the concept in contemporary thought is Richard J. Bernstein's *Praxis
and Action: Contemporary Philosophers of Human Activity* (Philadelphia: University of Pennsylvania Press, 1971).

23. Gutiérrez, *Theology of Liberation*, p. 15.

24. Ibid., pp. 8–10.

25. Ibid., pp. 21–42.

26. Ibid., p. 53.

27. Ibid., p. 72. Gutiérrez traces the term "New Christendom" to Maritain's
work *True Humanism* (New York: Charles Scribner's Sons, 1938) and asserts that
this helped give rise to the modern parties of "socio-Christian" inspiration (p. 59,
notes 7 and 11).

28. Gutiérrez, *Theology of Liberation*, p. 84.

29. Ibid., p. 88.

30. Ibid., pp. 101–31.

31. Ibid., p. 168.

32. Gutiérrez's proposals for a spirituality of liberation encompass pp. 203–8;
his basic understanding of a "spirituality" is as follows: "Spirituality, in the strict
and profound sense of the word, is the dominion of the Spirit. . . . A spirituality is a
concrete manner, inspired by the Spirit, of living the Gospel; it is a definite way of
living 'before the Lord,' in solidarity with all men, 'with the Lord,' and before men"
(pp. 203–4).

33. Ibid., p. 215. Here Gutiérrez buttresses his position with the interesting
remark of Paul Ricoeur that "only utopia can give economic, social, and political
action a human focus." The reference given is to Ricoeur's article, "Tâches de
l'éducateur politique," in *Esprit* (July–August 1965):90.

34. Gutiérrez, *Theology of Liberation*, p. 232. With regard to the much disputed
question of the relationship of Jesus to the Zealots, Gutiérrez believes that "Jesus
kept his distance from the Zealot movement. The awareness of the universality of
his mission did not conform with the somewhat narrow nationalism of the
Zealots. . . . The message of Jesus is addressed to all men. . . . In this he was even
more revolutionary than the Zealots . . ." (p. 227).

35. Ibid., p. 262.

36. Ibid., p. 301. After an insightful discussion of the meaning of Christian
poverty (pp. 287–302), Gutiérrez ends wryly with the comment that "the absence of
a sufficient commitment to the poor, the marginated, and the exploited is perhaps

the fundamental reason why we have no solid contemporary reflection on the witness of poverty."

37. *Cristianismo y tercer mundo* (Madrid: ZYX, 1973).

38. The description of the four approaches is given on pp. 17–34; the theological analysis of them occupies pp. 37–83.

39. Ibid., pp. 85–109.

40. The book is entitled *Praxis de liberación y fe cristiana* (Madrid: ZYX, 1974). The shorter version is called "Evangelio y praxis de liberación" and appears in *Fe cristiana y cambio social*, pp. 231–45.

41. Cf. especially the chapter "Hacia una iglesia del pueblo" in *Praxis de liberación y fe cristiana*, pp. 45–55. Articles by Gutiérrez that have appeared in English include the following: "Jesus and the Political World," *Worldview* (September 1972):43–46; "Liberation and Development," *Cross Currents* (Summer 1971):243–56; "Liberation Movements in Theology," in *Concilium 93: Jesus Christ and Human Freedom* (New York: Herder and Herder, 1974), pp. 135–46; "Liberation, Theology and Proclamation," in *Concilium 96: The Mystical and Political Dimension of the Christian Faith* (New York: Herder and Herder, 1974), pp. 57–77; and "Faith as Freedom: Solidarity with the Alienated and Confidence in the Future," *Horizons* (Spring 1975):25–60. His most recent books are *Líneas pastorales de la Iglesia en América Latina*, 2nd ed. (Lima: CEP, 1976) and *Teología desde el reverso de la historia* (Lima: CEP, 1977).

42. Segundo Galilea, "Liberation as an Encounter with Politics and Contemplation," in *Concilium 96*, p. 20.

43. Cf. *Hacia una pastoral vernácula* (Barcelona: Nova Terra, 1966).

44. *Contemplación y apostolado* (Bogotá: Indo-American Press, 1972).

45. Ibid., p. 12.

46. *Espiritualidad de la liberación* (Santiago: ISPAJ, 1973).

47. Ibid., p. 7.

48. Ibid., pp. 8–10.

49. Ibid., p. 18.

50. Ibid., p. 19.

51. Ibid., p. 36.

52. Other articles of Galilea include "Liberation Theology began with Medellín," *LADOC* (May 1975):1–6; and "Spiritual Awakening and Movements of Liberation in Latin America," in *Concilium 89: Spiritual Renewals* (New York: Herder and Herder, 1973), pp. 129–38. The "militant-contemplative" synthesis closely approximates the fusion of the "neo-mystic" and the "neo-militant" that Harvey Cox proposes in *The Feast of Fools* (Cambridge: Harvard University Press, 1969). For an interesting adaptation of liberation theology to Ignatian spirituality, see José Magaña, *A Strategy for Liberation: Notes for Orienting the Exercises toward Utopia* (Hicksville, N.Y.: Exposition Press, 1974).

53. *Opresión-liberación: Desafío a los cristianos*, p. 76 and also p. 138.

54. *Jesucristo el liberador* (Buenos Aires: Latinoamérica Libros, 1975). The text quoted here is the Spanish translation of the third Portuguese edition. Boff's book has recently been translated into English as *Jesus Christ Liberator: A Critical Christology for Our Time* (Maryknoll, N.Y.: Orbis Books, 1978). Other works on Christology include: Héctor Borrat, "Para una cristología de la vanguardia," *Víspera* 17 (1970):26–31; Ignacio Ellacuría, "The Prophetic Mission of Jesus," and "Jesus' Own Consciousness of His Mission," in *Freedom Made Flesh: The Mission of Christ and His Church* (Maryknoll, N.Y.: Orbis Books, 1976), pp. 23–51 and 53–79; Jon Sobrino, "El Jesús histórico: Crisis y desafío para la fe," *Estudios Centroamericanos* (April 1975):201–24. The latter article has been incorporated into Sobrino's *Cristología desde América Latina: Esbozo a partir del seguimiento*

del Jesús histórico (Mexico City: Ediciones CRT, 1976). This book is an original and creative work that should have great influence; however, I did not obtain it in time to give it the careful treatment here that it deserves. An English translation now exists: *Christology at the Crossroads* (Maryknoll, N.Y.: Orbis Books, 1978).

55. *Jesucristo el liberador*, p. 59.

56. Ibid.

57. Ibid., pp. 59–60.

58. Ibid., p. 60.

59. Ibid.

60. Ibid., p. 61.

61. Ibid. In the same vein, Boff notes that "faith does not proclaim another world, but a *new* world" ("Salvation in Jesus Christ and the Process of Liberation," in *Concilium 96*, p. 87). He has also presented the Latin American approach elsewhere in a very succinct manner: "Without reflection, praxis is blind; without praxis, reflection is empty" ("¿Qué es hacer teología desde América Latina?" in *Liberación y cautiverio*, p. 144).

62. Among the books Boff has published are the following: *O evangelho do Cristo cósmico* (Petrópolis, 1970); *Die Kirche als Sakrament im Horizont der Welterfahrung* (Paderborn, 1972); *O destino do homem e do mundo* (3rd ed.; Petrópolis, 1974); *Vida para além da morte* (3rd ed.; Petrópolis, 1974); and *A vida religiosa e a Igreja no processo de libertação* (Petrópolis, 1975).

63. "¿Qué es hacer teología desde América Latina?" *Liberación y cautiverio*, p. 131.

64. Bernard Lonergan, *Method in Theology* (New York: Herder and Herder, 1972). For example, José Comblin advances one "suspicion" and two objections against Lonergan (*Liberación y cautiverio*, pp. 517–19). I shall not attempt to summarize these, but the tone can be captured in the following quote: "I believe that none of the medieval theologians nor any other one would have spent even a quarter of an hour doing theology, if theology were what Fr. Lonergan says it is, that is, the study of a system of meanings (*significados*) in order to move to another system of meanings" (p. 518). See also the remark of Assmann in the same volume: "Personally I am not situated in the system of Lonergan: he was my professor in Christology and the Trinity, but I think I have realized that his theology does not lead to history . . ." (p. 296).

65. Ignacio Ellacuría, "Posibilidad, necesidad y sentido de una teología latinoamericana," *Christus* (February 1975): 12–16, and ibid. (March 1975):17–23.

66. Raúl Vidales, *Cuestiones en torno al método en la teología de la liberación* (Lima: Secretariado latinoamericano, 1974).

67. Ibid., p. 1.

68. Jon Sobrino, "El conocimiento teológico en la teología europea y latinoamericana," in *Liberación y cautiverio*, pp. 177–207. I have treated this article at greater length in "Theological Method: The Southern Exposure," *Theological Studies* (December 1977):709–35.

69. Ibid., p. 181.

70. Ibid., p. 189.

71. Ibid., p. 185.

72. Ibid., p. 189.

73. Ibid., p. 187.

74. Ibid., p. 192.

75. Ibid., p. 195.

76. Ibid., p. 201. Sobrino adds here that he believes Moltmann's book *The Crucified God* is of great importance because it marks the introduction of the epistemological break into European theological thought.

77. Ibid., p. 207. I would repeat that Sobrino's article could lead to an extraordinarily fruitful dialogue with European and North American theologians; however, it should be considered in its entirety since it is considerably more nuanced and tightly reasoned than a mere summary indicates.

78. *Marx y la biblia: Crítica a la filosofía de la opresión* (Salamanca: Sígueme, 1971). The English translation is *Marx and the Bible: A Critique of the Philosophy of Oppression* (Maryknoll, N.Y.: Orbis Books, 1974). Both personally and in his writings, Miranda has an extremely forceful approach, as a few characteristic quotes from his book will indicate: "One of the most disastrous errors in the history of Christianity is to have tried—under the influence of Greek definitions—to differentiate between love and justice. . . . Love is not love without a passion for justice" (English translation, pp. 61–62); "if the West calls Marx utopian, it must first give up its pretense and call the gospel utopian" (ibid., p. 225). See also by the same author *El ser y el mesías* (Salamanca: Sígueme, 1973) and *El cristianismo de Marx* (Mexico City, 1978). The English translation of *El ser y el mesías* is *Being and the Messiah* (Maryknoll, N.Y.: Orbis Books, 1977); an English translation of *El cristianismo de Marx* is forthcoming from Orbis Books. An example of western reaction to Miranda may be found in the rather acerbic review of *Marx and the Bible* by John L. McKenzie in *Journal of Biblical Literature* 94 (1975):280–81.

79. J. Severino Croatto, *Liberación y libertad: Pautas hermenéuticas* (Buenos Aires: Mundo Nuevo, 1973). His articles in the Argentinean periodical *Revista Bíblica* include the following: "El Mesías liberador de los pobres" (32, 1970): 233–40; " 'Liberación' y libertad" (33, 1971): 3–7; " 'Dios en el acontecimiento,' " (35, 1973): 52–60; " 'Hombre nuevo' y 'liberación' en la carta a los Romanos" (36, 1974): 37–45; and "Las estructuras de poder en la Biblia" (37, 1975): 115–28.

80. A good example of this combination is Castillo's article, "Confesar a Cristo el Señor y seguir a Jesús: Ortodoxia y ortopraxis desde la perspectiva de Marcos," in *Christus* (December 1975):19–31. Castillo like other Latin Americans emphasizes the concrete "following" of Jesus. On the relation of orthodoxy and orthopraxis, he concludes that "to know Jesus does not precede following Jesus; rather both realities constitute necessary dialectical categories" (ibid., pp. 29–30). Another promising newcomer in the field of biblical studies is Francisco López Rivera. See his recent *Biblia y sociedad: Cuatro estudios exegéticos* (Mexico City: CRT, 1977).

81. In the article already cited, "El Jesús histórico: Crisis y desafío para la fe," Sobrino concludes as follows: "In the resurrection of Christ there appears the definitive promise of the goal toward which we are traveling; but it is in the historical Jesus that there appears the way to make that journey. To go to God means to make God real in history, to build his kingdom, and we only know that from Jesus and not from any abstract concept of divinity" (ibid., p. 224).

82. In addition to the works cited earlier, Dussel's books include: *Hipótesis para una historia de la Iglesia en América Latina* (Barcelona: Estela, 1967); *Historia de la Iglesia en América Latina: Coloniaje y liberación (1492–1972)* (Barcelona: Nova Terra, 1972); and *Caminos de liberación latinoamericana: Interpretación histórica de nuestro continente latinoamericano*, 2 vols. (Buenos Aires: Latinoamérica Libros, 1972–73).

83. *Para una ética de la liberación latinoamericana*, 3 vols. (Mexico City: Siglo Veintiuno, 1973).

84. *Ama y haz lo que quieras: Hacia una ética del hombre nuevo* (Buenos Aires: Escatón, 1972). The book is a valuable reinterpretation of Christian ethics from a liberation perspective. One quote may serve to illustrate the "praxis" orientation: "Faith is a new *reality* which has invaded our world, a new *situation* in which we have been placed, a new *power* which may be seen in its actuation, a new *form of*

existence which has been made accessible to us'' (ibid., p. 46, italics are the author's).

85. ''Visión del cambio social y sus tareas desde las iglesias cristianas no-católicas,'' in *Fe cristiana y cambio social en América Latina,* pp. 179–202. Míguez's most recent works in English are *Christians and Marxists: The Mutual Challenge to Revolution* (Grand Rapids, Mich.: Wm. B. Eerdmans Publishing Company, 1976), and *Room to Be People* (Philadelphia: Fortress Press, 1979).

86. *A Theology of Human Hope* (Washington D.C.: Corpus, 1969). See especially his last chapter, ''Theology as a Language of Freedom,'' pp. 159–68. The Spanish edition of this work is *Religión: ¿Opio o instrumento de liberación?* (Montevideo: Tierra Nueva, 1970).

87. *Tomorrow's Child* (New York: Harper and Row, 1972), p. 187.

88. *Christianity and Crisis* (17 September 1973): 173–76. In this very compact and closely reasoned article, he rejects North American ''Christian realism,'' and his basic argument is that ''realism's revolt against utopias is a sign that it participates in the revolt against transcendence that characterizes Western civilization'' (ibid.). Another important article of Alves is ''Theology and the Liberation of Man'' in *New Theology No. 9* (New York: Macmillan, 1972), pp. 230–50. In this essay he has presented a now famous biblical definition of truth as related to praxis: ''Truth is the name given by an historical community to those historical acts which were, are, and will be, effective for the liberation of man. Truth is action'' (p. 237).

89. *Opresión-liberación: Desafío a los cristianos,* p. 106. The terms he uses are ''prólogos en busca del coraje'' and ''el coraje con armas primitivas.'' Assmann is very prolific and perhaps the most radical of the liberation theologians; many of his major orientations can be found in outline in a series of articles he published in the Uruguayan monthly, *Perspectivas de Diálogo:* ''Fe y promoción humana'' (August 1969):177–85; ''Iglesia y proyecto histórico'' (October 1970):239–47; ''Teología política'' (December 1970):306–12; and ''El aporte cristiano al proceso de liberación de América Latina'' (June 1971):95–105.

90. ''Notes on Moral Theology: April–September 1975,'' *Theological Studies* (March 1976):112.

91. *The Crucified God: The Cross of Christ as the Foundation and Criticism of Christian Theology* (New York: Harper and Row, 1974). I will give references to this edition, since Míguez Bonino's own references appear to be to the German original or to a Spanish translation.

92. *Doing Theology in a Revolutionary Situation,* p. 146.

93. *The Crucified God,* p. 329.

94. *Doing Theology in a Revolutionary Situation,* p. 174.

95. Ibid., p. 148.

96. Ibid., p. 95.

97. Ibid., p. 149.

98. ''An Open Letter to José Míguez Bonino,'' *Christianity and Crisis* (29 March 1976). Moltmann also expresses his differences with Rubem Alves, Juan Luis Segundo, and Gustavo Gutiérrez in the letter, but these will not be considered at the moment. The German theologian says he has broken off the dialogue with Assmann because of the latter's recently proclaimed policy of ''incommunication'' with Europeans. It may be noted that Assmann had published criticisms of Moltmann very similar to Míguez Bonino's several years earlier; see *Opresión-liberación: Desafío a los cristianos* (1971), pp. 119ff.

99. ''An Open Letter to José Míguez Bonino,'' pp. 57–59.

100. Ibid., pp. 59–60. Moltmann also refers to a similar suggestion made by J. B. Metz in a recent article: ''Kirche und Volk oder der Preis der Orthodoxie,'' *Stimmen der Zeit* (11, 1974):797–811.

101. Moltmann, "An Open Letter To José Míguez Bonino," pp. 60–62.

102. Ibid., p. 62. Over a year before Moltmann's remarks on a "world-theology," I argued for the same thing in the course of an analysis of liberation theology: "Beyond the consideration of any specific area's transient historical situation, a process has been initiated in which the hitherto voiceless majority of mankind can be heard and respected as an equal partner in the global articulation of Christianity. In brief, the age of theological imperialism is over, and a new era is beginning" ("Today's New Task: Geotheology," in *America* [18 January 1975]:29).

103. Bridgetown, Barbados: CADEC, 1971.

104. Ibid., p. 8.

105. Manley's speech was given at a plenary session of the World Council of Churches Fifth Assembly in Nairobi, Kenya, in November of 1975. It was published in *Ecumenical Review* (January 1976):49–65; the quotes from Medellín are found on pp. 64–65.

106. "The Christian Left at Detroit," *Ecumenist* (September-October 1975): 81–100.

107. *Religion and Alienation: A Sociological Reading of Theology* (New York: Paulist Press, 1975). Other book-length studies that could serve as models for future theological work in North America include Marie Augusta Neal, *A Socio-Theology of Letting Go: The Role of a First World Church Facing Third World Peoples* (New York: Paulist Press, 1977), and John C. Haughey, ed., *The Faith That Does Justice: Examining the Christian Sources for Social Change*, Woodstock Studies 2 (New York: Paulist Press, 1977).

108. See especially "Reflections on 'Liberation Theology' " in *Religion in Life* (Autumn 1974):269–82. Brown has recently expanded these reflections and reviewed the whole field of liberation theology in *Theology in a New Key: Responding to Liberation Themes* (Philadelphia: Westminster Press, 1978).

109. "Reflections on 'Liberation Theology,' " p. 273.

110. See especially Herzog's book, *Liberation Theology: Liberation in the Light of the Fourth Gospel* (New York: Seabury Press, 1972). His recent articles include "Liberation Hermeneutic as Ideology Critique?" *Interpretation* (October 1974):387–403; "Which Liberation Theology?" *Religion in Life* (Winter 1975):448–53; and "Liberation and Imagination," *Interpretation* (July 1978): 227–41.

111. See references to Elizondo's writings in Chapter One, n. 77.

112. Francis Fiorenza, "Latin American Liberation Theology," *Interpretation* (October 1974):441–57, and "Political Theology and Liberation Theology: An Inquiry into their Fundamental Meaning," in *Liberation, Revolution and Freedom: Theological Perspectives* (New York: Seabury Press, 1975), pp. 3–29; John Coleman, "Vision and Praxis in American Theology," *Theological Studies* (March 1976):3–40; Rosemary Ruether, "Latin American Theology of Liberation and the Birth of a Planetary Humanity," in *Liberation Theology: Human Hope Confronts Christian History and American Power* (New York: Paulist Press, 1972), pp. 175–94; Phillip Berryman, "Latin American Liberation Theology," *Theological Studies* (September 1973):375–95; Monika Hellwig, "Liberation Theology: An Emerging School," *Scottish Journal of Theology* 30 (1976):137–51; Glenn R. Bucher, "Toward a Liberation Theology for the 'Oppressor,' " *Journal of the American Academy of Religion* 44 (1976):517–34; and David R. Peel, "Juan Luis Segundo's 'A Theology for Artisans of a New Humanity': A Latin American Contribution to Contemporary Theological Understanding," *The Perkins Journal* 31 (Spring 1977):1–9.

113. Brown, "Reflections on 'Liberation Theology,' " p. 277. In a similar vein

Glenn R. Bucher has commented rather ironically that "it is safe to suggest that liberation theologies will continue to frequent the theological scene for some time since they do not arise from the 'edge' but from the emerging, vast human 'center' only misperceived by some as the edge" ("Toward a Liberation Theology for the 'Oppressor,' " p. 519).

CHAPTER THREE

WHAT IS A CHRISTIAN?

A common procedure in western theological inquiry is to search for the origins of new theological movements in other developments that preceded these movements and that provided the seminal ideas for the new direction. Thus, for instance, the origins of liberation theology are sometimes traced to the Second Vatican Council, especially to its Pastoral Constitution on the Church in the Modern World in 1965. Another hypothesis consists in viewing liberation theology as an "application" to Latin America of the political theology that arose in Europe during the decade of the sixties.

In this chapter and the following one, I will analyze several works of Juan Luis Segundo that were published as early as 1962 and that were the product of lectures delivered in the two years preceding that date. I believe that such an inquiry will demonstrate that the historical analyses mentioned above are oversimplifications or even distortions of the facts. For in these early works Segundo was already presenting basic theological ideas along liberation lines that were prior to and independent of both Vatican II and European political theology. The important conclusion is that the liberation movement is indigenous to Latin America and possesses a dynamism and originality that is peculiar to that continent. Segundo, moreover, is certainly the most prolific representative of the movement, having produced fifteen books as well as numerous articles in a wide variety of publications over the past two decades. After I had surveyed the general contours of liberation theology, therefore, a study of his writings appeared to open up the most promising path forward for advancing theological dialogue in the Americas. In this chapter, I will begin with a brief introduction on Segundo and afterwards proceed to the investigation of his early books.

Background and Method

Segundo was born in Montevideo in 1925 and has spent most of his life working in Uruguay.[1] After entering the Society of Jesus, he completed his philosophical studies in neighboring Argentina. Ordained to the priesthood in 1955, he received his licentiate in theology in 1956 from the University of

Louvain. In 1963 he obtained a Doctorate in Letters from the University of Paris, submitting for this degree a study of the thought of Nicolas Berdyaev and a two-volume work on ecclesiology.[2] Segundo founded the Peter Faber Center for social and theological studies at Montevideo in 1965, and in the following year began publication of a monthly entitled *Perspectivas de Diálogo*, which served as an official organ of the Center. The periodical was abruptly suppressed by the Uruguayan government in 1975, and soon afterward the Center was closed by Segundo's religious superiors.

It is important to note that Segundo has not been employed as a university teacher in Uruguay, although he has taught as a visiting professor in the United States. Much of his theology has been elaborated in dialogue with colleagues at the Peter Faber Center and with communities of lay Christians; this has contributed to an underlying pastoral orientation that pervades most of his published work. Clearly then his writing is not directed primarily to the academic community nor is it dominated by the interests or methods of that community. His audience is rather adult members of the church in his own country and the rest of Latin America, while his interest has been to contribute to the continuous religious and intellectual maturation of that audience.

An "Open" Theology

A possible way of organizing a study of the thought of Segundo would be the one usually employed in a systematic theology. One could search for the fundamental systematic contents that dominate the author's corpus of writings, isolate these in a suitable framework, and then select further texts from all the various stages of his work that support, amplify, or clarify the basic structural elements that have been discovered.

I believe, however, that a more fruitful approach for understanding his thought consists in treating it from the outset not as a systematic theology but rather as an "open" theology. By using this term, I mean to stress the fact that in his approach methodological principles that allow for constant growth and development take precedence over a systematically organized body of theological contents. His most extensive work (a five-volume series) is thus accurately described in the original Spanish title as an "open theology for an adult laity."[3]

Consequently, I will attempt to adapt to the approach of an open theology throughout the present dialogue. Beginning with the author's earliest works, I will discuss the major themes that occur, leaving their subsequent development to the chapters that follow. In this process an entire book or article will as much as possible be considered in its totality, since this appears preferable to the selection of scattered texts from a number of diverse writings. The chapter divisions, moreover, are not intended as systematic outlines but as functional heuristic devices that appeared to be suitable for understanding the main avenues that Segundo has investigated thus far. Since he is at present in mid-career as a theologian, it would seem reasonable to suppose that an analysis of his work written ten or fifteen years from now would manifest a quite different pattern of organization.

In this connection Jon Sobrino has recently drawn attention to the interesting fact that the distinguished German theologian Karl Rahner had been actually producing a transcendental theology for almost thirty years before proceeding to a detailed analysis of his transcendental method.[4] I believe that Segundo, too, has been using his own method (referred to by him as the "hermeneutic circle") for the past fifteen years and has only recently produced a detailed analysis of it. Since the late articulation of method in Rahner did not prevent the understanding of his earlier work, I believe the same can be said of Segundo. Consequently, a thorough discussion of the latter's method and hermeneutic will be postponed to a later chapter of this book.

Also, at the end of this and subsequent chapters, I will present some of my own reflections on how the ideas presented may be of value in theologizing from my own historical situation, that is, from the developed nation that is the United States of America. It should be stressed that I do not intend to work out these reflections in any detail in the present volume. They can thus best be understood as preliminary sketches for future theological elaboration and development.

With that background we can now turn to a discussion of Segundo's earliest writings. Two of these works were first delivered as public lectures in 1962 and are entitled *Pre-Christian Stages of Faith: The Idea of God in the Old Testament* and—a complementary work—*The Christian Understanding of Humanity.*[5] His first theological work to appear in printed form was also published in 1962 as *The Function of the Church in the Reality of the River Plate.*[6] In these books the author comes to grips with a very fundamental theological issue: what is the basic Christian message? The question can also be paraphrased from different perspectives. How are we to understand the God revealed progressively in the history of the Old Testament and definitively in the life, death, and resurrection of Jesus Christ in the New Testament? Or, how does this revelation affect our conception of the human person, that is, what is the Christian understanding of the person? Finally, in briefest form, the question is expressed in our chapter heading: "What is a Christian?"

In seeking answers to the above question, I will first examine the work *Pre-Christian Stages of Faith.* Here Segundo establishes a fundamental principle that continues to be employed and developed even in his latest work: the Bible must be understood not merely as a "sacred history revealed by God to certain writers" but also, on a much more profound level, as "the education in faith of God's chosen people, provided by him in the different stages of that same education."[7] Thus it is essential for

Segundo to discern the various stages of this vast educational process in the Old Testament, for he views it as functioning as an essential propaedeutic for understanding the radical novelty of the revelation contained in the New Testament. It may be noted in passing that he considers the same educational process to be the continuing central function of Scripture within the ongoing history of the Christian churches.

In delineating the stages mentioned, Segundo utilizes the generally accepted results of scriptural scholarship that the Old Testament contains various levels of redaction or editing of the sacred history by the Yahwistic, Elohistic, Deuteronomic, and Priestly schools[8] as well as similar processes of reinterpretation in the prophetic and sapiential movements. From this perspective he distinguishes *four* stages in the development of the Old Testament, which he considers critical for the understanding of God and of the human encounter with God. In each of the four levels, an attempt is made to discern authentic religious elements and also to point out some deficiencies or immature elements that are involved. Moreover, the entire process must not be understood as a series of abrupt and unrelated transitions but as a dialectical movement in the course of which previous conceptions are purified and then integrated into new syntheses. After the analysis of each level, the author presents a brief survey of the contemporary church and indicates the various modalities in which these pre-Christian conceptions continue to exist, at least on the level of practice, in the lives of modern believers.

The Sacral Stage

The first of the stages is to be found in what are generally considered to be the earliest redactions of the Old Testament: the Yahwistic source, composed in Judah in the ninth century B.C., and the Elohistic account, written not too long after this in the southern kingdom of Israel.[9] After an analysis of several texts from this period, Segundo concludes that at this point God is not yet understood as the universal, all-powerful being with whom we associate that term today. Rather his power appears to be confined within the territory of Israel (as in the story of Cain: Gen. 4:13 ff.), and other deities are considered to be existing outside this sphere of influence.

Furthermore, Israel's encounter with God within this framework is understood to take place primarily in the sphere of the terrible and the mysterious or inexplicable. Specific examples of these characteristics of the encounter are analyzed, including the attitude of Moses with regard to the burning bush (Exod. 3:1ff.), the fear of the people after the proclamation of the decalogue (Exod. 20:18–19), and the death of Uzzah for accidentally touching the ark (2 Sam. 6:3ff.). Since God in this conception is totally removed from the realm of the familiar and the secular, it follows that the human encounter with him must necessarily be mediated by utilization of the nonfamiliar and the nonsecular, that is, through sacred spokesmen, sacred places, sacred objects, and sacred rituals. Human freedom and indeed any human intentionality are all but lost sight of within this perspective; rather the overwhelming emphasis is focused on carefully prescribed cultic gestures, in the proper time and place, in order to please and win over the favor of the deity. In summary, holiness or purity in this view is transmitted by physical contact, and even an accidental violation of sacral regulations, as in the case of Uzzah mentioned above, could result in the death of the offender.

Although at first glance this may appear to be a bizarre and primitive form of religious understanding, Segundo is careful to point out the authentic element it contains:

We must understand that, in the evolution of conscious human existence, it is very difficult for something of great importance, which totally surpasses humanity, to develop in any other way. . . . Certainly the first stage is still almost totally exterior, but this is the inevitable law of all human education: gradually to penetrate into the interior by means of the sensible.[10]

On the other hand, he also adverts to the severe limitations of the approach, since the divine appears to be alienated from ordinary human existence, and humanity seems doomed to the use of various forms of "sacred magic" in the attempt to exercise influence on the caprice of an arbitrary divine power.

But this analysis of the basic attitudes of the first phase of religious consciousness must not be seen as possessing mere antiquarian or historical interest; rather Segundo emphasizes that the attitudes are present, in varying degrees of intensity, in the religious understanding and practice of the contemporary church. This is seen to be especially true with regard to the sacraments, where "we are told that the interior is required, true; but existentially it is considered of lesser importance. A fundamental, habitual intention is required of doing what the church does. However, what demands greater attention, since they are crucial for the efficacy of the sacrament, are the conditions for its validity."[11]

Although the sacraments are most exposed to the danger of sacred magic, the same phenomenon can appear in other areas, such as in the realm of dogma and morality. Thus external adhesion to exact dogmatic statements is sometimes assigned more religious importance than interior understanding or a vital assimilation of their meaning. And in the ethical sphere, a kind of moral magic has often developed, whereby we ask precisely what is commanded and what is allowed by authorities, without proceeding further to inquire into the rationale of the actions and of their bearing on our relationship with God and with human beings.

Segundo concludes the discussion of the first stage by summarizing the profound limitations of such conceptions in the contemporary world. By stressing externals and ignoring humanity's capacity for freedom and love, they can create a type of infantile Christianity, leaving human beings defenseless before the great problems of existence and suffocating what are more and more clearly recognized as the best and most profound qualities of the human person. In addition, such attitudes are bound to crumble before the inroads of the pervasive scientific mentality that is gradually penetrating everywhere; the unhappy result is that "one moves from this primitive religion to no religion at all or, what is worse, to a personality split between the scientific and the superstitious."[12]

The Covenant Stage

The second stage of religious understanding in the Old Testament extends from the period just discussed until the time of the exile; included in it are a first group of prophets, the account of the reform of Josiah, and a subsequent group of prophets.[13] In this period God is still not understood as universal but as the God of Israel; the religious attitude involved could be categorized as "monolatry" rather than real monotheism. The notion of the covenant is most characteristic of this phase and adds a more personal and moral dimension, as can be seen in the note of "fidelity" to Yahweh demanded of Israel by the covenant. Basically, the covenant concept includes two elements: the awareness of a divine vocation approved and sustained by a divine power, and the conviction that the decisive element in this historical destiny is moral conduct. In the covenant relationship Israel's role is seen as one of obedience to the commandments, while Yahweh fulfills his part by guiding the events of history; basically, then, Yahweh's image at this period is really that of a "moral providence." Meanwhile, in the prophets, there is an attitude of scorn for religious practice that does not touch the heart of human beings, that is, "for ritualism without a soul and without justice."[14]

Quite clearly this period represents a much closer approach of God to the center of human existence than had been possible in the previous phase. At the same time there is established an identification between religion, the task of humanity in history, and the interpretation of history that has been decisive ever since in the thought of the West.

In contemporary times this type of religious understanding has often resulted in the formation of an active or "conquistador" type of Christian; that is, it furnishes the spirituality underlying the concept of the "crusade." "Crusaders" are seen as the recipients of the plan of God which they have to realize in history; they thus divide the world neatly into the friends or enemies of God, depending on whether the others support or oppose their own plans. God is understood as preoccupied with the first group while the latter one is tolerated up to a certain point. After that point is reached, any means may be employed to crush the latter group, since one is fighting for the cause of God.

A more subtle version of this mentality also exists, basing itself on an understanding of the covenant. For implicit in the concept of the covenant at this stage is the belief that favorable events demonstrate that one has fulfilled one's moral obligations under the covenant; on the other hand, disastrous or unfortunate happenings are taken as a sign of moral failure. The upper classes in Christian countries have often applied this understanding to their own situation of wealth, explaining it by the fact that "God has blessed us," that is, "God has rewarded us" for our upright morality. And of course, he has done the opposite for the sinful lower classes.

The limitations of this religious outlook are readily apparent: "The incompatibility between the very notion of God and, on the other hand, a divine interest localized in a particular group of people, becomes increasingly evident, especially since psychology shows how easily aggressivity toward those outside our clan is disguised with noble motives."[15] Another limitation arises from the simple fact of historical experience. For history bears witness that events are not as simple as this version of the covenant pretends; thus there arise the disillusionment and bitterness of those Christians who discover that God does not always award victory to those who display his banner. The realization of this fact plays as important a role in undermining faith in the second stage of religious understanding as did the intrusion of scientific consciousness in the first period.

The Justice Stage

In his analysis of the third stage,[16] Segundo surveys a vast expanse of literature, which encompasses the periods of the exile and restoration and also includes a third group of prophets, the priestly redaction, and the Hebrew sapiential books. The profound advance in the understanding of God in this period results in his being understood now as the *only* God as well as the creator of the heavens and the earth; the frequent use of the phrase "all flesh" clearly shows that human beings and everything else are understood as creatures. Moreover, great stress is placed on the infinite holiness of God and the absolute need of his creature, resulting in both a longing for God and yet a fear in his presence.

In the Hebrew wisdom literature, however, the critical question is raised with regard to God's justice: if he is indeed just, what explanation is there for the obvious fact that the wicked prosper while the righteous suffer? The question receives its supreme embodiment in the Book of Job, and Segundo summarizes the answer as follows: "How then do we explain the providence and justice of God? It cannot be explained. It is precisely the transcendence of God which makes his providence a mystery and his justice a mystery."[17]

Again there are obvious advances in this stage of religious understanding, for it frees the conception of God from all particularism while his transcendence is clearly recognized. Thus, too, a kind of dialectic between the stages becomes apparent. In the first stage God appeared as remote and unapproachable; in the second stage he drew nearer through the covenant, but in a certain sense *too* near, for the people of Israel thought that by means of the covenant they could control God and the events of history. Now, in the third stage, there occurs a kind of backward step, brought about by the clear recognition of God's transcendence. The result is an extraordinarily "pure" religion involving total surrender to God, for the human person "understands himself or herself as totally needing God and totally incapable of understanding the ways of the Most High. Finally, adoration and religious fear, that is, the acceptance of creatureliness, become characteristic of religious wisdom."[18]

Segundo believes that this type of religious consciousness is extant today but not in as massive a way as was apparent in the first two stages. Indeed, it maintains the position of being "true Christianity" in direct opposition to the fanaticism or superstition of the masses. Its approach consists in dividing the world neatly into two planes: there exists the horizontal, historical, or profane dimension, where humanity acts; and parallel to this is the vertical or sacred plane, where God acts in his own mysterious ways. Thus the foreseeable in life is envisioned as the human and the unforeseeable as the divine. From this perspective the inequality between rich and poor, for example, is understood as resulting from the mysterious will of God, in the same way as the occurrence of health or sickness. Within Catholicism it can result in an outlook wherein "Christians separate what is religious and vertical from all that is achieved horizontally in history, that is, from the profane. And they give supreme importance, at least theoretically, to the first element. It does not matter how people live, so long as they say yes to God by means of the moral life and the sacraments."[19]

It follows from this that the truly religious action is considered to be that of the cleric, whose primary concern is with the sacred dimension. Also the only true evil in the world from this perspective is sin itself; the historical evils that afflict human beings must be borne with religious patience, since they are such only in appearance. And the spirituality that results from this is typically individualistic. The ordinary layperson, without sacred powers, possesses no possibilities for religious acts other than prayer, a personal spiritual life, and worship, but even in worship the communal element is often viewed as a disturbing distraction.

In the rest of life the religious element is represented as the acceptance of the will of God, which is believed to be manifested by vertical happenings at random, such as the directions of a spiritual guide, inspirations, and various "signs" of the will of God. In summary, the basic outlook of this form of religious consciousness can be characterized as "passivity."

Segundo believes that the acceptance of contingency is a valid element of authentic religion; but when this element becomes dominant, the result is that:

Humanity, with its innate creative power, with its unavoidable destiny toward history and toward society, either frees itself from the religious and places the essence of itself into its historical task together with the rest of those outside religion, or it establishes two often contradictory compartments in its life, between its mission and the individualistic and interior religion by which it relates to God.[20]

The Wisdom Stage

In the fourth and last stage of Old Testament religious understanding, the author restricts himself to a single work, the Book of Wisdom.[21] But this is considered to be an extremely important book, for it presents a solution to the problem that threaded its way through the Hebrew wisdom literature and reached its definitive expression in the Book of Job. Moreover, the book is important for its delineation of the conceptual background of the Pharisees, who constituted the most "religious" group at the time of Christ.

Once again in this stage, the separation between God and humanity in a preceding period is here replaced by his much closer approach to human existence. This nearness involves a purification of the understanding of divine transcendence, which in the previous stage appeared to leave humanity in a lost and disoriented position, since now it becomes clear that the transcendent God does indeed seek justice and, in fact, the whole universe is ordained to that end. At the same time an advance is made in understanding the importance of humanity's central faculty, freedom. The absolutely crucial importance of freedom in the attainment of human destiny is stated and emphasized; correlatively, evil ceases to be an insuperable obstacle in the face of this freedom. Lastly, it is at this stage that faith affirms for the first time that life will definitively triumph over death so that the most deeply rooted desire of human beings for immortality is enabled to glimpse its realization.

The resemblance of these ideas to current elements of Christian spirituality should be immediately obvious. Yet Segundo is at pains to point out that we are still in the presence of a pre-Christian spirituality and that thus, despite its notable advances, this view falls short of a fully Christian perspective. Its limitations are pointed to in three principal areas.

First of all, it leads to the perception of human existence as basically a *test* or *trial*. And eventually this culminates in a radical relativization of present human values, which are viewed as merely provisory; the only ultimate values are eternal. Closely connected with this is another attitude, namely, that human freedom is envisioned as essentially *noncreative*. The purpose of life is to fulfill the law written in human nature, and in this crucial enterprise freedom introduces the very dangerous element of risk; it follows then that the less liberty there is, the less risk will be entailed in achieving one's destiny.

A last attitude that evolves from this type of spirituality is a posture of *inhibition* or *resignation* before the problems that human existence poses. Nonbelievers use all the means at their disposal, including unscrupulous ones, to arrive at their goal of success in the present life. Compared to them, religious persons appear almost as victims; although it is true that their triumph will be vindicated in eternity, in the meantime they must organize their whole life around the central virtue of patience.[22]

As was mentioned earlier, this lengthy analysis of Old Testament ideas is considered to be a necessary propaedeutic for an understanding of the New Testament, that is, for an understanding of the essence of Christianity. As Segundo expresses it at the conclusion of *Pre-Christian Stages of Faith,* "to speak of the limitations of this fourth pre-Christian stage is to speak of Christianity, since it is only the marvelous novelty, the Good News of the message of Christ, that enables us to understand what is still lacking in the spirituality we are studying."[23] Consequently, I will now attempt to clarify that Good News in the two volumes already cited.

The Great Commandment

As its title indicates, Segundo's book, *The Function of the Church in the Reality of the River Plate,*[24] is concerned with elucidating the contemporary role of the church in Uruguay and Argentina, the two countries that border on that river. However, this ecclesiological question immediately presents a serious problem, since he finds two distinct—and opposed— conceptions of the church operative among committed Catholics in the two countries. How is one to determine which of these positions is authentic or, to probe more deeply, how is one to know whether either one of them is? The only possible solution to the quandary is described thus: "Keeping in mind those elements of the analysis of our situation, let us look at what is for the church the source of its true mission: the truth revealed by its founder, Jesus Christ."[25] Thus, after an initial chapter that analyzes the problem noted above, the second chapter of his book is devoted to a return to the New Testament sources, in order to seek there the fundamental significance of what it means to be a Christian.

In this task it becomes immediately apparent that two distinct lines of thought appear in the sources, which appear to correspond with the opposing ecclesiologies mentioned above. For the first position Segundo advances a "text of capital importance" since it contains the last command of Christ before he returns to the Father: "And [Jesus] said to them, 'Go into all the world and preach the gospel to the whole creation. He who believes and is baptized will be saved; but he who does not believe will be condemned' '' (Mark 16:15–16). To show that this perspective is not peculiar to Mark, he also notes that, in a conversation with Nicodemus, Jesus reiterates the absolute need of faith three times in the course of a few verses (John 3:14–18). Again, in the Acts of the Apostles, when the jailer asks Paul and Silas, ''What must I do to be saved?'' the reply of these early ministers of the gospel is the same, ''Believe in the Lord Jesus Christ and you will be saved, you and your household,'' and they all believed and were baptized that same evening (Acts 16:30–33).[26]

Turning to the second line of thought, Segundo first comments on a text that is also of central importance—Christ's last sermon on the judgment of human history in Matthew 25:31–46—and attempts to discover there what is ''the ultimate, decisive value.'' He paraphrases the judgment on human existence as follows:

What will decide one's eternal destiny? It could not be otherwise than one's religious attitude, that is, the attitude which human beings have adopted toward Christ (God). But will this attitude before Christ be one of adoration, of faith, of belonging to his true church? No, the gospel tells us that the Judge will ask whether one has given food to the hungry, a glass of water to the thirsty, whether one has given assistance, consolation, companionship.[27]

In an attempt to integrate the two lines of thought, Segundo believes that this integration can be achieved only if one of them is understood as basic and central to the Christian message while the other is viewed as subsidiary to it. To determine which one is primary, he first examines the writings of St. John. In John's effort to synthesize what he had seen, heard, and touched (1 John 1:1), he twice employs the striking expression, ''God is love'' (1 John 4:8,16). While admitting that the word love has been debased in countless ways in the course of time, Segundo still insists on its absolute centrality in the New Testament: ''God is love, and when the author inspired by him wrote this word, he took it from our language and from our human experience. He decided that this experience was better than any other to describe what took place in the interior of God and what the Word had communicated to us.''[28] Thus, John's conclusions are perfectly logical: ''He who does not love does not know God'' (1 John 4:8); and also ''we know (by experience) that we have passed out of death into life, because we love the brethren'' (1 John 3:14).

And if it is true, Segundo continues, that God is the *origin* of all authentic love, it is also true that he is the *object* of it. In establishing the latter point, he cites the great twofold commandment in Matthew 22:37–40, and notes that ''it is certainly extraordinary that the obligation to love God, infinite Goodness, and to love an imperfect creature can be compared and declared to be similar.'' It is even more extraordinary when we return to St. John and discover that one of the two great commandments is relegated to second place, and that it is not the one pertaining to humanity but the one concerning God: "If anyone says, 'I love God,' and hates his brother, he is a liar; for he who does not love his brother whom he has seen, how can he love God whom he cannot see?" (1 John 4:20). The conclusion is clear:

We are not in the presence of a love tested by the profundity of its intention, called supernatural because it is not natural. We are before a love which puts its demands before our eyes. And this love, which is the pattern and test of the other, is love for the neighbor, for the person visible at our side in history. For St. John, for the Christian message, all love for the invisible God will be suspect unless it is tested by the love of the brother.[29]

Consequently, on the night he was betrayed, Christ left to his church not two commandments but a single one: "This is my commandment, that you love one another as I have loved you" (John 15:12).

Segundo summarizes his case by asserting that "the great religious revolution of Christianity has been the abolition of the profane—and that, not in favor of the religious, but in favor of that very area which we call profane." Or, to put it more exactly,

that which is primarily religious, according to the Christian message, is that which goes to God by means of the effective love which people have for each other, even when behind this love there is no awareness of the religious values which it contains. How can we call profane or temporal the bread which satisfies the hunger of God? How can we call profane the technology which serves to heal God? Or the structures which offer or do not offer to God in our brothers a life with meaning and dignity, instead of the existence of an animal?[30]

Integration of Love and Freedom

A further expansion of these ideas from a different perspective and starting point has been advanced by Segundo in the third work mentioned at the beginning of this chapter, *The Christian Understanding of Humanity*.[31] In this book the author is intent on fostering a "dialogue of the living" with those currents of contemporary thought which he considers to be most vital and dynamic, that is to say, with existentialism and Marxism. He adopts as the focal point of dialogue the image of humanity in each system (for Christianity, this would entail a parallel image of God); moreover, he attempts to discover the image on the level of each approach's authentic sources (that is, what *should be* the image), not on the level of a contemporary sociological analysis (that is, what is the *actual* image now). His reason for adopting such a choice is presented at the outset: "One of the most decisive factors hindering every kind of dialogue is that all speak of their own system in terms of what it should be, while they suppose the system of the adversary to be nothing but its *sociological realization*."[32] Thus, for example, Christians might view themselves in dialogue with Marxists as true disciples of Christ in conversation with assassins of Budapest, and the same could hold true for the Marxists.

In seeking to delineate the authentic Christian image of humanity, Segundo paraphrases in summary form the basic insights that were discussed in the previous section. He is intent on distinguishing this image from certain ones proposed in classical "religion," asserting that in Christianity "God is love, and all effective love is transformed into an absolute value, into the only true and absolute value in human existence." Moreover, he places great emphasis on what he calls the "materialism" of Christian charity and insists that "in authentic Christianity no problem is solved by substituting any form of sacred magic for the responsibility of efficacious love."[33] He refers, also, to an anecdote concerning the French novelist Jean Giono, which appears to have impressed him deeply, for it is repeated in some of his other works. When asked why he rejected Christianity, Giono replied: "I do not want to be one of those people who walk across a battlefield with flowers in their hands." In this metaphor, the battle refers to the struggle of human existence, and the flowers to Christianity considered as an absolute value, which relativizes the struggle. Segundo appears to reject such an image as strongly as Giono; what bothers him most about it is not its underlying egotism but its utter lack of reality.[34]

The real advance in this work, however, lies in the deepening of the notion of freedom and the clarification of its essential relationship to love in the Christian image of humanity. The author notes that, even in the early church, submission to the institution as well as to the laws of nature constituted a serious problem; consequently, St. Paul struggled for years to convince his listeners that "for freedom Christ has set you free; stand fast therefore, and do not submit again to a yoke of slavery" (Gal. 5:1). The dialectical tension this creates within the institutional church will be discussed in the following chapter.

With regard to the laws of nature, a situation of slavery can also occur, since "the structures, the laws of the universe can appear as established by God independently of human beings, as a superior power that is proper to God."[35] Again, Paul's struggle was to convince his hearers that the world had been given totally and definitively to human beings, as in his repeated assertion that "all things are yours" in the First Letter to the Corinthians, 3:21–22. This clearly entails a certain resemblance to the Promethean myth of taking the world from the gods to turn it over to human beings; the basic difference, however, lies in the fact that "it is God himself who has given the world to humanity. . . . Human freedom is worth more than all the structures of the universe."[36]

Toward the end of *The Christian Conception of Humanity*, a more profound understanding of the Christian notion of freedom is attained by a comparison with the two main currents of contemporary thought mentioned earlier. Existentialism's basic objection to Christianity (as in Sartre's *The Flies*) is centered on its purported denial of human liberty, a charge which Segundo believes to be false, at least on the level of principle. He then proceeds to point out the individualistic emphasis that is the basic weakness of existentialism[37] and emphasizes what he considers to be the transcendence of this weakness in the Christian sources: "Christian liberty is radically social. Humanity is free when it spontaneously gives itself, in love, to other persons."[38]

Marxism, too, rejects existentialism, for the latter is seen as the ultimate consequence of bourgeois ideology, and it is clear to the Marxists that "you can't achieve the revolution while holding on to your own little piece of ground." Thus Marxism is clearly closer to Christianity through its emphasis on the social dimension of humanity. But at this point Segundo returns to the concept of personal freedom and poses a penetrating question to the Marxists: "Is it possible to achieve it [the revolution] without previously taking into account the most profound alienation, which is the loss of humanity's creative power in these same social structures?"[39] It should be noted that this question is intended not to settle the issue but to further the dialogue and to bring it to richer and more complex levels. A fuller treatment of the Marxist-Christian relationship will be taken up in Chapter Nine of this book.

At this point, we may attempt to summarize the basic understanding of the Christian message that has been presented thus far. It is by efficacious love that humanity shares in and reflects the inner life of God, who is love. But to accomplish this task, human beings must be free, free *from* all forms of slavery, including religious ones, and free *for* the loving service and reconciliation of their brothers and sisters. And it is precisely for such freedom "that Christ has set us free" (Gal. 5:1). To use Segundo's own synthesis, "human freedom is creative, but it has the true meaning of freedom only when it is realized in the love which is the gift of self to the community"; yet at the same time "the destiny of human beings is social, but in such a way that they can be free and creative in the social area."[40]

If we move for a moment from the level of principles to that of the actual contemporary situation, the question may be raised as to whether this understanding of freedom is evident in ecclesiastical practice today. Segundo believes that it is not and that the reason for this lies in the fact that the western church after the time of Constantine was converted into the gigantic "machine for making Christians" that we call Christendom. In the process, social pressures, and not a personal and profound adhesion to the original sources, became the normal reason for becoming and remaining Christian.[41]

Recently, however, the technological revolution has radically changed the course of this process, and we are now witnessing the disappearance of the last remnants of Christendom. Segundo believes that the most significant reality of modern times is the appearance, through technology, of mass communications, whereby "everyone lives in contact with everyone else" and "everyone suffers the impact of everyone else." Paradoxically, he ends his book with a statement of profound hope in this situation, for "only in a world such as this, which technology makes possible, could real Christianity become more identified with the original Christianity. . . ."[42]

Reflections from the First World

The foregoing summary should serve to highlight some of the salient features which characterize Segundo's "open" theology in his earliest works and which continue to be operative up to the present. Clearly, his approach is profoundly *historical,* accentuating the fact that God's self-revelation and the human response to it constitute an ongoing process throughout history. It is a historical drama, moreover, in which the exercise of human love and freedom plays a profoundly creative and not merely a conformist role. The stages of revelation, both in the past and the present, are also characterized by an essential *dialectical* interaction throughout the historical process. And the human pole of this dialectic embraces a number of key elements: an analysis of the "reality" or sociopolitical situation; a consideration of the actual praxis of Christians under the guidance of the Spirit; and a continuing dialogue with vital currents of thought or systems of meaning that have interacted with Christianity in the course of history.

With regard to the possible value of Segundo's ideas in these early works for the North American situation, I would judge that the primary contribution lies in his unswerving insistence on the *essentials* of what it is to be a Christian. For him the God revealed in Jesus Christ is not a Greek "unmoved mover," but a God whose very essence consists of love; moreover, it is only by the self-transcending love of others that human beings are enabled to share in and to reflect the very life of the Christian God. The Good News of Christianity, therefore, is that the life, death, and resurrection of Jesus Christ have liberated human persons from the slavery of sin, alienation, and egotism, and thereby liberated them for a life of service, justice, and love.

Consequently, the relevance for our own situation would be to insist that these basic essentials continue to *function as such* in every sphere of the life of the church, including catechetics, liturgy, preaching, counseling, spirituality, action programs, and—perhaps most importantly—theology. In other words, the necessary tasks of investigating other areas and solving other problems should never be allowed to overshadow or detract from the paradoxical simplicity and profundity of the Good News of God's liberating action in Jesus Christ. In this regard, the "pre-Christian" stages discussed above can function just as well in our own situation for discerning the ideologies of egotism and group interest that have distorted the Christian ideal in the past and that will continue to do so in the future.

To many in North America, however, the stress on the centrality of love of neighbor as the expression of the love of God may appear irreverent or exaggerated. But that precise attitude provides all the more reason for stressing the fundamental importance of the concept in our own situation. To further such an emphasis, therefore, I would like to make the point here that the concept has recently been defended by theologians in the West as well as by those in Latin America.

An excellent focus on the issue may be found in an article by Kieran Quinlan with the provocative title, "Is Love of Man the *Only* Way to God?"[43] Quinlan begins by asserting that "for several years now Karl Rahner and other prominent Catholic theologians have been advancing the theory that only in loving his neighbor, and in no other way, can man love God."[44] After examining the biblical evidence and the problems the thesis raises in systematic theology, Quinlan comes to the conclusion that for Rahner "not only is love of neighbor first *in practice,* but that *it is itself the basic act of love of God.* It is not merely psychologically first, but *ontologically* so."[45] In concluding, he also draws attention to the novelty of the unity doctrine: "It *is* new, it *does* pose a challenge, less perhaps to our inclination to search anxiously for answers and refutations, than to finding out where our hearts *really* lie."[46] While supporting Quinlan's analysis, I would add the observation that the "novelty" he mentions is not some form of doctrinal development but rather a retrieval of the astonishing novelty of the message of the New Testament.

Our last aspect of love of neighbor in the contemporary situation concerns its relationship to the quest for justice. In the works cited in this chapter, Segundo does not analyze the relationship in depth, although a strict correlation seems implicit in the concrete examples he has chosen. Also, the Catholic bishops of the world in the synod of 1971 advocated a strict correlation, as in their assertion that "Christian love of neighbor and justice cannot be separated," that "love implies an absolute demand for justice," and finally that "justice attains its inner fulness only in love."[47] But once again the bishops did not attempt to provide a detailed theological justification for these assertions.

Because of this lack of theological foundations, a recent series of articles by Ignacio Ellacuría, a Spanish Jesuit working in Central America, appears to me to be of great importance.[48] The articles present a detailed and profound synthesis of the scriptural proofs as well as the theological rationale for the assertion that love and justice cannot be separated. A discussion of Ellacuría's thought would move beyond the limited purposes of this book. I will conclude, however, by stating my judgment that his ideas are absolutely crucial, if indeed "action on behalf of justice and participation in the transformation of the world'' are to become—in the lived existence of the church and not merely in documents—''a constitutive dimension of the preaching of the gospel.''[49]

NOTES

1. This brief curriculum vitae was derived mainly from book jackets and other similar references. At the time of my writing, Segundo's attention was taken up with pressing work and with various forms of persecution, so that a fuller account of his life was impossible. Perhaps the brevity of this account may stand as a testimony of the very different and dangerous circumstances in which theologians work in Latin America.

2. *Berdiaeff: Une réflexion chrétienne sur la personne* (Paris: Montaigne, 1963), and *La cristiandad ¿una utopía?*, 2 vols. (Montevideo: Mimeográfica "Luz," 1964). Segundo had earlier published a more philosophical work: *Existencialismo, filosofía, y poesía: Ensayo de síntesis* (Buenos Aires: Espasa-Calpe, 1948).

3. *Teología abierta para un laico adulto*, 5 vols. (Buenos Aires: Carlos Lohlé, 1968–72).

4. Jon Sobrino, "El conocimiento teológico en la teología europea y latino-americana," *Liberación y cautiverio: Debates en torno al método de la teología en América Latina* (Mexico City: Comité Organizador, 1975), p. 192.

5. Juan Luis Segundo, *Etapas precristianas de la fe: Evolución de la idea de Dios en el Antiguo Testamento* (Montevideo: Cursos de Complementación Cristiana, 1962); *Concepción cristiana del hombre* (Montevideo: Mimeográfica "Luz," 1964). The latter volume contains conferences given at the Universidad de la República of Montevideo in February 1962. Since writing this chapter, I was able to obtain a printed edition which combines both these works: *¿Qué es un cristiano?* (Montevideo: Mosca, 1971).

6. Segundo, *Función de la Iglesia en la realidad rioplatense* (Montevideo: Barreiro y Ramos, 1962).

7. Segundo, *Etapas*, pp. 6 and 9. The educative role of Scripture is treated in considerably more detail in Segundo's most recent book, *Liberación de la teología* (Buenos Aires: Carlos Lohlé, 1975), especially in "Las ideologías y la fe," pp. 111–40.

8. Cf. the classic treatment of this process in Gerhard von Rad, *Old Testament Theology I: The Theology of Israel's Historical Traditions* (New York: Harper and Row, 1962). Segundo's brief survey of the historical traditions is given on pp. 11–19 of *Etapas*.

9. Segundo, *Etapas*, pp. 19–32.

10. Ibid., p. 29.

11. Ibid., p. 30. This conception of the sacraments as well as his view of a more authentic version are treated at length by Segundo in *Los sacramentos hoy* (Buenos Aires: Carlos Lohlé, 1971).

12. Segundo, *Etapas*, p. 32. Segundo also notes here that "the scientific propaganda by which the Communist world tries to uproot religion affects in reality only this type of religion, which, however, is widely diffused."

13. Ibid., pp. 32–47.

14. Ibid., p. 39.

15. Ibid., p. 47.

16. Ibid., pp. 48–71.

17. Ibid., p. 68. In discussing the Book of Job, Segundo draws attention to what he calls "perhaps the strongest words that occur in Scripture": "It is all one; therefore I say, [Yahweh] destroys both the blameless and the wicked. When disaster brings sudden death, he mocks at the calamity of the innocent (Job 9:22–23)" (*Etapas*, p. 64).

18. *Etapas*, p. 69.

19. Ibid., p. 70.

20. Ibid., p. 71.

21. Ibid., pp. 71–82.

22. Ibid., p. 81. Segundo also observes that this fourth type of pre-Christian spirituality has a special attraction for women. He traces this to the division of labor in western society, whereby men undertook active and creative roles outside the home while women were entrusted with domestic tasks "in which patience and hope as well as humility play a predominant role" (p. 82).

23. Ibid., p. 81.

24. *Función de la Iglesia en la realidad rioplatense*. The Spanish word "realidad" is difficult to express exactly in English; in addition to the idea of physical area, it also connotes "the contemporary situation," that is, the economic, cultural, and political reality.

25. Ibid., p. 30. Scattered references to Segundo's Christology may be found throughout my book, but he has not yet produced a synthetic Christology. Recently, however, he has stated that this will comprise his next major theological work.

26. Ibid., pp. 30–31.

27. Ibid., p. 31.

28. Ibid., pp. 32–33. Another eloquent statement of the divine origin of all love is the following: "This love, as old as the world, this love which has determined all the sacrifices, all the loyalties, all the silent acts of charity, all the simple, enduring, and pure unions since humanity has existed—the Christian message tells us that all this has a divine origin, that it is a supernatural possibility placed in our souls by the One who gave us his life" (p. 33).

29. Ibid., p. 34.

30. Ibid., p. 35.

31. Segundo, *Concepción cristiana del hombre*. It may be noted that the "Christian image of man" is not considered a fixed concept but one open to development and change: "In a certain sense, Catholic thought concerning humanity does not exist. . . . One can say that the twenty centuries of Christianity have been nothing but a progressive exploration, both speculative and practical, of this enigma which is humanity, starting from the basic truths which Christianity believes to have been revealed by God" (p. 4). The author also states rather bluntly that "if Christianity claimed to be the fixed and prefabricated answer once and for all to the problems of all human beings of all times, it would be the most gigantic spiritual tyranny in history" (p. 5).

32. Ibid., pp. 6–7.

33. Ibid., p. 17. The basic idea is also expressed in a more concrete manner: "If one does not know the technique of making bread, that person is up against a closed door which no rite will open for him" (p. 16).

34. Ibid., p. 20. As regards the specific contribution of Christianity in this task of efficacious love, Segundo believes that it provides "a greater awareness and a greater certitude about that direction, a greater responsibility to help others to travel that path, and a greater hope of what awaits the travelers at its conclusion" (p. 19).

35. Ibid., p. 27.

36. Ibid., p. 28.

37. "It is strange that existential phenomenology has not produced a serious analysis of love and of solidarity" (p. 31).

38. Ibid., p. 32.

39. Ibid., p. 34.

40. Ibid., p. 31. These elements are considered to comprise the twofold "revolution" of Christianity.

41. Ibid., p. 37. In this respect, the remark of the French sociologist A. Desqueyrat is cited: "When a religious existence no longer finds support in the social milieu, which is what is happening at present, then it is no longer possible except in a personal, heroic, and internalized form" (*La crisis religiosa de los tiempos nuevos* [Pamplona: Desclée, 1959], p. 77).

42. Segundo, *Concepción Cristiana*, pp. 39–40. Earlier, Segundo had noted that technology tends to reduce the decisions of liberty to an automatic "second nature," but that, nevertheless, technology possesses "no intrinsic force contrary to liberty" (p. 38).

43. Kieran Quinlan, "Is Love of Man the *Only* Way to God?" in *Catholic Mind* (February 1978):29–37. The work originally appeared in *Doctrine and Life* (August 1977).

44. Quinlan, "Is Love of Man the *Only* Way to God?," p. 29. The most important article for Rahner's thought on the issue is "Reflections on the Unity of the Love of Neighbor and the Love of God," in *Theological Investigations VI* (Baltimore: Helicon Press, 1969), pp. 231–49. Rahner also considers the problem in briefer compass in "Why and How Can We Venerate the Saints?" in *Theological Investigations VIII* (New York: Herder and Herder, 1971), pp. 3–23.

45. Quinlan, "Is Love of Man the *Only* Way to God?," p. 37. Italics are the author's.

46. Ibid. Italics are the author's.

47. *Justice in the World*, Second Synod of Bishops, no. 34, in Joseph Gremillion, *The Gospel of Peace and Justice: Catholic Social Teaching Since Pope John* (Maryknoll, N.Y.: Orbis Books, 1976), p. 520.

48. Ignacio Ellacuría, "Fe y justicia: I," *Christus* (August 1977):26–33; "Fe y justicia: II y III," ibid. (October 1977):19–34. A briefer treatment of the problem may also be found in Jon Sobrino, "La oración de Jesús y del cristiano," *Christus* (July 1977):25–48; see Sobrino's *Christology at the Crossroads* (Maryknoll, N.Y.: Orbis Books, 1978), chapter 5: "The Prayer of Jesus." I intend to take up these ideas in much greater detail in future publications.

49. *Justice in the World*, no. 6, in Gremillion, *Gospel of Peace and Justice*, p. 514.

CHAPTER FOUR

THE MISSION HAS A CHURCH

The North American sociologist Joseph H. Fichter recently concluded an article on the role of the churches in the United States with some rather startling assertions. "What I see," he wrote, "as the absorbing future work of the American churches is the attempt to transform the concupiscent institutions of the larger society. . . . *I see no other force, outside of religion, that will intelligently challenge the institutionalized inequalities and discriminations of Western society.*"[1] If Fichter is correct—and I believe he is—then the need for more profound theological reflection on the church appears to be vital. In this chapter we will attempt to seek light for such a reflection by an investigation of Segundo's ecclesiology.

Furthermore, the preceding chapter, concerned with the meaning of Christian existence, leads logically in this direction. That is to say, it leads us to ask how persons who share such an understanding of Christianity organize their relationships so as to realize it in their corporate existence and also to transmit it to others. In short, we are led to an analysis of the meaning of a structured Christian community, that is, to an ecclesiology. The analysis will entail an examination not only of such a community's relationships with regard to its own members but also with regard to the secular society in which it is situated.

In this chapter, therefore, I will consider three early works of Segundo that are concerned directly with such a problem. It should be emphasized that ecclesiology is a central concern of the author—perhaps the major one in all his writings—and that it is elaborated in various ways in most of his later writings.

Opposed Visions of the Church

The first work to be considered has already been cited in the previous chapter: *The Function of the Church in the Reality of the River Plate.*[2] As the title indicates, the purpose of the book is to analyze the role of the church in the context of Uruguay and Argentina. However, the basic insights appear to merit consideration for an understanding of the church in other areas of the world, including our own. Illustrations that have only

69

topical or dated reference will not be considered, although references to them will be provided for the interested reader.

The book first considers two basic—and radically opposed—views concerning the function and what Segundo calls the projected "triumph" of the church in the two countries mentioned. Although the authentic religious motivations of the persons who espouse such views are respected, the author believes that both positions are incomplete and are based on a partially distorted understanding of Christianity. It should also be noted that he limits himself to the outlook and actions of those who are apostolically active, and thus he does not consider in his analysis those who are merely superstitious in their religious understanding nor those who consider religion as "an individual passport for eternal life."[3] In the process of criticizing the two positions, the author advances his own mediating position, and then develops the more profound implications of his view, especially in his final chapter.

A succinct summary of the opposing views is presented quite early in the book: ". . . Either they will say that the function of the church is the only one that has an absolute value, and that consequently other problems have to be placed on an inferior level, or they will accept the fact that the function of the church is one among many others, all of which are important and necessary."[4] Segundo considers the first—or what I will call the absolute—position to be better grounded theologically, basing itself on such straightforward texts as Mark 16:15–16: "And [Jesus] said to them, 'Go into all the world and preach the gospel to the whole creation. He who believes and is baptized will be saved; but he who does not believe will be condemned.' " The role of the church, through faith and sacraments, is thus a life or death matter for all of humanity, in comparison to which such secular matters as the Alliance for Progress, to cite one example, are of no lasting importance. The absolutist asks, in strict logic, "Would Christ's institution of a visible church and his declaration of its absolute necessity make any sense, if people were saved outside the church as well as within it?"[5]

The second, or relative position, is not as strongly founded theologically, contenting itself with references to charity or to the Incarnation as God's insertion into human history. Rather it appears to flow from a certain type of "apostolic instinct," which desires to take with utmost seriousness, not only humanity's good intentions but the actual *efficacy* of human tasks in history. Thus the absolutist position seems to them to result in a kind of duplicity or playacting that is inauthentic, since it does not take terrestrial reality seriously.

Concrete examples of the two positions in the churches in Argentina and Uruguay are then analyzed in detail on three levels: pastoral practice, socioeconomic structures, and the political order.[6] Of more general interest, however, is the author's observation that the two positions are intimately related to divergent views of a theology of history, which results in differences in understanding such key areas as the role of the laity in the church, relations between church and state, possible collaboration with non-Catholics in a pluralistic world, and so forth. He also notes that, in actual practice, the two positions are often to be found commingled in any number of combinations and compartmentalizations and cites a well-known text of Pierre Teilhard de Chardin that alludes to the same phenomenon.[7]

In a chapter entitled "The Religion of Authentic Love," Segundo begins his criticism of both the absolute and relative positions by means of a return to the sources of Christianity in the New Testament. First, he notes that there actually exists in the New Testament a double line of thought that appears to coincide with the two conceptions just mentioned. The absolutist view may be clearly discerned in texts such as Mark 16:15–16 and John 3:14–18. In a much longer discussion, moreover, texts which would appear to support the relativist position are analyzed, for example, the judgment scene in Matthew 25:31–40 and a verse from 1 John 4:20: "If anyone says, 'I love God,' and hates his brother, he is a liar, for he who does not love his brother whom he has seen, cannot love God whom he has not seen."

It would be inappropriate at this point to repeat the ideas on the meaning of Christianity that were discussed in the previous chapter. It will be sufficient to note several of the basic conclusions Segundo draws from his analysis of the great commandment of charity in the New Testament: "The great religious revolution of Christianity has been the abolition of the profane—and that, not in favor of the religious sphere, as the first position would have it, but in favor of the absolute religious value of that very reality which we call profane." In the same context, he insists that "the primary religious reality, according to the Christian message, is that which goes to God by way of the effective love which human beings have for one another, even when, behind this love, there is no awareness of the religious value which it includes."[8] According to Segundo, these principles undermine both of the positions under discussion. That is immediately obvious for the first position, since the absolute values are diametrically opposed; the relation of the principles to the second position, however, is somewhat more complex.

For the stumbling block for many with a relativist outlook lies in the institutional church itself. It often seems to them that it would be easier to achieve their task of dialogue and transformation of the nation with the spirit of Christ alone and without the burdensome elements of the institution. Thus there arises "the strange compromise of the autonomy of the secular."[9]

Segundo's basic reply to this is that the church is necessary as an aid to the task of efficacious love in history, for by its preaching (cf. Rom.

10:14–15) and sacraments it brings to conscious awareness what the rest of humanity can only know spontaneously. This knowledge, moreover, is given for the service of humanity in what is seen to be a common journey. In brief, "the church as a visible and hierarchical society is at the service of all humanity for the goal which humanity is spontaneously seeking."[10] Thus the failure to appreciate its own message is seen as the fundamental flaw of the relativist position and of its theory of the autonomy of the secular: "Not to recognize that exigency, not of the institutional church, but of the Christian message which it transmits, not to recognize the absolute value of Christianity as the inspiration and meaning for all human history in general and for our countries in particular, in this lies the error of the second position."

A Third Vision of the Church

In this way the two apparently opposed strains of New Testament thought mentioned earlier are reunited and harmonized. Segundo stresses, however, that the two realities—the church as a small, visible community and the much broader expanse of all humanity which it serves in a common history—must be maintained in a state of continual tension. What this amounts to, at bottom, is a dialectical relationship between the two realities. If the dialectical tension between them is maintained, the process goes forward; if it is lost, the process is halted. It is precisely "that tension without which the church would have no reason for existence, would be neither ferment nor salt: possessing an absolute value, it is at the service of humanity on the one effective level of the love of God, the level where the authenticity of humanity is at stake, as it faces the sorrow, the hunger, the ignorance, the loneliness, and the alienation of our brothers and sisters."[11]

Segundo attempts to deepen the understanding of the above dialectic in his last chapter, entitled "Christianity and the Masses." He draws here a distinction between "minorities" and "masses," which will continue to function as a key concept in much of his later theological reflection. We will first examine the concept of "masses" and then attempt to see its relationship to the church, which for Segundo is a "minority" by its very essence.

Since the concept is of such importance, it is absolutely essential to stress at the outset that he does not use the word "masses" to designate the popular classes or the proletariat or, indeed, any one group of people as opposed to another. Rather, the word is used in the sense of "mass man" or "mass society," that is, it refers to "persons who are especially characterized by the ease with which they follow the crowd, assimilate propaganda, allow themselves to be led by psychological or social mechanisms. . . ."[12] The phenomenon of "mass man," then, cuts across all social strata, levels of education, etc.

The basic characteristics of this phenomenon include, first of all, *simplification,* the pursuit of simple and direct solutions to all problems, however complicated. This is accomplished by the temporal variety of the simple, that is, *immediacy,* the search for swift and immediate solutions rather than long-range and complex ones. The combination of the two is clearly exemplified in the activity of the demagogue (lit., "leader of masses"), "who promises results that are too immediate through means that are too simple."[13]

Moreover, although this phenomenon of "mass man" has always existed, it is greatly amplified in the contemporary world by what are aptly termed "mass media" or "mass communications," with the result that "in the present world there is a daily increase in the means [*medios*] intended to organize masses, to direct masses, and to manipulate masses."[14] In a certain sense, the phenomenon is essential to human existence, for without mass behavior there would be no continuity in groups, and therefore no continuity in the course of human history. It is clear, too, that one could not speak of a science of sociology without taking into account mass behavior, since this provides the foundation for what are called sociological laws.

Segundo begins his discussion of the relationship of the Christian message to all this by means of an analysis of the prologue of the gospel of St. John. In John 1:9 (Christ the Light "was coming into the world"), he notes that the expression "world" is used in a neutral sense, a general term to denote the earth and human existence. However, in the very next verse, with the phrase "the world knew him not," the word takes on a negative sense: the world is now envisioned as the "mass" of humanity that rejects the Word. Those who say yes to the Word will comprise a minority, one that will know him, his plan, and his moral law, so that through them he may penetrate more profoundly into human existence. Yet the question still remains: if the mass of human beings (the world) says no to him, how can Christ say in John 16:33 ". . . I have overcome the world"?

In answering this, Segundo turns to St. Paul and analyzes a number of texts related to Christ's lordship over the world, including 1 Cor. 15:28, 2 Cor. 5:17, Col. 1:15–20, Eph. 1:9–10, 19–23, and Rom. 8:19,22. A fair summary of this discussion is found in the following text:

Thus, history for St. Paul can be nothing but the road along which all the beings of the universe, directed by the grace of Christ . . . travel toward a goal when the whole of history will reveal its mystery. Therefore, as we have seen, Jesus wished through his revelation that we might know beforehand this meaning of history in order to aid those who journey with us. And so he wished, as Paul writes to the Ephesians, "to have us know the mystery of his will, according to the purpose which he set forth in Christ as a plan for the fulness of time, to unite all things in him, things in heaven and things on earth" (Eph. 1:9–10).[15]

Within this broad perspective of world history, Segundo is able to integrate the concept of mass man. First of all, the Constantinian period, which so deeply affected the European church, and through it, many other parts of the world, is seen by him as an unusual development and not the normal dialectic of masses and minorities in Christianity. Basically, the institutions of society in the Constantinian period were turned into mechanisms for creating and maintaining Christians: ". . . they made it easy and advantageous to embrace an ideal which was, in itself, the most difficult and complex in the world."[16] But given the changes of the past century, especially in the mass media, the Constantinian framework has all but disappeared, and the situation has returned to normal (that is, as in the norm of the New Testament). The result is that "from now on Catholicism must be proven to all people, by having recourse to that which is most profound, most personal, and most heroic in it, and in open struggle with all the other systems which claim to explain and orientate people's lives."[17]

On the local level of the countries of the River Plate, Segundo appears intent on persuading its Catholics to cease bemoaning the de-Christianization of their lands and yearning for the halcyon days of Christendom. Instead of this ideal, which in any case is impossible, he proposes to them a new vision and a new motivation to commit themselves to the Christian transformation of the history of their countries.[18]

A much more profound analysis of the authentic meaning of the church in history is to be found in a later two-volume work entitled *Is Christendom a Utopia?*[19] The first volume concerns itself with the historical and sociological *facts* of the relation between Christendom and Christianity; the second volume approaches the same subject from the viewpoint of *principles*, that is, the teaching of the New Testament and especially of John and Paul. This work was written as a doctoral dissertation under the direction of Paul Ricoeur and its ideas are extremely compact and nuanced; consequently, it is impossible to summarize all the insights and details, and I will offer here merely an overview of the general argument.

Historical and Sociological Facts

To begin with, it is necessary to clarify the signification of the title mentioned, which more literally reads *Christendom—A Utopia?* By using this terse phrase, the author wishes to highlight an extremely important question: is Christendom as it developed in the West after the time of Constantine the ideal situation (utopia) that the church should strive to achieve in all times and places? In the first volume, he proposes an answer to this question in five stages, which correspond to his five chapters.

The first chapter, "Christendom and Christianity," is concerned with the distinction between these two concepts. A descriptive definition of Christianity is given as "that which can be transmitted only by personal conviction," while Christendom is seen as "that which is transmitted along with the institutions of civil society, and which is lost along with them."[20]

For Segundo, it is historically certain that "the masses in the West did not enter the church by the personal conversion of each of its members"; rather mass conversions took place on the basis of decisions by those who possessed authority. Among other examples, the action of Henry VIII is cited, which led the whole of England into a religious schism lasting up to the present moment. The authorities also created social institutions for this purpose, resulting in a kind of "second nature," which would render a Christian commitment both habitual and convenient for the masses.[21]

If we turn to the contemporary world, however, it is obvious that Christians are more and more "uprooted" from the effect of such institutions by the process of civilization, and the result is a trend to massive de-Christianization. At the same time, the phenomenon exists of a minority choosing to become and remain Christian, not because of institutions, but on the basis of an interior, personal conviction; this group, consequently, is not affected by the above-mentioned de-Christianization. Summing up, then, a basic difference between Christianity and Christendom is that the progress of civilization is *neutral* with regard to the former, but *negative* as regards the latter. Thus it becomes clear that Christendom does not comprise the authentic realization of Christianity for all time, and we are left with the task of determining just what that authentic realization is in actuality.[22]

Segundo addresses this question in a second chapter, which is entitled "Christianity and the Masses." The basic question at this stage is: are Christianity and Christendom actually *compatible* or, to put it another way, is Christianity as an ideal intended by its very nature to strive for universal acceptance? In the contemporary situation, the question may be phrased more concretely as follows: "In the competition between ideals of life which seek the adhesion of the masses, does Christianity still have probabilities,"[23] that is, probabilities of mass acceptance. Segundo believes that the answer to the question thus posed must be no; there is no probability that a majority will embrace Christian ideals, which are mediate, long-range, and complex, for the majority will always tend to solutions characterized by immediacy and simplicity. To put it another way, Christianity demands an adhesion that is "personal, heroic, and internalized," which is by its very nature a minority phenomenon.

Segundo notes that many contemporary theologians refuse to face this problem squarely; they appear instead to rely on some vague hope that it will somehow go away, and choose to speak of a religious *crisis,* a word which the author considers to be a mere tranquilizer. At least at the present moment in history, then, he insists that there is a basic incompatibility between Christianity and mass membership.

This leads into a third stage, which is discussed in the chapter on "Masses and Determinism." Here Segundo asks whether the incompatibility applies only to the present situation of contemporary life or whether it implies something deeper, something that necessarily applies in every situation. The answer given is rather complex, involving as it does the philosophical foundations of sociology as a science, and it will be sufficient to provide the author's own summary: " . . . The undeniable existence of sociology as a science tells us of a determinism or, if you wish, of determinisms, without which scientific knowledge would lack an object and any possibility for progress. Well then, what does a determinism that is not total mean, unless it refers to a *majority* of modes of conduct that are similar?" Furthermore, the connecting link between these similar modes of behavior is the idea of *simplicity,* so that " . . . if sociology advances, it is because all its working hypotheses suppose that the conduct of majorities is structured according to the plan of the greatest simplicity, whether this be with regard to the system of means and ends or with regard to time (immediacy)."[24] The conclusion is that Christianity is minoritarian because of the very structure of human social existence and that it is fundamentally opposed to mass membership.

But this leads to an even more basic question:

How can we unite this radical opposition with the pretension of Christianity to historical universality? Should not Christianity reach the masses? In other words, is not the alternative we are proposing the *particularization* in a small select group of the influence of Christianity, in spite of the fact that it claims a total universality in history?[25]

To answer this, it is obviously necessary to enquire into the conditions of a historical universality that is not massive, that is, that does not strive for a majority in its membership.

This problem constitutes the fourth level of analysis in a chapter entitled "Determinism and History." At this stage, Segundo's basic effort is an extremely ambitious one: to discern the meaning of history, that is, the basic law that undergirds the irreversible development of history. The necessity of this derives from the previous chapter, where "one could get the idea of a Christianity directed toward a minority or an elite, in a word, of an aristocratic Christianity."[26] Only by comprehending more profoundly the basic thrust of history can this misunderstanding be overcome and the true nature of the church's universal role be illumined.

From the preceding analysis, it is abundantly clear that mass mechanisms make up an essential element of the historical process. On an individual level, of course, the person's liberty and authenticity must be respected; however, any "plan which seeks to achieve something on the level of collectivities must take into account the presence within these collectivities of mass man."[27] Otherwise, the plan would be a purely idealistic construct, which would promote disaster, rather than liberation, in human history.

On a very broad scale, Segundo then outlines what he considers to be the most basic elements that constitute historical progress in all times and all places. Fundamental to this thesis is the assertion that "we have never known a single people who, acting freely, have not opted, reasonably or not, sooner or later, for civilization." And civilization always involves three fundamental elements: tools, technology, and law. Tools are seen as providing some leisure from the daily struggle for survival; technology goes further and employs practical science to foresee needs and provide for them ahead of time; and law entails the joining of forces to achieve security and justice and to satisfy needs that exceed the possibilities of the individual. It is true that these elements occur in an immense variety of combinations; moreover, they are complicated, interdependent, and often opposed, but still "they are at the base of every movement in history."[28]

Furthermore, the historical accumulation of these elements can be characterized as a liberation, that is, they do not confer liberty, but have a positive role in facilitating its exercise. And the force that brings this liberation into existence is always a creative minority, for the process entails a mediation and complexity that will always be resisted by the mass-majority.

On the other hand, the minority cannot achieve a social change of any consequence unless it brings the masses along with it in the process. Thus, the minority must create a "facilitating environment" or type of artificial environment to achieve its goals; in a word, it must develop *institutions* which, "created by an active minority, are intended for the passive majority, in order to obtain from it the choice needed for its own good."[29] The author insists that no value judgment is being made on this process, but that nevertheless it constitutes the irreversible meaning of history: "By the interplay of institutions, in which converge masses and minorities, determinisms and liberty, history receives an intelligible meaning, without losing any of its radical unpredictability and ambiguity."[30] It should be added that institutions must always be subject to judgment, for they can obviously become retrogressive, criminal, or exploitative.

The dialectical interaction of masses and minorities is then utilized by Segundo to explain his understanding of the universal dimension of Christianity:

Christianity should not fear that this institutional second nature will eliminate its complex, heroic, and essentially minoritarian character. . . . In itself, Christianity will be no more difficult than it always was in its true profundity; however, by losing the supports that are foreign to this profundity, its transcendence and greatness will be able to appear more clearly.[31]

On the other hand, it cannot neglect its responsibility for the liberation of the majority, without becoming a "gnosis" for an aristocratic elite. Precisely how this responsibility is to be fulfilled is taken up in the last chapter, which is concerned with "History and Liberty."

A key to the discussion is presented immediately with the concept of "fallenness," which has been emphasized by contemporary philosophers, especially phenomenologists, as an accurate description of the actual condition of humanity. It is defined as a "universal negative tendency," which is freely chosen but not determining, that is, "a tendency which is always capable of being overcome in each particular situation, but which is never completely overcome in its total extension."[32]

Furthermore, Segundo holds that this tendency is not peculiar to the human person, but that it characterizes all being, even the physical and material. Much of the chapter is devoted to a metaphysical analysis of the concept on the various levels of being; in this effort, an absolutely central reality is that of *entropy,* that is, "the continual degradation of energy." On the level of physical science, this means that, in any physical change, the amount of energy remains invariable, but that it becomes less available for use after the change (the term "degradation," therefore, is only correlative to a human project of utilization). But he goes on to insist that the physical level is only one phase of entropy, for "the degradation of energy reaches all species of energy, even spiritual energies. Under other forms, entropy is coextensive with the real."[33]

The next step is to demonstrate the existence of the phenomenon on the biological level, where it is viewed basically as "that which triumphs over life, that is, death." Life, therefore, at its most profound level is the struggle against entropy, for "to obtain a victory over the degradation of energy, however slight and momentary, is not *one* of the activities of life, nor is it *one* of its aspects; it is, to put it simply, life."[34]

The phenomenon is also manifest in the psychic sphere, where "the degradation of energy appears as offering resistance to our desires, as a bridle on our impatience and greed. Everything that has value also costs something." The moral philosophies of the Stoics, the Epicureans, and Nietszche are analyzed as different attempts, more or less successful, to come to grips with this phenomenon, while failure to take it into account has sometimes resulted in a rather passive and conformist version of Christian morality.[35]

Segundo's own ultimate moral criterion centers on Sartre's notion of good and bad faith. Good faith results in a life which "does not come from law, but from ourselves, from our most profound being, from the being *that we had decided to be* through our actions. . . . In effect, liberty is not only the power to perform a certain act or not: it is the power to give a certain meaning to life, to give ourselves a being by means of our actions." The act of bad faith is seen as one which does not correspond to this unity; its degradation of liberty lies not so much in deceiving others, but rather in deceiving oneself. Thus, now on the level of anthropology, we encounter the most profound degradation of energy, namely, "the resistance to that free act which would totally commit a person to the type of life which he or she has freely chosen." On the metaphysical level of freedom, this is seen as pure negativity.[36]

The preceding metaphysical analysis is of primary importance for Segundo's basic thesis in this book; indeed, it forms the substrate of all his work, even the most concrete, since it exposes the basic reality within which one must reflect upon and live out the gospel. In concluding his first volume, he asks whether this negative tendency, this "transcendental illusion" which denies creativity in history, is not actually the ideal or utopia implied in the concept of Christendom. It should be recalled that, at this point in the analysis, he has refrained from value judgments and confined himself to the sociohistorical facts. However, such a judgment is needed to answer the above question; thus the author turns to the original sources of Christian revelation, that is, to the New Testament.

Exegetical Principles

In his companion volume on Christendom subtitled *Principles,* Segundo presents an extremely complex and nuanced exegetical analysis, focusing primarily on what he terms the "Christian phenomenology" of St. John and St. Paul. He devotes special attention to the dialectic of these authors, such as the Pauline "flesh" vs. "spirit" and the Johannine "world" vs. "truth" or "world" vs. "liberty," although many refinements of other terms are included. Because of the intricacy of the argument, it would be impossible to present it in detail at this point, so I will be content to present a summary in the author's terms, while encouraging specialists to consult the text itself.

Segundo begins his conclusion to the second volume by noting again that the key problematic confronting the contemporary church is that of the "crisis of Christendom." He goes on to suggest that it may be possible to see in this crisis a more profound and permanent element rather than a passing evil or a mere crisis of growth. That element is precisely the rediscovery of the vision of the church as a minority called to liberty at the service of the mass-majority, a vision that was the burden of his first volume.

But the question may be raised as to whether such a vision, based as it is on historical and sociological facts, is not "a *human* reduction, all too human, of the perspectives of faith. Do not the *principles* of Christian revelation demand Christendom as the only perfect realization of the Christian ideal in history?"[37] Segundo believes he has answered this by showing that the New Testament authors themselves believed that they were unfolding the "mystery" of God's plan for all of history, a plan, moreover, that was already under way and whose final result was certain.

He summarizes the two poles within which the plan is presented as follows:

On the one hand, Christianity (above all in John) knows that its message, since it maximizes the demands of liberty, cannot hope to obtain a yes from the mass, in the very measure in which it presents itself as it authentically is. On the other hand, Christianity does not aim at presenting itself in another way because (above all in Paul) it conceives a history within which both the determinism and no of the masses as well as the liberty and the yes of the minorities form part of one complex dynamism which terminates in Christ, the head of the cosmic Body.[38]

Thus Christianity is interested in the development of human institutions, since they are conditioning elements with regard to the exercise of real liberty and love, two terms which are synonymous in Christian thought.[39] And since according to revelation, God is both the source and object of all authentic love, it would be anti-Christian to attempt to direct institutions to a situation of diminution of liberty and love in order to achieve a mass adherence to Christianity. For such a Christianity would be emptied of its very substance.

Segundo then appends two further observations concerning the irreversible historical development that occurs on the human level by means of institutions, according to the New Testament. First of all, the development conduces to a progressive presence of the *hour* of judgment, for "the increasing dependence of all with respect to all others daily locates Christ the Judge more centrally in every human existence, and increasingly the universe refers to him in every act of authentic liberty."[40]

Second, he ends with a caution against identifying specific human groups with a yes or no, that is, with identifying them as minorities or masses. For these two elements "operate within each human existence and each one bears within itself a 'majority' and a 'minority,' flesh and spirit, a yes and a no. Moreover, the analysis of the thought of the New Testament forces us to consider as a victory of grace every emergence of a yes among the multitude of no's." For Segundo, in concluding, all this explains the imperturbable security with which John and Paul "expect of the entirety of history and of each existence in particular the superabundance of grace over and above the multiplication of sin."[41]

The discussion in the two volumes of *Is Christendom a Utopia?* is deliberately kept on a theoretical level, in order to construct a solid foundation for further reflection. Obviously, the conception of the church that is advanced contains enormous ramifications for every area of Christian existence, and a number of these will be developed in future chapters.

Remaining for the present on the theoretical level, it is clear that Segundo's view of the church has numerous parallels with the basic vision of Pierre Teilhard de Chardin. Although certain key quotations of Teilhard crop up frequently in the author's work, to my knowledge he has treated the relationship in detail in only one article, the concluding chapter of *From*

Society to Theology.[42] There he discusses the role of the church in evolution, beginning with an analysis of Teilhard's often quoted description of the church as "the reflectively Christified portion of the world . . . main focus of interhuman affinities through super-charity . . . central axis of universal convergence and exact point of encounter between Universe and Omega Point." In the rest of the chapter he sketches an outline of an ecclesiology in terms of evolution and from the perspective of the church in Latin America.

Comparisons and Conclusions

In contemporary ecclesiology, Richard P. McBrien has presented views that are similar to Segundo's. In his book *Church: The Continuing Quest*,[43] McBrien surveys three basic conceptions of the church in the light of Vatican II and subsequent developments. He believes that the "doctrinal-scholastic view," which flourished before the Council, is held by so few theologians today that it does not even deserve to be called a "probable opinion." The second position, which he calls "kerygmatic-biblical," does find some support, most notably in the works of Hans Küng; however, McBrien stresses that recently ". . . what is most significant to me is the change, on the part of Rahner and Schillebeeckx, from a generally kerygmatic-sacramental view of the church to a more historically and politically oriented eschatological view."[44]

McBrien himself supports this third form of "historical or proleptic eschatology," in which "the kingdom of God is central; the Church makes no sense apart from it"; moreover, he believes that most theologians today accept this in one form or other. Basically, this view "regards history as in process of becoming the Kingdom of God, and the Church as sign, instrument, and herald of this ongoing reality." In all his works, McBrien has insisted on a triad of essential functions of the church: proclamation (*kerygma*), a sign of community (*koinonia*), and service to humanity (*diakonia*).[45] The current emphasis on *diakonia*, it would appear, is not because the first two functions have ceased to be essential, but because such *diakonia* has been neglected in both the theory and practice of the church.

A similar approach has also been adopted in an important article published by Roger D. Haight.[46] His succinct statement of the key issue in current ecclesiology is the following: "When one passes from a common presupposition that there is no salvation outside the Church to the supposition that indeed the 'ordinary' way of salvation is outside the Church, one must also pass to a fundamentally different understanding of the nature and role of the Church."[47] Using a concrete, existential, and historical approach to theology, Haight proffers a convincing analysis of "mission" as the key symbol for the church's self-understanding today, a symbol "that both absorbs into itself the contemporary critique of the Church and responds to it confidently in a uniquely traditional and Christic way."[48] In summary form, he concludes, "As was the mission of Jesus, so the Church is sent to the world and for the world, especially the dispossessed, to help make all things new in the name of Christ."[49]

My only reservation with regard to Haight's view of the church is that it does not go far enough, that is, it does not attend sufficiently to *what the mission is*. That mission is clearly evangelization, and its basic features were defined in a synthetic and very nuanced manner in Pope Paul VI's apostolic exhortation *Evangelii Nuntiandi*.[50] Without going into detail, I believe that document breaks new ground in stating that authentic evangelization has three major aspects: verbal proclamation of the Good News; a life of personal witness to the Good News; and transforming social praxis in accordance with the Good News. The last feature is especially important: social praxis is here envisioned not merely as an ethical impera- tive of the gospel nor as a form of pre-evangelization, but as part of the evangelization process itself.

Without reviewing in detail the analysis in this chapter of Segundo's ecclesiology, I would suggest that it has the advantage of providing a thorough grounding for these views, both on the philosophical and on the theological or exegetical levels. Thus, it demonstrates clearly that such a view of the church is not a *new* development but actually the basic one from the beginning as well as the only one consonant with the historical and scientific evidence.

It is the situation of Christendom then that represents a distortion, or at least an abnormal condition, in the understanding of the church's role in history. The normal condition, and the one that is coming back into focus today,[51] is that of a creative minority dedicated to the service of the vast majority of humanity. But I believe we should not assert too cavalierly that the era of Christendom is over and done with; abundant evidence of its continued existence, especially in the *operative* mentality of Christians, is all around us in the church in the United States.

But Segundo's view also appears to me to go beyond the two positions mentioned above with regard to how the church will actually function in its "service" or "mission" to the world. The view clearly locates the church's role within the evolutionary perspective advocated by Teilhard de Chardin and finally adopted by the Second Vatican Council. And it places great stress on the role of secular institutions in providing a "liberating environ- ment" for humanity, as well as the church's role in the criticism and transformation of institutions. By "church" here I do not refer to the hierarchy or clergy but to the whole people of God. The adult laity men- tioned earlier would be the principal architects of the creative transforma- tion of institutions, since they are already present in all the institutions of society. Outside of exceptional circumstances, the hierarchy's role would be one of education and guidance along general lines, in a spirit of true service to the people of God.

Lastly, I believe that Segundo's views also provide a much needed theoretical underpinning for a whole series of developments in the praxis of North American Christians that has burgeoned in remarkable fashion since Vatican II. I refer to the creation of various "lobbies for justice," such as the Center of Concern, the Network of Catholic religious women, the Protestant-initiated organization Impact, various national and local chapters concerning "Peace and Justice," and many others.[52] If Segundo's views are valid, these groups can now be envisioned as fulfilling an absolutely essential function of the church, that is, participation in the struggle to humanize the local, national, and international institutions—social, economic, political, and cultural—that deeply affect the lives of every man and woman on the planet. Such organizations would no longer be looked upon as "fringe groups" or "mere activists," an optional addition to the church's real task, but rather as a central component of the church's role in the evolution of humankind. In other words, without such organizations or similar ones, the church would not authentically be the church.[53]

On the grassroots level of the ordinary Catholic parish, participation in such efforts appears to me to be a marginal phenomenon, although there exists abundant documentation in magisterial documents to support this activity. Rather the situation of the majority, both clerical and lay, appears to be that of Paulo Freire's "culture of silence." A further examination of this critical divorce between theory and practice will be taken up in the following chapter. Here I will close by voicing agreement with the succinct statement of Jürgen Moltmann: "What we have to learn . . . is not that the church 'has' a mission, but the very reverse: that the mission of Christ creates its own church."[54]

NOTES

1. Joseph H. Fichter, "The Uncertain Future of the Church in America," *Thought* (June 1975):131; italics mine. Fichter also notes that "historically we have moved from a Christendom which attempted a universal embrace of society to a situation where organized religion became a recognized institution alongside other major institutions of the cultural system. We are already in the next phase, and increasingly so, where the churches stand in judgment of the whole complex social structure of the modern world" (ibid.). While I agree with Fichter, I think that some very salutary observations on the limitations inherent to the church's role have been presented by Charles E. Curran in "Theological Reflections on the Social Mission of the Church," in *The Social Mission of the Church: A Theological Reflection*, ed. Edward J. Ryle (Washington, D.C.; Catholic University, n.d.), pp. 31–53.

2. *Función de la Iglesia en la realidad rioplatense* (Montevideo: Barreiro y

Ramos, 1962). Henceforth, if the context is not clear, I will refer to this book simply as *Función*.

3. Ibid., p. 6.

4. Ibid., p. 7.

5. Ibid., p. 9.

6. Details of these three areas relating to the situation in Uruguay and Argentina in 1962 and earlier may be found on pp. 13–27 of *Función*.

7. In the English edition of *The Divine Milieu* (New York: Harper and Row, 1965), the quote is as follows: "Depending on the greater or less vitality of the nature of the individual, this conflict is in danger of finding its solution in one of the following ways: either the Christian will repress his taste for the tangible and force himself to confine his taste to purely religious objects, and he will try to live in a world that he has divinised by banishing the largest possible number of earthly objects; or else, harassed by that inward conflict which hampers him, he will dismiss the evangelical counsels and decide to lead what seems to him a complete and human life; or else, again, and this is the most usual case, he will give up any attempt to make sense of his situation; he will never belong wholly to God nor wholly to things; incomplete in his own eyes, and insincere in the eyes of his fellows, he will gradually acquiesce in a double life" (p. 52).

8. Segundo, *Función*, p. 35.

9. This phrase occurs in the Pastoral Constitution on the Church in the Modern World (*Gaudium et Spes*). For an excellent brief analysis of the various ecclesiologies that were combined but not synthesized in Vatican II's decrees, see Richard P. McBrien, "The Second Vatican Council: A Study in Ambivalence," in *Church: The Continuing Quest* (New York: Newman, 1970), pp. 23–41.

10. Segundo, *Función*, pp. 46–47. In his study of J. B. Metz, Marcel Xhaufflaire stresses the same point with regard to European political theology: "The first thing that political theology has to say to the church is that it does not exist for itself. . . . Its reason for existence lies in its role of mediating the eschatological proclamation of salvation" (*La 'théologie politique': Introduction à la théologie politique de J. B. Metz* [Paris: Editions du Cerf, 1972], p. 53).

11. Segundo, *Función*, p. 50.

12. Ibid., p. 70.

13. Ibid., p. 74.

14. Ibid., p. 72.

15. Ibid., p. 68. It may be noted that this last text and the one from Colossians occur repeatedly in the writings of Pierre Teilhard de Chardin.

16. Segundo, *Función*, p. 75.

17. Ibid., p. 76. Cf. the remarks of J. B. Metz: "Since the late Middle Ages, but all the more definitively and irreversibly, man, his science, his culture, his economy, have moved out of the great all-inclusive edifice that was medieval Christendom and its theopolitical structure, in which theology and the Church possessed the key to every sphere of life" (*Theology of the World* [New York: Herder and Herder, 1969], p. 143).

18. A number of concrete applications to the actual situation in Uruguay and Argentina are presented in *Función*, pp. 71–77.

19. *La cristiandad ¿una utopía? I. Los hechos. II. Los principios* (Montevideo: Mimeográfica "Luz," 1964). In further references I will refer to these volumes as *Cristiandad I* and *Cristiandad II*.

20. Segundo, *Cristiandad I*, p. 87.

21. Ibid., pp. 3–4.

22. Ibid., p. 13.

23. Ibid., p. 20.

24. Ibid., p. 89.

25. Ibid., p. 90.

26. Ibid., p. 45.

27. Ibid., p. 46.

28. Ibid., pp. 56–57.

29. Ibid., p. 61. From a different point of view, Georg Lukács stresses the same point in *History and Class Consciousness* (Cambridge, Mass.: Harvard University Press, 1971), p. 299: "The organization is the form of the mediation between theory and praxis." Quoted in Jürgen Habermas, *Theory and Practice* (Boston: Beacon Press, 1973), p. 34.

30. Segundo, *Cristiandad I*, p. 65.

31. Ibid., pp. 66–67.

32. Ibid., p. 70. In the course of this chapter, Segundo notes the "profound identity" of what he is describing with the views of Karl Rahner in "The Theological Concept of 'Concupiscence,' " *Theological Investigations I* (Baltimore: Helicon Press, 1961), pp. 347–82.

33. Segundo, *Cristiandad I*, p. 71.

34. Ibid., p. 75.

35. Ibid., pp. 75–77.

36. Ibid., pp. 80–82. The references to Sartre are from the original French edition of *Being and Nothingness*.

37. Segundo, *Cristiandad II*, p. 96.

38. Ibid., p. 97.

39. See the comment of Karl Rahner in "The Future of Theology," *Theological Investigations XI*, p. 145: "Christianity consists in something more than a mere contemplation of essences or an attitude of passively waiting for the Kingdom of God. Rather it consists in bold decisions, in action, in transforming the world, and in these alone is the eschatological hope for the advent of the absolute future made real."

40. Segundo, *Cristiandad II*, p. 98.

41. Ibid., p. 99.

42. "La Iglesia en la evolución de un continente," in *De la sociedad a la teología* (Buenos Aires: Carlos Lohlé, 1970), pp. 155–73. Denis Goulet also quotes Teilhard in the context of liberation theology and Segundo's work in particular in *A New Moral Order: Development Ethics and Liberation Theology* (Maryknoll, N.Y.: Orbis Books, 1974), p. 111. The relationship involved deserves further study; at present it appears to me that Segundo's contribution is to translate Teilhard's vision (which remained on the scientific-technological plane of the developed nations) into the sociopolitical context appropriate to the developing world. See the comments along this line of Gustavo Gutiérrez, *A Theology of Liberation* (Maryknoll, N.Y.: Orbis Books, 1973), pp. 173–74.

43. For a basic statement on McBrien's views of the Church, see Richard P. McBrien, *Do We Need the Church?* (New York: Harper and Row, 1969).

44. Richard P. McBrien, *Church: The Continuing Quest*, pp. 64–65. Another important proponent of the historical-political emphasis is Gregory Baum, e.g., "Ecclesiology is not simply the theological study of the Christian church; it is the critical study, based on divine revelation, of what happens in human society. Ecclesiology is the study of the Spirit's presence to the sick society" (*Man Becoming: God in Secular Experience* [New York: Herder and Herder, 1971], p. 68).

45. This is especially developed in *Do We Need the Church?* In a later work, McBrien has boldly stated what his theories would entail regarding internal church renewal in *The Remaking of the Church: An Agenda for Reform* (New York: Harper and Row, 1973).

46. Roger D. Haight, "Mission: The Symbol for Understanding the Church Today," *Theological Studies* (December 1976):620–49.

47. Ibid., p. 630.

48. Ibid., pp. 648–49.

49. Ibid., p. 649.

50. Pope Paul VI, "Evangelization in the Modern World (*Evangelii Nuntiandi*)," *The Pope Speaks* 21 (1976):4–51. For an excellent analysis of the document, see Jon Sobrino, "Evangelización y Iglesia en América Latina," *Christus* (February 1978):25–44.

51. For an example of such an ecclesiology from a European perspective, see Jürgen Moltmann's *The Church in the Power of the Spirit: A Contribution to Messianic Ecclesiology* (New York: Harper and Row, 1977). Especially helpful is Moltmann's section on "Christianity in the Processes of the World's Life," pp. 163–89.

52. These organizations are meant only as examples; I mention them because I have had personal experience of their competence and effectiveness. The Center of Concern is located at 3700 13th St., N.E., Washington, D.C., 20017; Network operates from 224 D St., S.E., Washington, D.C., 20003; Impact has its office at 110 Maryland Ave., N.E., Washington, D.C., 20002; and the very active branch of the United States Catholic Conference now entitled "Department of Social Development and World Peace" has its headquarters at 1312 Massachusetts Ave., N.W., Washington, D.C., 20005. Some excellent examples of the depth of the work done by the Center of Concern may be seen in the following articles by the director, Peter J. Henriot: "Social Sin and Conversion: A Theology of the Church's Social Involvement," *Chicago Studies* (Summer 1972):3–18; "The Concept of Social Sin," *Catholic Mind* (October 1973):38–53; and "A Theology of Action for Social Justice: Applications in the Global Context," *Catholic Mind* (December 1973):31–45. Valuable collaborative works of the Center include "The Quest for Justice: Guidelines to a Creative Response by American Catholics to the 1971 Synod Statement, 'Justice in the World,' " (Washington, D.C.: Center of Concern, 1972); "Soundings: A Task Force on Social Consciousness and Ignatian Spirituality," (Washington, D.C.: Center of Concern, 1974); and "Detroit and Beyond: The Continuing Quest for Justice" (Washington, D.C.: Center of Concern, 1977).

53. In conclusion, it may be noted that this approach is not some form of new development but rather a retrieval of the most authentic traditions of the Bible. As an example, see the classic work of Gerhard von Rad, *Old Testament Theology II: The Theology of Israel's Prophetic Traditions* (New York: Harper and Row, 1965): ". . . one of prophecy's greatest achievements was to recapture for faith the dimension in which Jahweh had revealed himself *par excellence,* that of history and politics" (p. 182); ". . . these men [the prophets] tore open the horizons of world history to reveal perspectives of a vastness such as Israel had hitherto never imagined" (p. 343).

54. Jürgen Moltmann, *Church in the Power of the Spirit*, p. 10.

CHAPTER FIVE

PRAXIS VERSUS MAGIC

One of the most extraordinary developments in the theology of the past decade is the manner in which the question of praxis and its relation to theory has moved to the center stage of theological debate. Recently a number of penetrating articles by North Americans have focused on the issue,[1] and Matthew Lamb has gone so far as to assert flatly that "theory-praxis goes right to the core of the entire theological enterprise."[2] Most of the articles, however, have been clarifications of the parameters of the problem and not genuine examples of praxis-based theologizing. On the other hand, since praxis has constituted the linchpin of liberation theology since the beginning, it might legitimately be expected that that theology has a valuable contribution to make with regard to the actual doing of a praxis-oriented theology.

In this chapter then I will review some key publications of Segundo on this important issue. A variety of expressions will be utilized to describe praxis, depending on the different points of view that may be adopted with regard to it. Thus, it will be designated as "pastoral praxis" when emphasis is placed on the activity of hierarchy, clergy, and other church professionals. Orthopraxis constitutes a broader expression to encompass those actions of the entire ecclesial community that are in harmony with the message of the gospel; thus, it would be opposed to heteropraxis, in the same way as orthodoxy is opposed to heterodoxy. Lastly, the term "morality" is intended to place the accent on the conduct of the individual believer, although, in an authentic Christian context, this would involve essential social dimensions. These three approaches in Segundo's thought will now be examined, followed by a consideration of what might be called "counterapproaches," and which can be summarized under the heading of a fundamentally "magical" understanding of the Christian religion.

Pastoral Praxis

In discussing pastoral activity, it must be strongly emphasized at the outset that theology and pastoral praxis are much more intimately linked in Latin America than is the case in North America and Europe. In the latter areas, the two fields are often completely separated from each other or, when there is a union, the pastoral task is viewed as a mere practical implementation of a previously established body of theology. In opposition to such dualism, the Latin approach has been succinctly explained by Enrique Dussel:

> . . . since there is only one theology in the final analysis, this *logos* about God is also pastoral in nature from the very start. Everything I have said so far is also pastoral in one way or another, because speculative theology cannot really be separated from praxis. Theology must interpret God's revelation in day-to-day history. When it is separated from that history and turned into a distinct theoretical discipline, as happened in the past history of the Church, theology will inevitably become decadent.[3]

A sympathetic observer on the European scene, Claude Geffré, also adverts to this understanding when he notes that "a theologian who carries out his theoretical research work independently of actual commitment, as happens in Europe, is inconceivable in Latin America."[4]

However, granted that theology and pastoral activity are always closely linked in the Latin context, it is still possible and fruitful to focus on the latter activity in a more concentrated and specific way. I believe that Segundo has achieved this with greatest clarity in his book *Pastoral Activity in Latin America: Its Hidden Motives,*[5] which we will now consider.

To put it in briefest form, the thesis of this book is that pastoral practice ends up in opposing and even contradictory activities and goals, depending on the basic choice that is made between two opposed ecclesiologies, whether these be explicit or implicit. Neither of these two conceptions, it should be noted, are imposed as obligatory by the extraordinary magisterium or teaching authority of the church, although the entire book is a sustained and carefully reasoned argument for one of the ecclesiologies. However, no matter what choice one finally makes, I believe the careful delineation of alternatives is most helpful for a more profound and realistic discussion of pastoral strategy in any area of the world, and especially in North America.

The two basic options, which may be referred to as Option A and Option B, are radically opposed to each other with regard to three basic principles. Option A would adhere to the following: (1) "the church was established for the benefit of those who belong to it"; (2) "the universality of the church is quantitative, not qualitative"; and (3) "the church is always the best place for attaining salvation."[6] On the other hand, the fundamental assertions of Option B would include: (1) "the church was established in the world for the benefit of the rest of humanity"; (2) "the universality of the church is qualitative, not quantitative"; and (3) "the church is not always the best place to attain salvation."[7]

As noted above, Segundo presents a strong argument for the acceptance of Option B, not only because it is rooted in the message of the New

Testament but also because it is the only option that has a realistic future in the contemporary world. In reviewing his position, my attempt will be to select those elements with possible applicability to the North American scene.

In his initial chapter, "A Society Undergoing Change," Segundo presents a sociological background for understanding the person and the society to which pastoral activity is directed. As has often been noted, the society is one of rapidly accelerating urbanization, which brings with it uprootedness, insecurity, and a relativization of values in those who have been displaced. The author places particular emphasis on the fact that "every great modern urban concentration, even in the undeveloped nations, is *a consumer society*. And that holds true even if it has many people and little to consume."[8] Without entering into details of his exposition, consumption and its demands are seen as the new integrating factor in the cities, replacing the common worldview and shared values of the traditional society. Moreover, the consumption outlook and ethic are intensively propagated and continually reinforced by the powerful mass media, so that more profound questions of goals and means are relegated to the private sphere and finally relativized. The result is that "any profound idea is to a certain extent revolutionary for the consumer society and will be treated as such."[9]

Along with the above, he stresses the importance of the emergence of a "social consciousness," a phenomenon that is not often treated by European and North American sociologists. The appearance of this consciousness is attributed in part to the "discovery of the abyss which exists between those values which are said to direct society and those interests which control it in reality." This has led to the process called "conscientization," which is ubiquitous throughout the continent, and which Segundo describes as "that entire social mobilization designed to make known, in a manner less naive and more realistic and critical, the interplay of interests—above all, group interests—which are disguised by propaganda, promises, and types of paternalism in their united effort to maintain the society as it is." The author notes that there are different forms of conscientization at work in Latin America—Marxist, Christian, nationalist, etc.—but that they all have the common effect of further widening the chasm between traditional values and new conceptions of society and of the universe.[10]

In the following chapters Segundo continues his cultural analysis, but at the same time begins to interweave the question of the proper pastoral responses to the new situation. Again, as in other works, he empasizes a crucial reality that pastoral action must confront in the contemporary world, namely, the "destruction of the closed environment." This refers to the fact that the protective social structures and pressures that used to transmit Christianity from generation to generation in the past have either vanished or are in the process of disappearing. And the phenomenon applies not only to the large cities but also to the most remote rural areas, as these are progressively absorbed into the global net of mass communications. A very graphic example is given of the tiny village of Ars in France. In the period of the "closed environment," the Curé of Ars devised a pastoral strategy to extirpate the sin associated with dancing—he simply paid the only musician in town to leave. In that still tiny village today, however, although externally it appears the same, each family possesses its own "musician," thanks to the mass media. Ars, consequently, has been opened up culturally as if it were situated in the midst of a large city; indeed, "to it come, with great distinctness, the ideas, the styles of life, the different human values, of Paris, of New York, or of Moscow."[11]

This new situation, it is stressed, also affects deeply what are often considered to be the last bastions of the closed environment, that is, the family and the school. The author notes that "many statistics now show that children and young persons receive much more from the modern mass media—such as television—than from their families and schools." Day in and day out, the television messages produce their relativizing impact on whatever values and attitudes were inculcated by the school or the home; in this perspective, the attribution of blame to either of these for their purported failure to produce "committed Christians" appears extremely naive.[12]

Oddly enough, this phenomenon has not resulted in secularization or in massive abandonment of religious practices. The reason for this, in Segundo's view, is that religious rites, processions, etc., now function as a prime source of *security*—perhaps the only source—for the uprooted and insecure person who is bewildered by escalating change. Since, Segundo believes, the Christian must be characterized not by a search for personal security but by a greater responsibility for others, Segundo's own pastoral strategy would be to develop the kind of personal conviction that would lead to such responsibility. But here the difficulty looms: "A church overwhelmed by the task of offering religious security has neither the time nor the personnel to create new pastoral methods designed to replace the closed environment with a personal conviction."[13]

Thus only through a conviction that is personal and even heroic can the message of the gospel be presented to the consumer society. But how is conversion to such an attitude to be accomplished? It can only result, Segundo believes, "from a historical consciousness which, in accord with the gospel, is intent on the social signs of the times, in search of concrete symbols of liberation."[14] But this necessarily demands the existence of basic communities (*comunidades de base*), which were endorsed by the bishops at Medellín, and which are composed of "free adults, reflecting upon their faith and the existential and social consequences of that faith."[15] To summarize, "our hypothesis—and our hope—is that a personal and heroic conviction and a communitarian social meaning make up a *total* pastoral system for Latin America," a system, moreover, that "can accompany at the same pace the very rapid cultural transformations of the continent."[16]

But the church is prevented from undertaking such a task, because it has chosen to rely on political and economic alliances that furnish the social pressures and institutions for a pastoral goal of "a minimum of demands and a maximum of members." Paradoxically, in order to be the "church of the poor," it must first become "the church of the rich."[17] All this results in what Segundo calls a "vicious circle." For as was noted above, a personal conviction today necessarily involves a social consciousness. But in this precise respect, the present practice of the church is discredited because of its alliances with political and economic power. Thus the circle: these alliances are the result of not adopting a pastoral goal of personal conviction, while at the same time they make it impossible to arrive at such a conviction.[18]

But if such a vicious circle obviously holds out no hope for the future, why has Segundo's alternative not even been seriously considered? At this point the author develops what he considers to be the "hidden motives" mentioned in the subtitle of his book, which can only be touched on here in quite summary fashion. Basically his thesis is that certain radical steps would have to be taken to initiate the alternative pastoral approach, and that certain hidden obstacles are blocking this course of action.

One of the steps would entail moving from a religious faith and practice that is dependent on various kinds of pressure (including religious pressure) to a stance that honestly respects the freedom of the individual person. Another would mean abandoning an emphasis on protecting large numbers to concentrate on the task of developing creative minorities that would influence the rest of society. And the last step would issue in disentanglement from alliances with political and economic power, in order to emphasize the power of the gospel itself.[19]

The hidden reasons for not embarking on the above course can all be reduced to just one, fear, which has to be kept hidden because "fear is never respectable, no matter how reasonable it may be." This includes psychological fear, that is, fear of our own inadequacy when confronted with the freedom of other persons, whether they belong to the church or comprise those who are to be evangelized. In addition, there exists theological fear that without the protection of structures many people will not be able to attain their salvation. And, lastly, there is pastoral fear, that is, distrust in the power of the gospel alone to attract people, as it may have done in the past. These three together then comprise "the hidden but decisive motivations of most of the pastoral activity in Latin America."[20]

In his last two chapters Segundo attempts to present in more detail the positive elements of the pastoral approach he is advocating. One obvious step would be to recognize and eradicate the kinds of fear mentioned above. He also shows how his approach could result in a new program of evangelization, and presents the following description of such a task: "to communicate only the essence of the Christian message, to communicate it as Good News and, finally, not to add anything except at a pace that allows the essential element to remain just that."[21] Out of many helpful insights concerning the process, the following appear to be most important. Evangelization is primarily the task of the laity, with the priest's role being that of forming evangelical communities. One should be able to convey the Christian message in a short time, even half an hour, as happened in the early church. It should not consist of dead formulas, but rather be translated in a creative way that really will be Good News to people today;[22] this, of course, implies that we have first listened, that is, have tried to understand deeply the situation in which contemporary persons find themselves. And the values that are presented verbally should be seen to be in harmony with the actual decisions and undertakings that are manifest in the praxis of the Christian community.

The book concludes by reiterating that two different—and opposed—ecclesiologies are at the basis of the different pastoral approaches; moreover, it strongly supports Option B, as outlined at the beginning of this chapter, bolstering this decision with arguments drawn from the texts of Vatican II. With regard to the qualitative rather than quantitative universality of the church, he makes use of the biblical analogy of the church as leaven, noting that it is not the function of leaven to transform the entire mass of dough into leaven but rather into bread; thus the church is basically a transforming ferment for the rest of humanity. Those who are unable or do not wish to perform this function would be impeding the basic mission of the church, and from this follows the rather shocking statement that they would be more assured of salvation outside its boundaries.[23] Segundo ends with the warning that the two options can in no way be combined, and that a decision has to be made on the level of principles that have been clearly analyzed, "according to the ancient—and healthy—tradition of pastoral theology."[24]

Orthopraxis and Morality

If we move at this point from pastoral considerations to the question of orthopraxis mentioned earlier, a much broader vista opens up. A brief definition of orthopraxis would be Christian conduct in accordance with the gospel; obviously then it is not limited to the pastoral duties of the clergy but embraces the actions of all those who strive to lead a Christian existence. Clearly, too, orthopraxis is dependent for its authenticity on a correct understanding of Christian morality, that is, the norms that guide Christian action in the world. Thus I would now like to discuss the book

From Society to Theology, where Segundo analyzes the meaning of Christian morality at some length.[25]

He begins his analysis with a discussion of the role of intellect or understanding in the context of Latin American Christianity. It is important to emphasize strongly at the outset that he is not employing the word in some kind of elitist sense, but rather refers to the manner in which ordinary persons understand and mentally structure their own lives, whatever may be their level of culture. Keeping this in mind, he goes on to discern the same deep current of anti-intellectualism in Latin American religious understanding that Richard Hofstadter had pointed out in the history of both Protestantism and Catholicism in the United States.[26] The next step is to attempt to probe more deeply into the reasons underlying this strange phenomenon.

On the level both of morality and dogma, Segundo discovers that understanding of moral norms and religious truths is actually considered *dangerous,* because such understanding may place in jeopardy the one thing that is considered absolutely necessary, that is, one's eternal salvation. On the one hand, salvation can be obtained with far less risk if one merely assents to dogmas correctly *formulated by others* rather than attempting to internalize them or assimilate them personally.[27] On the other hand, the same holds true for specific commitments in history: "The function of understanding and the consequent introduction of the Christian message in the contingent, relative, and ambiguous realities of history appear as terribly dangerous for the one thing which really matters: salvation."[28] This fundamental opposition between intellect and salvation leads the author to inquire at greater length into the authentic meaning of "salvation" in the Christian sources.

In a rather long exegetical section Segundo analyzes the documents of the New Testament, especially the writings of St. Paul, to achieve a clearer definition of salvation. Of primary interest for the purpose of this chapter is to see how the basic Pauline insights are then translated into terms of Christian morality; therefore it will be sufficient to note in summary form Segundo's thesis that in Paul "salvation, without ceasing to be absolute, is realized within the construction of human history."[29] And the Christian morality that flows from Paul's understanding of salvation is seen to have four central characteristics.

1. First of all, Christian morality is fundamentally a *creative* morality. To the numerous cases of conscience proposed to him by the community at Corinth as to what acts were licit or illicit, Paul replies that " 'All things are lawful for me,' but not all things are helpful" (1 Cor. 6:12) and " 'All things are lawful,' but not all things build up" (1 Cor. 10:23). Correlating this with the teaching on morality in the Letter to the Romans, Segundo concludes that this provides the first, basic principle of Christian morality, and that it is "even prior to the commandment of charity or love, precisely in order

that the latter can be understood and followed to its ultimate consequences.'' Thus Paul rejects the Corinthians' question about the liceity of acts and substitutes instead the question of their suitability (as in the expressions ''helpful'' and ''build up'' in the texts cited above). As a consequence, ''this correction displaces the emphasis of morality from the *action in itself* to the *project,* which Paul calls 'building up,' '' because ''the Christian, precisely by being Christian, has a project to accomplish; and morality consists in accomplishing it efficaciously.'' According to St. Paul, then, it is precisely in this new way of posing the question that one discovers the radical newness of Christianity and its definitive break with the Law. To sum up, ''the morality . . . which is derived from the authentic concept of Christian revelation is a *creative* morality, that is, a morality which does not receive its precepts from the world but from the project which the liberty of humanity must impose on a world which belongs to humanity.''[30]

2. Another fundamental characteristic is that Christian morality is *developing* or *evolving (progresiva).* This becomes clear when one pinpoints the project referred to above:

To love and to love efficaciously is the only law of the Christian—no longer the law that pins labels of ''permitted'' or ''prohibited'' on actions, independent from each person; but rather the law that points out to the liberty of human beings their unique and authentic path: always, in circumstances that are personal and unique, to create a love that is historical as well as irreplaceable and unique. It is certain that we live ''for the Lord,'' but we know that this tendency of love does not exclude, but rather includes *necessarily* the concrete and historical love of the brethren (Rom. 13:8–10).

To sum up, ''Christian morality is not a morality of the licit and illicit, but rather a morality of what is suitable or not for the construction of love, for the efficacious gift of oneself.''[31]

In such a context, sin appears not as the practice of something illicit, but as ''the loss of liberty. For in reality, that which was expressed in creative love may give way to egoism.'' Thus, a broad and continuing purification of conscience is necessary, with the result that the Christian's moral behavior is in a continual process of development (cf. Rom 14:2–5 and 14:14). Since such a process clearly entails a certain relativity, Segundo's view concerning this characteristic should be stated in full:

Here we have a healthy and profound relativity, which takes into consideration the progressive maturation of humanity and the variety of human situations. On the other hand, since we have just seen the completely objective demands that a sincere and universal love entails, we will easily understand that this relativity is not a relativism. It points out the conditions of real progress in the creative moral conscience, which, to the extent that it loves, discovers more and more the dimensions of love that are profound, universal, and objective.[32]

3. In addition to the characteristics of development and evolution, Christian morality is also essentially *social*. Once again, this means that Christians are not absorbed in the question of the licitness or illicitness of actions; rather, "they build a community and guide their action according to the necessities of this community" (cf. 1 Cor. 10:24: "Let no one seek his own good, but the good of his neighbor"). Segundo emphasizes "the connection of this characteristic with the conception of salvation which we have presented. Once more, only such a conception of salvation, and the attitude which Paul calls faith that is related to it, can liberate humanity for this kind of creative, evolving, and social morality."[33]

In attempting to deepen the understanding of the social dimension of morality, Segundo utilizes the theological concept of the final judgment on human actions, referring especially to Matt. 25:31ff. and 1 Cor. 6:9–10. His emphasis is centered on the complexity, on the human level, that underlies such a judgment. For "all persons, in the course of their existence, have given and refused bread and water"; in other words, "if each of the sins which Jesus and Paul mention is a no to Christ and to the kingdom, are they not intermingled in each concrete person with other yes's achieved by love?" The author rejects a current solution to this problem, namely, that one's final act in life is decisive for judgment, on the grounds that it has no basis in the New Testament.

Segundo's own answer to the question is found in 1 Cor. 3:10–15, where Paul employs the image of a building constructed of materials that are either strong or brittle, depending on whether they result from love or egoism. He then concludes:

We have seen that the building is the building up of the body of Christ. In that process love builds and also endures. Egoism builds only in appearance and passes away. This is evidently the image of judgment which is in harmony with the Pauline concept of salvation and with the Pauline concept of a Christian morality that is social and located within history.[34]

4. Last, Christian morality is *significative*, "that is, the Christian is one who has regard for the conscience of the other, because his or her function is that of transmitting a message, and that message is transmitted in great part through his or her actions. Christian morality derives from the fact that actions are signs and that their signification bespeaks an intimate relation with the question of the other." To phrase it differently, as a Christian one has been entrusted with a light, a message, a revelation; thus one is "basically preoccupied, not only with what the other person is but also with what the other person thinks." The Christian's vocation—and that of the church—is to be a sign in the world and "above everything else their morality prevents Christians from 'being an obstacle to the Jews, to the Gentiles, and to the Church of God' " (1 Cor. 10:32). Lastly, this kind of significative morality must be one of dialogue, which includes a listening to

the signs of the times and a listening to other human beings.[35]

Accepting for the moment that Christian morality is meant to be creative, evolving, social, and significative, can we say that such a vision—and orthopraxis based on it—is truly *operative* in the majority of church members, here as well as in Latin America? This question brings us to the second, and negative, part of our analysis. For it is clear that this is not the operative morality of most Catholics; thus it is of utmost importance to search out the underlying reasons for this. What we are confronted with is not a failure to achieve high ideals (which is, after all, the human condition and will be always with us), but praxis that is based on the wrong ideals or, in other words, an operative heteropraxis that flows from an often unexamined heterodoxy. Throughout all his work Segundo is acutely aware of this situation, and intent on exposing its root causes. What follows, then, is a brief survey of his attempts from a number of different works.

Christianity and Magic

A fundamental concept in this area for Segundo is the notion of "magic"; that is, the surreptitious introduction of magical elements in the whole spectrum of Christian thought and practice constitutes an alienating intrusion that is exactly contrary to historical efficacy. He even goes so far as to state, with relation to the five-volume series *Theology for Artisans of a New Humanity,* that "the central concern of this whole series has been Christian liberty and its involvement in history; that is, the conquest of such magical elements."[36] Consequently, magic is defined by him as "looking for divine efficacy in certain procedures without any relation to historical efficacy."[37]

To be more specific, this magical tendency becomes evident in the field of dogmatic statements when, as discussed above, assent to formulations assumes greater importance than actual comprehension and assimilation of truths in relation to one's real existence. Segundo concludes that discussion by insisting that "it is not a question of formulas that are mysterious and efficacious in some mysterious way but of intelligible contents which are related to actual human endeavors. And although it is not basically concerned with books or courses or scientific investigation, this is a work of the intellect, it is a function of thought."[38] What he is opposed to is referred to as the "blank-check" approach to religious understanding, wherein "the faithful sign their name, and it is up to the church to fill in the exact formulas of faith and what they mean. But what efficacy does the blank check have? None but a magical one, since people's ignorance of its content means that it has no historical consequences."[39]

The alienating consequences of such an approach are also clearly stated:

If salvation consists in man's liberation in history and metahistory (*Gaudium et Spes,* no. 39), then this presupposes a God who is profoundly interested and involved in human history. But if we present God as some inaccessible being who is perfectly happy in his infinity no matter what happens in history, and what is more, as someone who kindly makes contact with human beings not in the space and time of history but in some separate, detached, cultic locale, then we are offering a magical escape hatch to Christians. And this image will speak much more forcefully to them than any episcopal document will.

A very succinct statement of this first aspect is the following: "Any orthodoxy that does not essentially point toward orthopraxy is magical."[40]

Exactly the same consequences can occur in the field of morality. For if moral teaching is understood as an already finished and complete instrument, independent of the real needs and experience of persons and societies, then it inculcates an ahistorical vision of the moral life, which is a typically magical procedure. As with dogma, this can also conceal an alienating function, for it often "inculcates conformity, based on abstract and atemporal considerations, with some *status quo* created to benefit very special interests." And this is especially detrimental in an era of rapid social change like our own, for "as it becomes advantageous and even necessary to replace 'natural' possibilities with new artificial possibilities, and as new images of societal life show up on the horizon as possible replacements for those which seemed to have stemmed from nature itself, a law that supposedly was sanctioned by God ahead of time increasingly shows up in its true light, i.e., as an evasion of history. And like every evasion of history, it is magical."[41] The earlier discussion in this chapter concerning authentic Christian morality should have already indicated why Segundo finds such a magical moral approach to be at variance with the prophetic tradition of both the Old and New Testaments.

It is the sacramental system, however, that provides the most potent and concrete vehicle for engendering and reinforcing magical attitudes. When a "bank-deposit" conception of the sacraments is adopted and translated into practice, then the sacraments are distorted and become instruments of domestication: "They almost always are alienated from people; they always alienate them."[42] It is not that Segundo opposes the very existence of sacraments; indeed, he views them as central to Christian existence. But in direct opposition to the "bank-deposit" approach, they must be construed as genuinely *dialogic,* preparing the Christian community to speak its liberating word in the history of humanity. Although I will not discuss the author's views on sacraments in detail, his approach is indicated in the following: "And so from birth to death Christians are associated through each sacrament with the perennial questions of humanity. And along with the communitarian commitment of their gestures they receive the response that God sends to those questions: the surety of victory over all the types of death that go to make up the life of human beings."[43] Thus, he concludes that ". . . the sacraments will be valid and efficacious, as Christ intended, to the extent that they are a consciousness-raising and motivating celebrating of humanity's liberative action in history."[44]

These divergent conceptions have resulted in what the author refers to as the present "crisis of the sacraments." However, he believes the impasse will not be resolved by further reform of the liturgy, because the roots of the crisis lie not in the sacraments but in the Christian community itself. The Eucharist, for example, often appears devoid of significance, not because it is a sacrament, but "because it does not flow out into any real community," or, to be more specific, "the act and fact of receiving communion does not unite people, reveal them to each other, or forge mutual involvement."[45]

What is radically at issue here is the manner of perceiving the relationship between sacraments and church. From one perspective the church is viewed as possessing value by reason of the sacraments it provides; from the opposite point of view the sacraments are assigned value only in function of the community that they create and set in motion. Segundo clearly enunciates his option for the latter position:

> . . . A community gathered together around a liberating paschal message needs signs which fashion it and question it, which imbue it with a sense of responsibility and enable it to create its own word about human history. This is precisely what the sacraments are about—and nothing else but that. Through them God grants and signifies to the church the grace which is to constitute it truly as such within the vast human community.[46]

The second position, moreover, involves a profound reappraisal of the one who stands in the epicenter of the system, that is, the priest or "man of the sacraments," whose position is also one of crisis. With regard to the administration of the sacraments, the solution to the problem appears *relatively* obvious: he must not allow the sacraments to become alienating gestures, leading people away from adult responsibility, but instead must make them "point up the specific mission of forming a community and leading it to its commitment in history."[47] The questions, however, of the priest's total lifestyle and the parish structure into which he is presently inserted present a much more formidable problematic, which is traced to a "crisis in the internal coherence of the Church."[48]

Sexuality and Original Sin

Aside from magical tendencies, there exist several other areas in the life of the church which Segundo believes often present obstacles to authentic orthopraxis and morality. These can be mentioned only briefly at this point.

One of these areas is sexuality, which is crucial, since "for the vast majority of human beings, liberation from egoistic and passive solipsism is possible only insofar as self-giving utilizes the sexual instinct."[49] Although traditional morality devotes a great deal of attention to sexuality, Segundo believes that it is often considered as a taboo rather than as a critical area of human existence that demands integration into the whole of one's psychic life. Sexuality comes to be perceived as the ultimate test of one's life project in a game plan established by God. The result of this approach is the following:

. . . the sexual part of what is called Christian morality has a debilitating effect on overall Christian praxis as well. Humanity's outlook on sexual matters is in large measure a solitary affair, particularly in the light of the surrounding eroticism of society. Now if its eternal destiny is constantly at stake in its attitude toward sexuality, then Christ's single commandment to love one another must drop into the background and suffer severe distortion. The Christian moral life is an eminently social one designed to create solidarity in society. But it is now devalued and turned into an individual struggle to preserve one's chastity.[50]

Another impediment to authentic orthopraxis involves the utilization that is often made of the doctrine of original sin. In practice, this is often converted into a very convenient prop and theological justification for some existing status quo. The recuperation of an authentic concept of original sin is a major thrust of the last volume in the *Artisans* series, entitled *Evolution and Guilt*. There Segundo observes that ". . . the image of an original fall that breaks up God's plan vitiates any and every attempt to attribute total and thoroughgoing value to the historical process."[51] In countering this conception, the author presents his own hermeneutic of John's gospel, concluding that the "sin of the world" proposed there does not consist in humanity's individual infraction of the law but rather in "the political negation of history."[52] Original sin must be perceived within a perspective of evolution, for "only an evolutionary outlook on sin and grace, entropy and love, violence and gratuitous giving, can hope to be in line with the message of the gospel." Indeed, this evolutionary outlook is stated flatly to be "*the key* to Christianity."[53]

Summary and Reflections

The issues discussed in this chapter seem to me to furnish abundant material for a critique of the fundamental principles underlying pastoral practice and Christian morality or orthopraxis in the churches of North America. As regards pastoral praxis, Segundo's analysis has the advantage of bringing great clarity for discernment of the ultimate objectives that underlie any pastoral strategy and of highlighting the decisions that must be made with regard to limited resources and personnel.

It appears to me, moreover, that Option B as described above is not only more in harmony with the source documents of Christianity but also offers the only possible way of forming men and women capable of transcending the consumer society, which is, indeed, the most thoroughly consumerized society in the history of the world. Five hundred commercial messages a day have been estimated as the average onslaught on the typical North American psyche, with each one propounding its own variant of the radically un-Christian message that "happiness is having." The result is the submerging or at least relativization of all other values. Only an adult, free decision and consequent praxis—heroic to the extent that one sets oneself directly counter to the prevailing values—appear to offer any hope of prevailing over this ubiquitous barrage.

It is also my judgment that Segundo clarifies some fundamental issues regarding orthopraxis or Christian morality, and that his extrapolation of such morality from the Christian sources is basically correct. Consequently, as regards the Catholic church in North America, the important question should be raised: is the orthopraxis or morality proposed at present one that is creative, evolving, social, and significative?

My own pastoral experience leads me to the conclusion that it is not. Often the need for security seems to dominate; that is, it is seen as far more secure to have someone else take responsibility for one's moral decisions rather than to exercise that often agonizing responsibility oneself. There is a great necessity in this country for a frank admission that the former behavior is the normal one of a child and at the furthest remove possible from that of an adult. Consequently, my own view is that a major task of Catholicism in this country is to exorcize such infantilism and to concentrate on the education of moral adults. Also, I believe Segundo has amply demonstrated above that such a morality necessarily involves an adult *understanding* of Christianity and of its relationship to the world.

This chapter may be concluded with a few references to contemporary praxis on the North American scene that may help clarify the above observations. Since the Catholic church here has devoted considerable (some would say obsessive) attention to sexual morality, a recent publication on human sexuality commissioned by the Catholic Theological Society of America may have considerable historical importance.[54] It may be left to experts in moral theology and to church authorities to assess the merits of this work on particular issues. But its basic thrust is the important point, for the book at least attempts to present a moral outlook that will foster a mature and integrated sexuality and that thus will transcend a mere catalogue of negative and external prohibitions. Granted that an integrated and adult sexuality is difficult to achieve in a highly eroticized culture, I believe that the attempt to do so constitutes the only realistic objective possible in an adult church.

Other examples of contemporary praxis may be mentioned which concern broadly social rather than interpersonal issues. The first concerns the abortion issue and the campaign for a constitutional amendment to restrict abortions. Again, I do not wish here to enter the thorny thicket of the strategic wisdom of this campaign. However, something else underlies this issue, which may have considerable historical reverberations. For a church formerly renowned for its "my country, right or wrong" attitude is now stating clearly that its country is wrong, and attempting in an organized way to correct the evil. And it should be kept in mind that the perceived evil does not pertain to the merely ecclesiastical sphere (as might be the case with religious freedom or aid to parochial schools) but rather affects the whole society. Clearly, too, a gigantic "conscientization" process could occur here that would have enormous consequences, for a pro-life attitude toward the unborn should logically be extended to a pro-life attitude toward those already born, that is, the poor, the oppressed, the suffering, who form the invisible underground of the affluent society, whether they live in it or in other parts of the world.[55]

Similar observations may be made regarding what I consider one of the most important movements in the North American church today: concern and action with regard to the problem of world hunger.[56] Not only is this a most appropriate reading and implementation of the signs of the times for citizens of the "breadbasket of the world," but it, too, has vast potential with regard to further conscientization. For if profit maximization is revealed as an inadequate "ethic" for a just distribution of the world's food resources, surely it is only a short step to ask if it is adequate for a just distribution of the other resources of the planet. For example, if each person were to receive adequate food, how are medical supplies and facilities at present distributed to ensure that that person does not die of sickness?[57] Or, if medicine is available, will it be effective when one's housing consists of a garbage heap?

A litany of further questions could be added, but these are sufficient to establish the fact that the world hunger movement has great potentialities for revitalizing American Catholicism. To employ Segundo's terms, it provides people with concrete experience of a morality that is creative, evolving, social, and significative, in a word, of a praxis that is Christian.

In conclusion, I would add a corollary concerning the objection that the activities just mentioned are misdirected, since they involve the "imposition of religious beliefs" on the rest of the nation. First of all, it is patently obvious that the nation referred to is a democracy and that the right to propose and argue for one's values is essential to the integrity and functioning of that system. The literal army of lobbyists in Washington are imposing their beliefs (religious or irreligious) on the nation also; yet there is little objection to this activity even when—as with the gun lobby—their objectives run counter to the will of the majority of the people. Moreover, an injection of such religious values as justice, solidarity, sharing, concern for the poor and suffering, could be seen as an extremely healthy antidote for a nation steeped—at times apparently swamped—in the basically egotistical values of consumerism.

The argument against the "imposition of religious beliefs" is thus exposed as a protective reaction of those who have their own interests to pursue in the system, which indeed is their right also in a democracy.[58] In rejecting the argument, and exercising their political rights to the full, American Catholics would be advancing toward a third form of maturity, which is really the logical outcome of a mature morality and a mature understanding of Christian existence. And that form is, in the fullest sense, political maturity.[59]

NOTES

1. The most helpful presentations include: Charles Davis, "Theology and Praxis," *Cross Currents* (Summer 1973):154–68; Matthew Lamb, "The Theory-Praxis Relationship in Contemporary Christian Theologies," *Catholic Theological Society of America: Proceedings of the Thirty-First Annual Convention* (New York: Manhattan College, 1976), pp. 149–78; Gregory Baum, "Critical Theology," in *Religion and Alienation: A Theological Reading of Sociology* (New York: Paulist Press, 1975), pp. 193–226; and David Tracy, "History, Theory, and *Praxis*," in *Blessed Rage for Order: The New Pluralism in Theology* (New York: Seabury Press, 1975), pp. 237–58. An excellent full-length study may be found in Matthew Lamb, *History, Method and Theology* (Missoula: Scholars Press, 1978). In this chapter I will confine myself to a more general discussion of the role of praxis. My views on more specific issues of the debate on method may be found in "Theological Method: The Southern Exposure," *Theological Studies* (December 1977): 709–35.

2. Matthew Lamb, "Theory-Praxis Relationship," p. 178.

3. Enrique Dussel, *History and the Theology of Liberation* (Maryknoll, N.Y.: Orbis Books, 1976), p. 157.

4. Claude Geffré, "A Prophetic Theology," in *Concilium 96: The Mystical and Political Dimensions of the Christian Faith* (New York: Herder and Herder, 1974), p. 12. In an earlier work Geffré proposed a helpful critique of political theology and related movements in Europe such as the theologies of hope and of history (*A New Age in Theology* [New York: Paulist Press, 1972]). His positive purpose there was "to show how much the Christian theology of today is seeking to move out from its cultural isolation by overcoming, in the very name of the Gospel, the false gulf between faith and modern reason, between the Church and the world, between the history of salvation and history pure and simple" (ibid., p. 9).

5. *Acción pastoral latinoamericana: Sus motivos ocultos* (Buenos Aires: Búsqueda, 1972). For a much briefer discussion of the same topic, see "Un nuevo comienzo pastoral," in *De la sociedad a la teologia* (Buenos Aires: Carlos Lohlé, 1970), pp. 29–59. After this chapter was written, *Acción pastoral* was published in English as *The Hidden Motives of Pastoral Action: Latin American Reflections* (Maryknoll, N.Y.: Orbis Books, 1978).

6. Segundo, *Acción*, pp. 70–71.

7. Ibid., pp. 126–29.

8. Ibid., p. 17.

9. Ibid., p. 22.

10. Ibid., pp. 22–26. The term the author uses in this section is "la conciencia social."

11. Ibid., p. 30. In *Sociedad* he also places great emphasis on "la destrucción de los ambientes cerrados" and uses the example of Ars; he also concludes in a similar

vein: "Because of the communications media, Ars today is a suburb of Lyons, of Paris, of Moscow, or of New York" (p. 32). The "Curé d'Ars," or St. Jean Baptiste Vianney (1786–1859), was appointed parish priest of Ars in 1818 and spent the rest of his life there. He was canonized by Pope Pius XI in 1925 and proclaimed patron of parish priests in 1929. See Henri Ghéon, *The Secret of the Curé d'Ars* (New York: Sheed and Ward, 1929).

12. Segundo, *Acción*, pp. 30–31.

13. Ibid., pp. 32–34.

14. Ibid., p. 39.

15. Ibid., p. 50. Segundo also notes that the priest is often an obstacle to base communities because "the reflection of lay persons is not based on the theology which the priest knows, but on real life and its problems" (p. 52). In the Medellín documents, the bishops state that ". . . the Christian base community is the first and fundamental ecclesiastical nucleus, which on its own level must make itself responsible for the richness and expansion of the faith, as well as of the cult which is its expression. This community becomes then the initial cell of the ecclesiastical structures and the focus of evangelization, and it currently serves as the most important source of human advancement and development" (*The Church in the Present-Day Transformation of Latin America in the Light of the Council* [Washington, D.C.: United States Catholic Conference, 1973], vol. 2, p. 202).

16. Segundo, *Acción*, p. 56.

17. Ibid., p. 44.

18. This is a summary of chapter 3, "Vicious Circle or Option?" pp. 45–59.

19. This paragraph summarizes chapter 4, "The Difficult Steps," pp. 61–77.

20. Ibid., p. 100. It would be impossible to include all the perceptive observations concerning these various forms of fear that Segundo advances in chapter 5, "The Cause of Concealment," pp. 79–100.

21. Ibid., p. 102. This definition is attributed to P. Seumois, an adviser to the Congregation for the Propagation of the Faith.

22. One suggestion that Segundo offers for explaining the life, death, and resurrection of Christ as "Good News" is the following: "On this earth no love is ever lost" (p. 106). He also notes that for acquiring a truth and not just repeating it like a parrot "it is necessary to make it one's own, and that means that one is given freedom and time to think about it and to mature. Furthermore, that one be given the opportunity to 'experiment' with it . . . to apply it to one's existence, even in an erroneous manner. . . . Thus is formed a Christian of *personal conviction*" (pp. 108–9).

23. Segundo is often accused of being "elitist" because of this view, but it appears to be logical: if the church is meant to be a visible, operative sign of God's love for the world, then those who are not committed to being this kind of sign should not belong to it. Here, as in other works, he uses the analogy of a bomb-disposal unit; persons who join it without the ability or commitment to do such dangerous work would be a menace to themselves and others (p. 129). In *Sociedad*, he answers the objection to elitism more explicitly: ". . . although the church is made up of persons who are weak and sinful, it has always understood that its duty of visibility placed limits on its desire of admitting or keeping the greatest possible number of members" (p. 42). In the same context, he notes that "the demands of visibility involve no connotation of puritanism, no intention of denying human weakness and forming a church of moral aristocrats," yet they remain "the absolutely necessary condition so that the message of the gospel may be the message of the gospel, in the mind of those who are to receive the message" (pp. 43–44). And he bolsters this by recalling the teaching of Vatican I that the visible life of the church comprises the fundamental argument for faith. On this issue, see Patrick J. Burns,

"Elitist Tendencies and Consumer Pressures in American Society," *Catholic Theological Society of America: Proceedings of the Twenty-Eighth Annual Convention* (New York: Manhattan College, 1973), pp. 47–69 and esp. p. 65, n. 25.

24. Segundo, *Acción*, p. 130.

25. *De la sociedad a la teología* is, in my opinion, the least unified of Segundo's books, with much of it consisting of articles previously published in journals. The section under consideration here is entitled "Intellect and Salvation," pp. 61–106. The book was published in Montevideo by Carlos Lohlé in 1970.

26. Richard Hofstadter, *Anti-Intellectualism in American Life* (New York: Alfred A. Knopf, 1963). He quotes Hofstadter to the effect that the intellectual content of Protestantism was watered down by denominationalism, revivalism, and fundamentalism. Catholicism, on the other hand, might have been expected to have had a contrary influence because of its preoccupation with dogma and richer theological tradition, but "the Catholic Church did not succeed in exercising that influence because of its excessive desire to adapt and to obtain the right of citizenship in American life" (*Sociedad,* p. 64).

27. Segundo, *Sociedad,* pp. 67 and 70.

28. Ibid., p. 75.

29. Ibid., p. 77. Segundo's basic exegetical approach will be analyzed in Chapter Six. In the present context, as in many others, he works out the detailed application of this approach in a spare and condensed form that is almost impossible to summarize. I intend to treat his detailed work in future publications; for now, the interested reader may consult pp. 78–94 for the actual exegesis. Also, it may be noted that Paul's vision is considered to be essentially the same as that of St. John, "in spite of the fact that John's profundity often conceals his radical novelty" (p. 84).

30. The discussion of creative morality occupies pp. 95–97. In Segundo's view, Paul was not merely a transmitter of the Christian message, but "he was a creator and his religious creation consisted in providing the message with means of expression that were more adapted to its own proper richness"; consequently, along with John, he appears as ". . . the first to construct a way of thinking that is directly Christian, so to speak, that is, a focusing of the totality of existence with regard to the new message" (p. 86).

31. Ibid., pp. 97–98. The moralist whom Segundo quotes most extensively here and in other works is Paul Lehmann, *Ethics in a Christian Context* (London: SCM, 1963). In this discussion, he cites passages from Lehmann's book (pp. 99, 101, 121–22), which basically revolve around the assertion that "Christian ethics is primarily concerned not with the good but with the will of God; it aims at maturity, not at morality" (Lehmann, p. 121).

32. Segundo, *Sociedad,* pp. 99–100.

33. Ibid., p. 101.

34. Ibid., pp. 102–3. A quotation that seems to be a favorite of Segundo's, since he utilizes it in other works, is appended here: "In short, maturity is salvation. . . . For maturity is the full development in a human being of the power to be truly and fully himself in being related to others who also have the power to be truly and fully themselves. The Christian *koinonia* is the foretaste and the sign in the world that God has always been and is contemporaneously doing what it takes to make and to keep human life human. This is the will of God" (Lehmann, *Ethics in a Christian Context,* pp. 99 and 101).

35. Segundo, *Sociedad,* pp. 103–4.

36. *A Theology for Artisans of a New Humanity:* vol. 4, *The Sacraments Today,* (Maryknoll, N.Y.: Orbis Books, 1974), p. 65. This was published in Spanish as *Los sacramentos hoy* (Buenos Aires: Carlos Lohlé, 1971).

37. Ibid., p. 63.

38. Segundo, *Sociedad,* p. 105. Again the author emphasizes that "we are not proposing a Christianity for intellectuals, but for people" (n. 11, p. 105).

39. Segundo, *Sacraments Today,* p. 64.

40. Ibid., pp. 64–65.

41. Ibid., p. 65.

42. Ibid., p. 102. A very interesting analogy is suggested in this "clarification" (pp. 100–04) between a correct approach to sacramental administration and Paulo Freire's approach to education; in brief, both activities should attempt "to move from deformation to information, from passivity to activeness, from being an object to being a subject, from false consciousness to true consciousness-raising" (p. 101).

43. Ibid., p. 74.

44. Ibid., p. 55. In this context Segundo quotes approvingly the definition of truth advanced by Rubem Alves, that is, "the name given by a historical community to those acts which were, are, and will be effective for the liberation of man" (from "Apuntes para una teología del desarrollo," *Cristianismo y Sociedad* 7 [1969]: 27).

45. Segundo, *Sacraments Today,* pp. 38 and 10.

46. Ibid., p. 99.

47. Ibid., p. 61.

48. Cf. the clarification "The 'Man of the Sacraments': A Life in Crisis," ibid., pp. 104–10. As regards priestly celibacy, Segundo notes that ". . . a man may 'sacrifice' his family and its just interests for the sake of a love that is directed toward the liberation of a whole society." However, he goes on to state that "priestly celibacy will be devoid of signification so long as the harsh requirements and creative risks of commitment are not visibly related to the priest's role" (ibid., pp. 86–87).

49. *Theology for Artisans of a New Humanity:* vol. 2, *Grace and the Human Condition* (Maryknoll, N.Y.: Orbis Books, 1973), p. 159.

50. Segundo, *Artisans 5: Evolution and Guilt,* pp. 92–93.

51. Ibid., p. 61.

52. Ibid., p. 56. The supporting exegesis of Johannine texts is given on pp. 51–56.

53. Ibid., pp. 113 and 159. Two other areas that could—and often do—alienate persons from historical responsibility include spirituality and education. Spirituality will be discussed in Chapter Eight. A concise statement of Segundo's views on education is contained in what he refers to as the "brilliant observations" of Richard Stith: ". . . Just as the community is grounded on an attitude of service, so the anti-community is grounded on an attitude of dominion and *control*. One who controls has no ear for any need, and feels that everything can be manipulated. . . . So he does not hesitate to label people in his desire to control and dominate them. The kind of knowledge required for an attitude of service is radically different from that required for an attitude of control. And the latter tends to eliminate the former. I think that perhaps the principle reason behind our loss of a community sense is the fact that we have allowed knowledge for the sake of domination to spread to the point where it has practically eliminated knowledge for the sake of service" (*Our Idea of God,* p. 143, n. 23; Stith's observations were published in *Perspectivas de Diálogo* no. 33 [May 1969]).

54. Anthony Kosnik et al., *Human Sexuality: New Directions in American Catholic Thought* (New York: Paulist Press, 1977). The emphasis on maturity throughout this work is summarized as follows in a postscript: "Human dignity and our vocations as Jesus' disciples require us to respond freely and out of conviction rather than from simple conformity to rules or the mere external imposition of authority. We hope that our reflections will help you form your conscience with a

better understanding of the teachings of Christ and the Church and in a way that enables you to respond to today's challenges freely and maturely, out of genuine conviction'' (pp. 241–42).

55. A classic statement of this viewpoint is to be found in Helmut Gollwitzer, *The Rich Christians and Poor Lazarus* (New York: Macmillan, 1970).

56. A key book in this area is Arthur Simon, *Bread For the World* (New York: Paulist Press, 1975). The book is also published by a Protestant firm, Wm. B. Eerdmans Publishing Company; the implications for ecumenical cooperation (and reunion) in this common project are enormous.

57. A catalyst for conscientization in these areas may be found in the book of Ivan Illich, *Tools For Conviviality* (New York: Harper and Row, 1973). In the context of a discussion of the misuse of medical ''tools,'' Illich observes that ''society can have no quantitative standards by which to add up the negative value of illusion, social control, prolonged suffering, loneliness, genetic deformation, and frustration produced by medical treatment'' (p. 9). He has considerably expanded and developed these observations in a recent book, *Medical Nemesis* (New York: Random House-Pantheon, 1976).

58. See the statement in this regard by Joseph A. O'Hare, in ''Of Many Things,'' *America* (31 January 1976):62. Referring to the abortion debate, he concludes: ''It is neither anti-Catholic nor un-American to argue against the bishops in this debate, but to question their right to be heard is a persistent form of bigotry.''

59. Another very important instance of the social praxis of Catholics in this country was the Call to Action conference held at Detroit on October 21–23, 1976. Since at this time the process of implementation is still underway, I have not treated it here. See *Handbook: A Call to Action* (Notre Dame, Ind.: Catholic Committee on Urban Ministry, 1976) and, for the resolutions, *Origins* 6 (nos. 20 and 21). In ''Detroit and Beyond: The Continuing Quest for Justice'' (Washington, D.C.: Center of Concern, 1977), the staff of the Center has summarized the conference in terms that parallel the objectives of this book: ''The call was . . . to a theology of relinquishment, to let go of privileges, to be critical of values held, ideologies, preconceptions, and, where indicated, theological understanding. Equally it was a call to a spirituality of liberation, to a freeing of the heart for loving service and for entry of the Spirit'' (p. 23).

CHAPTER SIX

THE STRUGGLE
FOR A LIBERATING THEOLOGY

Intimately connected with the issue of praxis analyzed in the previous chapter is the question of theological method. And as in the case of praxis, an intense debate on method has erupted in the past decade, encompassing both the northern and southern hemispheres of the world. Recent works by such authors as Bernard Lonergan, David Tracy, and Gregory Baum have had considerable influence in the North Atlantic nations,[1] while the centrality of the issue for Latin American theologians has already been surveyed in the second chapter of this book.

Like his colleagues, Segundo considers the question of method to be of the utmost importance, stressing that "the one thing that can maintain the liberating character of a theology is not its content but its method" and that "in this lies the best hope of theology for the future."[2] Consequently, the key issue of methodology will be discussed in this chapter and, from a different perspective, in the following one. Some articles of Segundo will first be considered, followed by the fullest elaboration of his method in *The Liberation of Theology*.

A Dynamic Learning Process

An illuminating example of Segundo's approach may be found in an early article on the Second Vatican Council entitled "Toward a Dynamic Exegesis."[3] There he expresses the view that the most important difference between "conciliar" and "postconciliar" theologians lies in the fact that the former employ a "static exegesis that only examines the solutions presented by the Council" while the latter operate with "a dynamic exegesis that examines the directions pointed to by the Council."[4] For it is clear to him that Vatican II, which combines clearly divergent theological conceptions, posed quite a number of problems that it left unresolved and that must continue to be confronted by the whole church.

In the article Segundo employs a dynamic exegesis with regard to the texts of *Gaudium et Spes* concerning two basic questions. The first of these asks whether the church is to be considered a perfect society, complete in itself, or rather whether an "interdependence of dialogue" defines its essential relationship to the world.[5] A second area of interrogation is concerned with the relation of human history and of human progress toward the arrival of the kingdom of God, a question that evoked different responses in different parts of *Gaudium et Spes*.[6] These issues are taken up in other parts of this book; our concern here lies in his emphasis that the approach to Christian sources must be a dynamic and not a static one.

Another article, published at approximately the same time, shows that this applies not only to conciliar documents but also and more importantly to the normative texts of Christianity, that is, to the Bible itself.[7] In the article Segundo offers an ecumenical critique of a work written by a group of Protestant authors. His major objection is to its approach to Scripture and specifically to a schematizing tendency in this regard. It is defined as "a tendency to compare, in a very simple and direct way, events of the world of today with ideas or images taken from the Bible."[8] The obvious difficulty with this is that thousands of years of enormous changes and ever-increasing complexity have elapsed since biblical times and that the schematic approach does not take this into account. One of the examples adduced is the contribution of José Míguez Bonino, which correlates in detail the similarities existing between the Judaizers in St. Paul's time and inhabitants of the western Christian world of today. Such an approach, Segundo believes, is incapable of illuminating new situations "in a world radically different from the biblical one."[9]

A more recent article returns to the same problem in connection with a Catholic book on the Bible, which was written in close collaboration with Paraguayan peasants.[10] Segundo's objection to this book is based on his fundamental hermeneutical principle that the Bible must be understood as a process of education; in the book, however, "the Bible loses its true nature as a process in order to become a message."[11] The literalism of the book's applications, he feels, leads inevitably to a conservative, and not to a creative or liberating, theology, again because the applications "represent a teaching, and not a learning how to learn."[12] The author notes that in this article he is merely pointing out the major features of the problem; for the promised nuances and refinements we must turn to *The Liberation of Theology*.

The Hermeneutic Circle

This book comprises a revised version of a series of lectures delivered by Segundo while he was a visiting professor at Harvard Divinity School in 1974. In it he is forthright in stating categorically the critical differences that distinguish a liberating theology from what he calls "academic" or "classical" theology, that is, theology as it is practiced in the centers of learning of the western world. Before considering those differences, it is essential to grasp his fundamental methodology, which is referred to as "the hermeneutic circle."[13]

The same term has been applied in the past to the exegetical approach of Rudolf Bultmann, but Segundo believes that his method corresponds better to the strict sense of the circle. On its most fundamental level, the method involves "the continuous change in our interpretation of the Bible, in function of the continuous changes in our present reality, both individual and social."[14] In order for present reality to change, one must be to some extent dissatisfied with it, and thus raise questions concerning it that are "so rich, general, and basic that they oblige us to change our usual conceptions concerning life, death, knowledge, society, politics, and the world in general."[15] And once these new and more profound questions are posed to the scriptural texts, it is essential that our interpretation of the texts change also, for otherwise the new questions would either receive no answer or answers that are conservative and useless.

This preliminary description of the method is further clarified by the delineation of four steps that are essential to its proper exercise:

First, our manner of experiencing reality, which leads to ideological suspicion; *second*, the application of ideological suspicion to the whole ideological superstructure in general and to theology in particular; *third*, a new manner of experiencing theological reality, which leads us to exegetical suspicion, that is, to the suspicion that current biblical interpretation does not take into account important data; and *fourth*, our new hermeneutic, that is, the new way of interpreting the source of our faith, which is Scripture, with the new elements at our disposal.[16]

The concept of "suspicion" used here is derived from Paul Ricoeur; it is based on Segundo's hypothesis that ideologies connected with current social conditions are unconsciously ruling our present theological ideas and pastoral practice.

It is also important to note that the first stage of the circle always involves the experience of a definite problem, and an act of will or commitment on the part of the knower to find a solution to the problem. Segundo concludes from this that "a hermeneutic circle always supposes a profound human commitment, that is, a consciously accepted partiality, based certainly not on theological criteria but on human ones."[17]

At this point, it is obvious that the hermeneutic circle is in need of considerable clarification, so that its procedures may be understood more precisely. To accomplish this, Segundo considers in some detail the works of four writers—Harvey Cox, Karl Marx, Max Weber, and James Cone; his objective is to determine whether they have succeeded in completing the four steps of the circle and, if not, to point out precisely at what point they have failed. In discussing these authors, I will merely select some key areas that appear to shed light on the understanding of the hermeneutic circle.

The Circle in Practice

The first example considered is the well-known best-seller of Harvey Cox, *The Secular City*.[18] In this work Cox is describing his own experience of the new realities of secularization and urbanization as well as the new approach to solving problems on a purely *pragmatic* level that these phenomena entail. He explicitly rejects the approach of Paul Tillich, who held that every person asks *ultimate* existential questions, and that Christian revelation provides an answer to these. Rather Cox appears to commit himself to the new pragmatic approach.

This brings us to the third step in the hermeneutic circle, where it would be logical to address new questions to Scripture from the perspective of pragmatic humanity. However, although such an interrogation could be fruitful in the opinion of Segundo, Cox does not take this approach. Rather his direction can be perceived in his analysis of The Girl or Miss America: "The Protestant objection to the cult of The Girl must be based on the realization that The Girl is an idol. . . .The values she represents as ultimate satisfactions—mechanical comfort, sexual success, unencumbered leisure—have no *ultimacy*."[19]

It is patent from this argument that Cox's method, when all is said and done, is identical with Tillich's. At the same time, although apparently his failure is at the third point in the circle, deeper reflection shows that he did not even complete the first stage; that is, he never *really* accepted or committed himself to pragmatic humanity, since ultimacy was seen as lacking in pragmatic humanity's values right from the outset. Since the partiality mentioned earlier is lacking, therefore, Cox has interrupted the hermeneutic circle at its very first point.

The second author treated, Karl Marx, can certainly not be faulted for such a lack of partiality, since his efforts were clearly directed over many years to a struggle with and on behalf of the proletariat. And in an attempt to explain why the masses of the proletariat did not achieve victory in the struggle, Marx advanced to the second point of the circle by elaborating his ideology of historical materialism. Segundo summarizes the essence of this theory in one sentence taken from *The Communist Manifesto:* "The ruling ideas of each age have always been the ideas of the ruling class."[20]

A key factor in any revolutionary process, moreover, must be the recognition of such an ideological superstructure by the revolutionary classes and its transformation on behalf of the revolution. But Marx did not apply ideological suspicion to the whole superstructure, not only because his social analysis was weak and superficial when applied to industrial societies but even more because he totally rejected any possible liberating function for religion. Thus Marx presents an example of failure at the second point of the hermeneutic circle.

The classic of Max Weber, *The Protestant Ethic and the Spirit of Capitalism*,[21] is next introduced as an example of failure to attain the third stage in the circle, that is, the suspicion of current biblical interpretation. Weber describes himself as an amateur theologian, but Segundo believes he was a brilliant one: "Amateur theologian that he was, Weber expounds dogmas correctly and interrelates them intelligently; moreover, he had an excellent grasp of the differences between the thought of Calvin and that of the two principal theologies of his time, the Lutheran and the Catholic."[22]

Although Weber has been termed the "Anti-Marx," Segundo believes that he actually complements and carries forward the work of Marx, for he attempts to uncover the religious ideologies of Calvinism that corresponded to the mode of production in the early stages of capitalism. As Weber himself expressed it, "We only wish to ascertain whether and to what extent religious forces have taken part in the qualitative formation and quantitative expansion of that spirit in the world."[23] An important contribution that he made, according to Segundo, was his utilization of psychology to ascertain the correspondence between certain religious values and their economic counterparts.

Although he moved a step beyond Marx, then, it must finally be acknowledged that Weber terminated the hermeneutic circle at its third point. For if one asks whether as a result of his work he saw the need for a new and more profound evaluation of Calvinism or whether he was motivated to undertake a more probing reinterpretation of Scripture, the answer is obviously no. To use Weber's own words, "we are concerned, not with the *evaluation,* but with the historical significance of the dogma."[24] Occasional exceptions to his detached stance occur, as when he notes that in Calvin's doctrine "the Father in heaven of the New Testament, so human and understanding, who rejoices over the repentance of a sinner as a woman does over the lost piece of silver she has found, *has disappeared.* His place has been taken by a transcendental being beyond the limits of human understanding."[25] However, in general, the desire for scientific objectivity constitutes an insuperable obstacle to a further development of the circle at its third point.

The last book considered, James Cone's *A Black Theology of Liberation*,[26] is adjudged to be the only one that successfully completes all four stages of the hermeneutic circle, although Segundo admits that its language is at times shocking and demagogic. In the first stage there can be no doubt that Cone is partial, that is, totally committed to the black community and its struggle for freedom. An important observation in this respect by Segundo is that "every hermeneutic involves conscious or unconscious partisanship. It adopts a partisan position even when it claims and believes that it is neutral."[27]

When he reaches the second point of the circle, Cone manages to achieve a high level of suspicion with regard to the whole American superstructure, including the dominant theology. This appears clearly in his charge concerning American white theology:

It has been basically a theology of the white oppressor, *sanctioning through religion* the genocide of Indians and the slavery of black people. From the very beginning to the present, white theological thought in the United States has been "patriotic," either by defining the theological task *independently of black suffering* (the liberal northern approach) or by defining Christianity as compatible with racism (the conservative southern approach). In both cases, *theology has become a servant of the state,* which has only meant death to black people.[28]

The central ideological weapon that Cone uncovers is white theology's pretense of "colorblindness," a ploy which manages to disguise the basic cause of oppression.

Cone moves to the third point of the circle, the suspicion of theology, by noting that, when the question of black liberation is broached to white theologians, they invariably "quibble on this issue and move from one point to another, always pointing to the dangers of *extremism on both sides.* In reality, they cannot make a decision, because others have really made it for them."[29] After noting that "the sources and norm [of theology] are presuppositions that determine *which questions are to be asked,* as well as what answers are given," Cone goes on to emphasize that "the manner of working of black theologians has to be such as to destroy the corruptive influence of white thought by building theology on the sources and norm that are *appropriate to the black community.*"[30] In summary, he believes that black theology must be founded on a double norm, "the liberation of black people and the revelation of Jesus Christ."

Finally, Cone arrives at the last point of the circle, that is, a new interpretation of Scripture based on the richer and more profound questions that have been raised. His hermeneutic is summarized as follows:

If we read the New Testament correctly, the resurrection of Jesus means that the Lord is also present today in the midst of societies, bringing about his liberation of the oppressed. He is not confined to the first century, and thus our talk of him in the past assumes importance only insofar as it leads us to an *encounter* with him today. As a black theologian, I want to know what God's revelation means here and now as the black community participates in the struggle for liberation.[31]

Segundo believes that Cone's interpretation is in accord with the biblical documents, where it is clear that there are divergences in God's message according to the different historical circumstances of his people. He also agrees with Cone in his departure from a false and alienating universalism and in his assertion that orthopraxis is more important than orthodoxy, that is, ''the truth is only truth when it is the basis for truly human attitudes.''[32]

Segundo voices some disagreements with Cone in the last point of the circle, for example, on the reasons why the biblical possibility of a vocation for redemptive suffering is excluded for black people. But these are incidental; his fundamental assertion is that Cone's book provides an excellent example of the methodology of the hermeneutic circle.

The author is also aware that his painstaking analysis of the circle may at times have appeared tedious and abstract. Thus he goes on to present several examples of the method that are more practical in import and that have perhaps already been utilized by the average intelligent Christian on his or her own initiative. Segundo observes that the "common sense" of such people should not be deprecated, for it can often make a significant contribution to necessary ideological criticism within the church.[33]

Contemporary Use of the Circle

The first example is related to sacramental practice. From the entire preceding discussion, it should have become obvious that "a liberating theology is of necessity a historical theology, based on questions that arise from the present," and that "only a Christian community with a keen historical sensibility can provide the basis for such a liberating theology."[34] However, the sacraments, and especially the Eucharist, stress exactly the opposite approach, and their emphasis on the same cycle of feasts, the same actions and texts, etc., fosters an ahistorical atmosphere. Considering that the main contact of most Catholics with their religion is through the Mass, the fact is that it "constitutes the polar opposite of a religion based on historical sensibility. With the exception of minor details, the Sunday Mass remains the same before and after a general disaster, an international crisis, or a profound revolution."[35]

Continuing his hermeneutic circle, the author is led to ideological suspicion of the emphases that are dominant in contemporary sacramental theology. The suspicion is expressed with characteristic bluntness: "Is it by chance that this conception and practice of the sacraments is perfectly adapted to the interests of the dominant classes and is one of the most powerful ideological factors in maintaining the status quo?"[36] This leads to the fourth point of the circle, that is, a new hermeneutic of the Christian sources, especially passages such as Hebrews 10:9–14. And the conclusion derived from the reinterpretation is that "religious efficacy is ruled out for any and every ritual, cult, or assembly, to the extent that such a ceremony supposes that the grace of God was not given once and for all, but that it must be won over and over again by means of religious rites."[37] The new understanding of the sacraments that should result from the above awakening from "ideological slumber" has already been discussed in Chapter Five.

Yet another example of the application of the circle has to do with the question of *unity* within the church. The preservation of unity is often viewed as a supreme value which must take precedence over any historical divisions that may actually exist among the members on basic issues. By thus making unity an absolute, however, the church is forced into the position of holding "that the issues of suffering, violence, hunger, and death are less critical than religious formulas or rites."[38] Moreover, the unity achieved takes place only on the level of language; for, if "one person conceives of a God who permits dehumanization, while another rejects such a God and believes only in a God who struggles unceasingly against such things," then the obvious conclusion is that they do not really believe in the same God nor share the same faith.[39]

Once again, the circle leads back to Scripture and a fresh look at texts that are often used to bolster the emphasis on unity at any price (such as 2 Cor. 5:18ff. and Col. 1:20), since they are concerned with "reconciliation." And it soon becomes apparent that the eschatological reconciliation mentioned in these citations is meant to be brought about by the real liberation of human beings and not by any "pious blindness" to real oppression or to the real remedies of oppression. Consequently, it would seem essential to be able to distinguish those who are suffering oppression and those who are causing it; moreover, this seems to have been perfectly clear to the writers of the New Testament, for "when did Christ reconcile himself with the Pharisees, or when did Paul reconcile himself with the Judaizers?"[40] In short, the circle is concluded with the realization that true reconciliation and unity can be achieved only in and through a real struggle for justice.

A last example of the circle involves a return to the understanding of God mentioned in the previous one. But it is not so much a question of the *concept* of God that is involved, which is the manner in which classical theology might formulate the question, but rather: "*What kind of God* lies behind the attitudes in the first two examples?" Here Segundo advances his belief that the understanding of God that evolved in the Christian West moved the question to a level that was far too simplistic. For use of the word "God" as the one certain sacred name may have solved the question of polytheism on a linguistic level, but it should be obvious that "using the same name does not guarantee that one is talking about the same person, especially when the descriptions contain contradictory traits."[41]

This serious problem was taken up by Vatican II in a well-known text that suggested the responsibility of believers for the phenomenon of atheism: "To the extent that [believers] neglect their own training in the faith, or teach erroneous doctrine, or are deficient in their religious, moral, or social life, they must be said to conceal rather than reveal the authentic face of God and religion."[42] However, the logical conclusions of this statement have not always been drawn with the same rigor that Segundo employs in his analysis. For the deficient attitudes and practices mentioned in the text must be based on a false understanding of God, that is, to put it bluntly, faith in a nonexistent God; otherwise, how could it make sense for believers to hide something that they clearly possess?

Segundo also believes that it is far too simplistic to place the blame for the immutable, impassible, self-sufficient image of God that developed in the West on the influence of Greek philosophy on Christian thought. This, when all is said and done, has not achieved much impact on popular thinking, but remains the province of comparatively few specialists. Rather ideological suspicion leads him to conclude that more generalized social and historical factors fostered such a development. For humanity's perennial tendency is to project its own real or imagined victory onto God; but "in the societies in which we live, economic and social competition is a condition of survival and eventually of victory."[43] Since my personal victory will inevitably entail diminution or suffering for others, I must cultivate the qualities of impassibility and self-sufficiency, and it is precisely those attributes that tend to be projected onto God. Thus two very different gods arose, of which "one was the authentic God of revelation, the other was an inauthentic and nonexistent god, which gave rise to atheism and was conveniently attributed to the influence of Greek philosophy."

Once again Segundo stresses that the worship of a nonexistent god is pure and simple idolatry; moreover, idolatry can not be exorcised by formal statements of orthodoxy, since "one can recite all the creeds in the history of Christian theology and still believe in an idol."[44] He concludes the circle by a fresh hermeneutic of scriptural texts such as Matthew 16:1–4. Here and in other places in the New Testament, Jesus accuses the most monotheistic people in the world at that time of idolatry, for they insisted on signs from heaven while refusing to acknowledge God's real liberative actions taking place before their very eyes.

Challenge to Classical Theology

Clearly the application of the hermeneutic circle extends much further than the above examples. Its use can be traced throughout the other chapters of *The Liberation of Theology* and, indeed, is discernible in all of Segundo's published works. As already noted, the important question of deideologizing will be examined in greater depth in the following chapter. For the present it would seem helpful to attempt to synthesize the differences that Segundo sees between this method and the usual ones adopted by classical or academic theology. In his introduction to *The Liberation of Theology*, he observes that liberation theology has evoked a certain academic contempt in the world centers of theological scholarship. As a reaction to this, his book involves a conscious effort to move to the attack and to confront the reigning methodologies in the world centers of theology, challenging them to justify their own procedures. It should be stressed, however, that this is intended to open up a dialogue, for it is meant "not as a nationalistic or provincial challenge but one that is properly and constructively theological."[45]

The basic difference between the two methodologies, then, is stated bluntly at the outset. For academic theology readily acknowledges that, in order to understand the biblical texts, it must employ many sciences that shed light on *the past,* such as history, cultural anthropology, ancient languages, form criticism, and so forth. However, at this point a curious anomaly becomes apparent: this theology declares itself independent of those sciences that seek to interpret *the present,* adducing as a rationale its need to preserve the autonomy of theology. In this vein, a theologian as progressive as Edward Schillebeeckx is quoted to the effect that theology can never be ideological, to which Segundo replies: "He appears to believe naively that the word of God is applied to human realities in a laboratory immune to all the ideological tendencies and struggles of the present."[46] By contrast, a liberating theology is obliged continuously to juxtapose the disciplines that are concerned with the past *as well as* those that interpret the present in order to understand the word of God as a real message addressed to us *here and now.* Such a conception, he believes, would "free academic theology from its atavism and chilly ivory tower, and remove its very foundation: the belief that it is a simple, eternal, and impartial interpretation or authorized translation of the word of God."[47]

At the conclusion of his book, Segundo returns to the same point with great vigor. He charges that academic theology, when it evades the problems of the present, is merely taking the easy way out. On the other hand, liberation theology "does not allow the theologian to set aside lightly—as academic theology often does— the great problems of today of history, biology, evolution, social change, and many others, on the pretext that they belong to other fields and disciplines."[48]

Another key methodological difference that is stressed repeatedly throughout the book concerns the question of the *partiality* of the theologian. It has already been noted that such partiality is considered essential for the proper use of the hermeneutic circle, both in its first point—a commitment to change reality, and its third point—a commitment to change theology. The liberation theologian accepts this need for commitment explicitly and consciously. On the other hand, "academic theology can ignore its unconscious partiality, but the very fact that it poses as impartial is a sign of a conservative partiality in its very point of departure. . . . The most academic theology is intimately, though perhaps unconsciously, linked with the psychological, social, or political status quo."[49] Thus an adamant denial of the myth of theological neutrality must be considered a basic foundation stone in Segundo's or any other theology of liberation.

A very important corollary of this view is that partiality must also apply to the usually taboo area of politics, since "every theology is political, even one that does not speak or think in political terms." Again, what is sought is a conscious and explicit recognition of this unavoidable reality. Segundo's judgment on the refusal to do so is severe: "When academic theology accuses liberation theology of being political and of engaging in politics, thus pretending to ignore its own relation with the political status quo, what it is really looking for is a scapegoat for its own guilt complex."[50]

Also, the so-called political theology of Europe is considered to be fundamentally divergent from a liberation approach. For it makes the attempt to derive political options from theological sources and concepts, "whereas the theology of Jesus derives theology from openness of heart to the most pressing problems of human beings, going so far as to suggest that one cannot recognize Christ or eventually know God, except from the perspective of a commitment to the oppressed."[51] In Segundo's view the approach of seeking theological signs from heaven is clearly the method of Pharisaical theology, and yet it is so widespread that "it is difficult to find a theologian, even a highly intelligent one as Rahner undoubtedly is, who does not turn the real order of things and problems upside down."[52]

Summary and Conclusions

The replies of theologians in the West to this challenging book of Segundo will have to be awaited. In the meantime we may inquire as to the possible implications a methodology such as that of the hermeneutic circle might entail.

Aside from the many nuances in the method which can stimulate theological dialogue, I would advance my own view that its principal contribution lies in the foundation it provides for a *theology of change* and, more specifically, a theology of social change. The need for such a theology becomes evident if we reflect on some texts from the Second Vatican Council. In *Gaudium et Spes* the bishops emphasized: "Today the human race is passing through a new stage of its history. Profound and rapid changes are spreading by degrees around the whole world. . . .Hence we can already speak of a true social and cultural transformation, one which has repercussions on man's religious life as well."[53] Somewhat further on may be found one of the most crucial statements of the council, namely, that "the human race has passed from a rather static concept of reality to a more dynamic, evolutionary one,"[54] to which is appended a host of recommendations regarding the church's adaptation to this new reality.

A similar emphasis emerges with even greater urgency from the Medellín documents of 1968. One of the clearest statements of it may be found in the position paper prepared for that conference by Marcos McGrath, then bishop of Santiago de Veraguas, Panama. There he recalls that "during the composition of *Gaudium et Spes*, bishops and experts from all over the world were systematically questioned. To the question, 'what is it that most characterizes your country?' the invariable answer was, in one form or another, the same: *change."* The bishop then proceeds to state flatly that change is "the great sign of our time, perhaps the principal one."[55] In the same year, moreover, the encyclical *Populorum Progressio* appeared, and has been succinctly described by José Comblin: "What *Populorum Progressio* demands both in the national and international order is a total subversion of the established order, a radical change in the most basic principles of society as it is."[56]

Despite this widespread recognition of the need for change, there is one glaring deficiency in all these documents. A knowledgeable observer of the Latin American scene, Phillip Berryman, puts his finger on the problem when he asserts that Medellín "is notably silent on *how* its ambitious aims are to be realized in society at large and in the Church itself."[57]

In short, the church has made the crucial move from a posture of uncritical identification with the prevailing values and goals of contemporary society to a stance of prophetic criticism. But to use the terms of Paulo Freire, it must "announce" as well as "denounce" in its dialogue with the modern world; that is, it must offer new visions and concrete proposals for social change, in addition to its critique of the existing order. For we can suppose that our contemporaries will soon grow weary of a carping negativism and constant denunciation if they turn to the church for enlightenment and aid in the common task of constructing a more human world.

To be sure, *Gaudium et Spes* and recent encyclicals contain positive elements in addition to their criticisms, although these are often advanced on a quite general level. It seems to me that the great task at the moment is to continue this positive line with ever greater specificity in the solutions proposed, thus taking the risk of concrete historical options that will embody the desired changes. And in fulfilling such a task, a fundamental necessity is that the church's conscious relationship with its normative charter documents, the Scriptures, be one that is open to social change, and not one of reaction and paralyzing conservatism. If its social teaching and action are to be effective in the long run, in other words, they must be grounded on a biblical hermeneutics that fosters creative and imaginative change.

It is precisely on this level of a profound exigency in basic theological method that Segundo's hermeneutic circle appears to offer great promise for the future. It provides the kind of "social preunderstanding" for the interrogation of Scripture that is so badly needed today, in the same way that Bultmann provided an "existential preunderstanding" on the level of the individual believer. The method can and should be submitted to a penetrating critique by theologians. But the only ultimate refutation of the circle, in my opinion, would be the elaboration of a more effective, creative, and liberating alternative. Until that appears, the hermeneutic circle offers the best hope for the church as it confronts the challenge of change in one of the most decisive epochs in its history.

NOTES

1. Bernard Lonergan, *Method in Theology* (New York: Herder and Herder, 1972); David Tracy, *Blessed Rage for Order: The New Pluralism in Theology* (New York: Seabury Press, 1975); and Gregory Baum, *Religion and Alienation: A Theological Reading of Sociology* (New York: Paulist Press, 1975).
2. Juan Luis Segundo, *Liberación de la teología* (Buenos Aires: Carlos Lohlé, 1975), p. 192. All references and my translations are from the original Spanish edition. An English translation, which appeared after this chapter was written, is entitled *The Liberation of Theology* (Maryknoll, N.Y.: Orbis Books, 1976). Cf. Alfred T. Hennelly, "The Challenge of Juan Luis Segundo," *Theological Studies* (March 1977):125–35.
3. "Hacia una exégesis dinámica," *Víspera* (October 1967):77–84.
4. Ibid., p. 78.
5. Ibid., pp. 78–80.
6. Ibid., pp. 80–83.
7. "América hoy," *Víspera* (August 1967):53–57. The book referred to is *América hoy: Acción de Dios y responsabilidad del hombre* (Montevideo: II Consulta Latinoamericana de Iglesia y Sociedad [ISAL], 1966).
8. Segundo, "América hoy," p. 56.
9. Ibid., pp. 56–57.
10. "Teología: Mensaje y proceso," *Perspectivas de Diálogo* (December 1974):259–70. The book under consideration here is identified only as *Vivir como hermanos* and is by José Luis Caravias.
11. Segundo, "Teología," p. 265.
12. Ibid., p. 269.
13. A very interesting parallel to Segundo's approach may be found in the article of Frederick Herzog, "Liberation Hermeneutic as Ideology Critique?" *Interpretation* (October 1974): 387–403. Although Herzog is in dialogue with North American and European theologians in this work, many of his conclusions are strikingly similar to Segundo's.
14. Segundo, *Liberación*, p. 12. Cf. the remarks of Wolfhart Pannenberg: "The insight that it is no longer possible for a present-day interpreter naively to identify himself with the primitive Christian texts—unless by means of a self-deception—makes it possible for the first time to seek the continuity of the Christian tradition in the *way* in which, from its inception, ever *new* forms of its interpretation were released" (*Basic Questions in Theology,* vol. 1 [Philadelphia: Fortress Press, 1970], p. 145.)
15. Segundo, *Liberación,* p. 13. The concept of "ideological suspicion" is also emphasized by Jürgen Moltmann as, for example, when he observes that "political hermeneutics sets out to recognize the social and political influences on theological institutions and languages in order to bring their liberating content into the political dimension and to make them relevant towards really freeing men trapped in certain vicious circles" (*The Crucified God: The Cross of Christ as the Foundation and Criticism of Christian Theology* [New York: Harper and Row, 1974], p. 318).

16. Segundo, *Liberación*, pp. 13–14.

17. Ibid., p. 18. Philip J. Scharper has stressed this partiality in a general article on liberation theology, where he notes that "these theologians of liberation have attempted to read the Scriptures through the prisms of the poor. That, in itself, represents a radical departure in theologico-scriptural methods. We are perhaps unaware of the fact that most of the theologians—Protestant and Catholic—who have had such a heavy influence on American theologians and American theology have tended to be, almost by definition, members of the upper middle class, indeed forming something of a social and intellectual elite" ("The Theology of Liberation: Some Reflections," *Catholic Mind* [April 1976]:45).

18. Harvey Cox, *The Secular City: Secularization and Urbanization in Theological Perspective* (New York: Macmillan, 1965). The discussion of Cox covers pp. 14–18 of *Liberación*.

19. Segundo, *Liberación*, p. 16; Cox, *Secular City*, p. 197.

20. Segundo, *Liberación*, p. 20. The quotation of Marx is from "Manifiesto del Partido Comunista," in Marx-Engels, *Obras escogidas en dos tomos*, vol. 1 (Moscow: Progreso, 1971), p. 37. The treatment of Marx occupies pp. 19–25 of *Liberación*.

21. Max Weber, *The Protestant Ethic and the Spirit of Capitalism* (New York: Charles Scribner's Sons, 1958).

22. Segundo, *Liberación*, p. 28.

23. Ibid; Weber, *Protestant Ethic*, p. 91. On this text, Segundo observes that "at least in theory, it is difficult to find a more genuine expression of the thought of Marx with regard to ideological analysis in relation to historical materialism."

24. Segundo, *Liberación*, p. 31; Weber, *Protestant Ethic*, p. 101.

25. Segundo, *Liberación*, pp. 32–33; Weber, *Protestant Ethic*, p. 103. In an indirect way, Segundo himself does not hesitate to pass judgment on Weber, for he asks pointedly: "One might well wonder whether it is not even more inhuman to understand this network of implications without passing any judgment, than it was to have created it in the belief that it was in basic harmony with the sources of revelation" (*Liberación*, p. 32). His treatment of Weber covers pp. 26–34.

26. The references here will be to the Spanish translation of Cone's book, *Teología negra de la liberación* (Buenos Aires: Carlos Lohlé, 1973).

27. Segundo, *Liberación*, p. 34.

28. Ibid., pp. 37–38; Cone, *Teología negra*, p. 18.

29. Segundo, *Liberación*, p. 39; Cone, *Teología negra*, p. 87.

30. Segundo, *Liberación*, pp. 39–40; Cone, *Teología negra*, pp. 38–39.

31. Segundo, *Liberación*, pp. 42–43; Cone, *Teología negra*, p. 46. Segundo adds that this is an essential hermeneutical principle, for "the value of this orientation in achieving a richer interpretation of Scripture consists in the rediscovery of the pedagogical principle that guides the whole process of revelation: God himself appears to be different according to the different situations of his people." Segundo devotes pp. 34–45 to the analysis of Cone's book.

32. Segundo, *Liberación*, p. 44. He adds that " 'doing the truth' is the revealed formula for this priority of orthopraxis over orthodoxy when it is a question of truth and of salvation."

33. The following examples were first presented in the paper, "Las élites latinoamericanas: Problemática humana y cristiana ante el cambio social," in *Fe cristiana y cambio social en América Latina: Encuentro de El Escorial, 1972* (Salamanca: Sígueme, 1973), pp. 203–12.

34. Segundo, *Liberación*, p. 48.

35. Ibid., p. 49.

36. Ibid., pp. 49–50. Another articulation of this question, which is central to all

areas of Segundo's theology, follows immediately afterwards: "Would it be too offensive to acknowledge that sacramental *theology* has been more influenced by unconscious social pressures than by the gospel itself?"

37. Ibid., p. 50.

38. Ibid., p. 51.

39. Ibid. His conclusion is that "therefore a common faith does not exist in the church: the only thing shared in common is the formula used to declare the faith. And, since the formula doesn't identify anything, are we not justified in speaking of a formula that is *empty* vis-à-vis the decisive options of history?"

40. Ibid., p. 53.

41. Ibid., pp. 53–54. Segundo believes that Karl Barth would have agreed with him on this crucial theological issue; however, he goes on to note that "Barth was always more sensitive to the danger of ideology stemming from philosophy than to the danger of ideologies that are intimately bound up with sociopolitical struggle."

42. *Gaudium et Spes,* no. 19, in Joseph Gremillion, *The Gospel of Peace and Justice: Catholic Social Teaching Since Pope John* (Maryknoll, N.Y.: Orbis Books, 1976), p. 258.

43. Segundo, *Liberación,* p. 56. A related development is discussed with great acumen by William Coates in *God in Public: Political Theology Beyond Niebuhr* (Grand Rapids, Mich.: Wm. B. Eerdmans Publishing Company, 1974). A good summary of his thought is the following: "Freudianism and existentialism are essentially individualistic and subjective creeds which exalt the person or the self over history, without at the same time offering a challenge to the shape of history. Both movements are now in a state of exhaustion precisely because they built on the weakest aspect of bourgeois ideology: the self in its ahistorical capacities. When, therefore, a large number of Christian thinkers linked up with these two schools of thought in the hope of providing a contemporary vehicle of interpretation for the Gospel, they succeeded only in arriving at the same dead-end at the same time" (p. 110).

44. Segundo, *Liberación,* p. 56. A further discussion on this important question of the image of God will be initiated in chapter eight in connection with Christian spirituality. More recently, Segundo has again utilized the circle to uncover the ideology behind the campaign for "human rights" conducted by the United States government. As a result of systematic economic oppression, he insists, "the tragedy of the situation is that those who shape and control the defense of human rights are (despite undeniable good will in individual cases) the very same ones who make such rights impossible on three quarters of the planet" ("Derechos humanos, evangelización e ideología," *Christus* [November 1978]:34).

45. Ibid., pp. 9–10.

46. Ibid., pp. 11–12. Dorothee Soelle has pointed out a similar focus on the past with regard to the theological method of form criticism: "In actual practice the sociological aspects of the method are almost always confined to antiquity—to the first-century church—and are rarely applied to the modern situation" (*Political Theology* [Philadelphia: Fortress Press, 1974], p. xiii).

47. Segundo, *Liberación,* p. 25.

48. Ibid., p. 266.

49. Ibid., p. 18. In his *Theory and Practice* (Boston: Beacon Press, 1973), Jürgen Habermas insists that "no theory and no enlightenment can relieve us of the risks of taking a partisan position and of the unintended consequences involved in this" (p. 36). He also explains the task of critical sociology as asking "what lies behind the consensus, presented as a fact, that supports the dominant tradition of the time, and does so with a view to the relations of power surreptitiously incorporated in the symbolic structures of the systems of speech and action" (pp. 11–12).

50. Segundo, *Liberación,* p. 88.

51. Ibid., p. 95.

52. Ibid., p. 90. Segundo has also stressed the importance of the hermeneutic circle for all theological education in "Perspectivas para una teología latino-americana," *Perspectiva Teológica* 9 (January–June 1977):9–25.

53. *Gaudium et Spes,* no. 4, in Gremillion, *Gospel of Peace and Justice,* p. 246.

54. *Gaudium et Spes,* no. 5, in Gremillion, *Gospel of Peace and Justice,* p. 247.

55. Marcos McGrath, *The Church in the Present-Day Transformation of Latin America: I. Position Papers* (Washington, D.C.: Latin American Bureau—USCC, 1970), pp. 85–86. The bishop also notes that "never have changes been so rapid and radical as those of today. They have already placed man 'in a new period of history' (*Gaudium et Spes,* no. 4); and we can imagine what it is initiating: that the changes that are forthcoming will be even more extraordinary than those we have witnessed to date."

56. José Comblin, *Théologie de la révolution* (Paris: Editions Universitaires, 1970), p. 227.

57. Phillip Berryman, "Latin American Liberation Theology," *Theological Studies* (September 1973):363.

CHAPTER SEVEN

IS CHRISTIANITY AN IDEOLOGY?

It should be apparent from the preceding chapter that the exercise of ideological suspicion constitutes an essential element in the hermeneutic of liberation theology. It would seem, therefore, that a more profound understanding of the concept of "ideology" itself should prove helpful in a further clarification of the liberation approach.[1] Such an analysis will also provide the foundations for a reply to one of the most common lines of attack against Latin American theology: that it reduces faith to an ideology or, at the very least, that it hopelessly confuses faith and ideology.

Two Meanings of Ideology

A recent article by Segundo on this issue may serve as a beginning for the analysis.[2] In it he presents a phenomenological analysis of faith and ideology as they actually operate in the concrete existence of the human person. It is important, first of all, to note the very diverse meanings that are often applied to the term "ideology." The more usual connotation is a pejorative one, referring to a mental mechanism that serves certain class, race, or other interests by concealing or sacralizing a given situation. Much of the discussion in the previous chapter was concerned with ideology understood in this way. However, the term can also be understood in a more *neutral* sense, that is, as a person's basic system of goals and values, plus the means to achieve them. And this neutral sense applies to both religious and secular areas, since "every person, consciously or unconsciously, chooses to structure his or her life in accordance with a system of values. . . . The system which gives coherence to a life is a component of human existence."[3]

In developing this neutral conception of ideology, Segundo makes use of a play of Albert Camus entitled *Caligula* as a parable of the human situation. The Roman emperor in the title is absorbed with the problem of human happiness, and especially with the fact that few people, as the end of life draws near, believe that they have actually attained such happiness. He comes to the conclusion that people do not attain their goal of happiness because they permit various distractions and affections to divert them from the path that leads to it. And so Caligula, using the semiomnipotence of his position as emperor, decides to eradicate all affections and emotional bonds by destroying the persons to whom he is attached, even the woman he loves, "not in order to be cruel, but to be free."[4] In the end, however, this monstrous and inhuman course of action does not succeed in bringing him happiness but rather indifference and finally death.

Segundo then proceeds to draw a number of conclusions from the play. The first lies in the fact that "no one can choose a path in life, knowing beforehand that it is a satisfactory one." From this it follows logically that the human choice of a goal for one's life always originates "in faith in other persons, through whom we perceive that certain values are worth living, because they promise a satisfactory and happy life."[5] And perhaps the most important conclusion is that, again in the concrete order of human existence, faith and ideology are identified, that is to say, "both organize life with regard to a meaning which is worth the effort; both indicate what is important and what is not; both point out the price that must be paid for happiness,"[6] and as noted above, both depend on faith in other persons. As a result, any attempt to separate faith and ideology, making the first an absolute and the latter relative, would entail ignoring the basic structure of human existence.

Segundo also, it should be added, adverts to the relatively recent discovery "that explicit denominations of faith and ideologies (I am a Christian, a Marxist, a liberal, and so forth) do not separate us as much nor do they unite us as much as the operative and unconscious ideological structures."[7] Consequently, although Christians are often exhorted to a unity that transcends ideologies, it is not actually faith that unites or separates them, but the different specific ways in which faith is translated into ideologies. We will return to this important point later.

While faith and ideology cannot be separated in practice, this does not mean that they cannot be distinguished. Through an analysis of the development of both faith and ideology in the human experience of childhood, adolescence, and maturity, including the various crises involved, Segundo arrives at several bases for distinctions. For one thing we can recognize an ideology by its lack of pretension to an absolute objective value, that is, it is as valid as the arguments that are used in its support. On the other hand, we can recognize a faith precisely by such pretension to an objective absolute value, that is, it claims to be based on an encounter with the objective source of all truth. A second distinction lies in the fact that faith entails a stronger relationship to the *goal* (signification), while ideology points more directly to the *means* to achieve the goal (efficacy). Nevertheless, it is strongly emphasized that "efficacy and signification are distinguished, but they are inseparably related and mutually influence each other in the quest for the realization of humanity."[8]

Ideology and the Bible

The basic ideas of the article on faith and ideology have been considerably elaborated and integrated with other key conceptions in *The Liberation of Theology*. Of special interest at this point is the implication of the ideas for an understanding of the Bible and, indeed, of the whole process of divine revelation.

Segundo first refers to the fact that liberation theology is known to have displayed a decided preference for the Old Testament in general and for the Exodus event in particular. The latter choice is obviously influenced by the very strong political and liberating elements that are characteristic of the Exodus narrative. Moreover, the New Testament, at first glance, appears to minimize or even exclude the idea of political liberation from the Christian message. Thus "Jesus seems to center his message on a liberation in interpersonal relationships, forgetting almost completely—and perhaps excluding—liberation with respect to political oppression."[9] And the same appears to be true of Paul and the other New Testament writers.

In his reply to this, Segundo first rejects the theory that has been advanced recently in both Europe and Latin America that Jesus was connected in some way with the Zealots, a revolutionary group opposed to the Roman Empire. Rather he believes that the really oppressive force at that time in Palestine was not Rome but rather the Jewish theocracy, which controlled the actual lives of the people by means of the sacred law. By undermining the very foundations of that law, Jesus was seen as a dangerous political enemy and was put to death precisely on that basis.

However, whatever the merits are of the latter hypothesis, Segundo wishes to move to a more profound level in the understanding of Scripture. Ultimately this is based on the understanding of the sacred texts as the process of education already mentioned in Chapter Six. It must also be stressed that God actually revealed himself to people preoccupied with their particular historical problems, so that "only in relation to the problems which represent the questions of the community can we understand who this God is who answers."[10] The educative process directed by God therefore involved different questions and different answers corresponding to the different periods of history.

These considerations lead to the further question of the relationship that exists between the revelation of God in the Old Testament and the revelation of Jesus in the New. Oddly enough, Segundo believes that "this question, which is so simple and so essential, is far from having received a clear answer in the course of twenty centuries of Christian life. And this fact has conditioned the whole of theology."[11] An example of the problem may be seen in the fact that the same God who ordered the Israelites to slay their enemies in Deuteronomy 7:14 ff. later on speaks through Jesus with an exhortation to turn the other cheek to aggressors (Matt. 5:39).

The attempts to explain the relation between the Testaments have moved in opposite directions. The theory of *continuation* stresses the fact that Jesus contributes another link in the process of divine revelation, all of which is seen as true (cf. Matt. 5:17–18). The whole of Scripture, therefore, appears as a great divine plan, and Jesus comes not to change it but to bring it to fulfilment. This would, however, entail a certain purification of the Law, which retained some elements that were gross and materialistic.

The theory of *correction,* on the other hand, looks to texts such as Mark 7:19, where, in opposition to former prophets, Jesus breaks with the Law and declares all foods to be clean. It also lays emphasis on teachings with regard to the gratuity of love, as in Luke 6:27–36, where Jesus would seem to be correcting the Old Testament passages that called for the extermination of the enemies of Israel.

Until recently, another position that mediated the above extremes was popular. It was entitled the *sensus plenior,* or fuller sense, of Scripture, and was prevalent in Catholic circles. According to this theory, it was Jesus who revealed the true and full meaning of the persons and events of the Old Testament, a meaning that had not been understood even by the writers of those documents. Segundo does not find this or the previous explanations to be valid, for the basic question still remains: how can there be unity of faith when a radical correction of divine revelation has occurred?

He proposes his own solution to the problem by returning to the idea of continuity, but at the same time making a clear distinction between two elements: one permanent and unique, that is, *faith,* and the other changeable and varying according to different historical circumstances, that is, *ideologies.* To summarize, the God revealed in the two Testaments is always known through a series of responses to different historical events; thus the unchangeable faith is always incarnated in changeable ideologies, which constitute "a bridge between the conception of God and the problems of history."[12] In one specific set of circumstances, then, God was understood to call for the slaying of neighboring peoples; in another and different historical situation, his message was one of nonresistance to evil.

If this argument is conceded for the moment, a further question crops up: what is the relation of the Bible to contemporary situations, such as the phenomenon of widespread oppression in Latin America? One way to seek a theological answer to this would involve searching the Scriptures for the paradigmatic situations which most resemble contemporary events and accepting these as the correct faith response for today. But such a procedure appears antiscientific and unreal, inasmuch as "the search for similar situations in cultures separated by twenty or thirty centuries, especially when we consider the acceleration of history, loses meaning day by day."[13] Instead, Segundo proposes an alternative:

The other option consists in inventing what could be today the ideology employed by a contemporary gospel. What would the Christ who appears in the gospels from two thousand years ago have said today, confronted with our problems? If the faith is one in spite of historical diversity, then there must exist today, just as in the past, an ideology that expresses it by extending a bridge between it and our situation.[14]

In clarifying this position, Segundo makes use of the language of communications theory. He distinguishes between simple learning, or proto-learning, which involves the acquiring of additional information, and learning how to learn or deutero-learning, which would enable one to multiply knowledge in new situations.[15] From this perspective, he holds that "the ideologies present in Scripture pertain to the first level: they are answers learned vis-à-vis definite historical situations. By contrast, faith is the total process to which humanity submits, and this process entails learning, in and through ideologies, how to create the ideologies needed for new and unexpected historical situations." To summarize with the examples mentioned earlier, "to escape from slavery through struggle is one experience, just as to turn the other cheek is another. Whoever has gone through both experiences and reflected on them has learned how to learn."[16]

The above approach is considered helpful in solving, or at least clarifying, two other basic problems in liberation theology. One of these is concerned with the question of the continuation of revelation. Although classical theology speaks of revelation as a "deposit" that closed with the death of the last apostle, it is clear in the teaching of St. John that revelation was destined to continue after the physical departure of Jesus (cf. John 16:12–14). There it is asserted that the Spirit of truth will make known the "many things" that Jesus did not reveal, since his hearers were incapable of understanding them at that time. Moreover, this entailed "not a better comprehension of what was already said, but a learning of new things."[17] Once again, it is a question of deutero-learning, or learning how to learn, which by definition is the contrary of a deposit.

Secondly, the approach demonstrates that it makes no sense to separate faith and ideologies; for without ideologies faith is as dead as the faith without works referred to in the Letter of James (2:17) and for the same reason—both are totally impracticable. After reviewing Paul's teachings on the essentials of the Christian moral life, Segundo presents the following summary of his position: "Faith then is not a universal and atemporal summary of revelation once it has been divested of ideologies. On the contrary, it is maturity for ideologies, it is the possibility of fulfilling fully and conscientiously the ideological task on which the real liberation of human beings depends."[18]

Ideology in the Churches

The process of deutero-learning described so far must of necessity be carried out within the framework of a community, which brings us to the question of the relationship that exists between ideology and the historic Christian churches. In considering the various problems involved, the first point to be stressed is that Segundo considers liberation theology to be ecumenical on a profound level, not only with regard to Christians but to all people of good will. As a result, he is at pains to consider both Catholic and Protestant perspectives, noting that "liberation poses problems of such magnitude that Christians of whatever denomination feel closer to those who have made the same option in history than they do to members of their own denomination."[19] And as will be seen later, his hope is for a creative synthesis of doctrines that have thus far been divisive in the history of Christianity.

A key problem regarding ideology in the Catholic church is stated bluntly at the outset, namely, that "in the past, the church adopted ideologies which, because of their immersion in the status quo, were not seen as ideologies but as plain common sense."[20] However, the Medellín conference introduced a new factor in the equation for the Latin American church, since the bishops there supported ideologies that were in direct contradiction to the status quo. In short, the church was challenged to free itself from ideologies in the *pejorative* sense mentioned earlier, but at the same time to free itself *for* ideologies in the *neutral* sense, which Segundo believes is the only way that the faith can actually be incarnated in history.

But this mélange of old and new concepts still awaits a full harmonization in the Latin American church, although exactly the same situation is visible in the documents of Vatican II. One of Segundo's favorite paradigms for this situation may be found in a draft document of the bishops of Chile, entitled "The Gospel, Politics, and Forms of Socialism,"[21] which he considers to be a truly historical statement with regard to the relation of faith and ideology. He is amazed at the manifest inconsistency in the bishops' teaching, because "on the one hand the document asserts that the church cannot choose sides and on the other hand it asserts that socialism in Chile is not a real alternative to the existing capitalist system."[22] The mental process underlying this choice seems to be based on the assumption that the existing situation (whose abuses they had often denounced previously) did not constitute an ideology, but rather purely and simply reality. This leads Segundo to the wry comment that "the great sin of 'Christians for Socialism' is that there does not exist a party of 'Christians for Capitalism.'"[23]

The crucial element determining the bishops' opposition is clearly seen as the factor of atheism implied in a socialist or Marxist system. Since this would totally imperil an understanding of the church as the ordinary means of salvation, the bishops who held this conception were bound to reject the socialist alternative. In Segundo's view, this also entailed the abandonment of the guidelines of Vatican II, Medellín, and other documents with regard to the church's role in the humanization of the modern world. Since they were embarrassed by these documents, the bishops did not want to enunciate explicitly the ecclesiocentric view of the church that actually comprised the underlying ideological structure of their document.

The unwillingness of the bishops is sharply illustrated if we turn to a recent Protestant work that was written in opposition to liberation theology.[24] In this book, C. Peter Wagner is also anxious to emphasize the transcendence of faith with regard to ideologies. And because he is not hindered by Catholic magisterial teaching in the elaboration of his arguments, the great value of this work lies in its clear exposition of the principles of an alternative ecclesiology. Wagner's basic points can be stated here only in their briefest form:

1. The function of the church consists in the *individual reconciliation* of all persons with God. . . . 2. Among the different functions of the church, the *salvation of souls* has priority. . . . 3. The work of Christ is reduced to his action by means of the Gospel *within the church*. . . . 4. The *unity of the church* and belonging to it is more important than any socioeconomic-political option. . . . 5. The "theology of the radical left" does not take into account the *dualism of the Bible* and particularly the *negative supernatural powers* that rule this world. . . . 6. Finally, there exists *no universal promise or plan of salvation*, but only a salvation that operates through evangelism and individual conversion.[25]

Segundo is positively grateful to Wagner for thus spelling out his position in such detail; moreover, its importance for the Catholic church lies in its lucid exposure of the real theological ideology that lies behind much opposition to liberation theology. Segundo notes rather ironically that "the bishops of Chile would have performed a real service to the church if they had made these same six points explicit, instead of trying to arrive at the same conclusions while hiding, in a more sophisticated manner, the true underlying theology of their document."[26]

Ideology and Eschatology

Another central problem regarding the church and ideology centers around the important concept of eschatology, or "the transcendence of everything in history." Segundo considers eschatology as tending toward a reality that is more profound and definitive than the church itself, namely, the kingdom of God. The differences in eschatology among all the Christian churches, he believes, may be reduced fundamentally to "the different conceptions they hold concerning the relation between the events and actions of history on the one hand and the kingdom of God on the other."[27]

Since the Reformation, he goes on to add, the Catholic position has tended to stress above all the notion of *merit* as a condition of entering the kingdom. What is of primary importance in this view is the effort that is expended and the proper intention directed to God; the merit of an action, therefore, has no direct relationship to its efficacy in history. Moreover, this sharp divergence between religious and secular spheres of value led logically to the creation of a "theology of two planes," one supernatural and the other completely natural.

However, in the past few decades the theologian Karl Rahner and others developed an opposing position that stressed the single supernatural vocation and destiny of all persons. And this viewpoint was adopted in its essentials by the Second Vatican Council, leading to the recognition that "what grace produces in the interior of the Christian has exactly the same value as what the same grace produces in all men of good will (cf. *Gaudium et Spes,* no. 22)."[28] This teaching, then, effectively undercut the theological foundations of the "two planes" theory and, in Segundo's view, opened the way for liberation theology.

While it rejected the Catholic notion of merit, Protestantism created its own version of the distinction of planes by adopting Luther's theory of the "two kingdoms." Segundo believes that this conception "formed the politicotheological base for the whole edifice of the Reformation."[29] Without it the reformers would have been unable to secure the armed support of the powerful princes, and the whole movement would have foundered. The two kingdoms idea, moreover, is closely related to other basic Lutheran doctrines, such as justification by faith alone and *soli Deo gloria,* glory to God alone. Segundo holds that essentially they reduce faith to "the confident and at the same time passive acceptance of a plan fixed by God alone for the destiny of each individual and for the construction of his eschatological kingdom."[30]

In comparison to the Lutheran position of justification by faith alone, the Catholic doctrine of justification by works in accordance with the moral law may not appear distinctively Christian. The important principle it did stand for, however, was "freedom *for* something definitive and even eschatological: the building of the kingdom."[31] Conversely, Segundo believes that the Lutheran side defended an essential element of Paul, freedom *from* the law and its preoccupations, although it was deficient in freedom *for* the kingdom. He is also convinced that a synthesis was (and is) possible: "The third conciliating element, that is, liberty for the construction of the kingdom, which could have reconciled Catholic legalism and Lutheran passivity, was left aside. The controversy, moreover, hardened both extremes even more, instead of leading to a fruitful and liberating synthesis."[32] Thus Segundo remains hopeful that a theology of liberation can be founded on a profound reconciliation and mutual correction in the two lines of thought.

The above analysis also helps to clarify the differences between liberation theology and the European "political theology." Segundo feels that the latter school is deeply influenced by the Lutheran emphasis on justification by faith alone; thus its language tends to avoid any terms that might suggest a causal link between historical activity and the construction of the eschatological kingdom. He applies the same criticism to the Catholic theologians in the school, who tend to "overlook the true aspect that the Catholic church defended at the time of the Reformation."[33]

Political theology does have an initial liberating function, especially through its key concept of hope, for "the future is freed from the weight of the past. Faith permits people to imagine new possibilities and to escape the allurements of the established order." But despite this imagination and creativity at the beginning, Segundo charges that it eventually ends up as a politically neutral theology. By its relativization of all historical projects, it throws cold water on the *enthusiasm* that is necessary for any movement for social change, "not only on the false ideological enthusiasms created by the status quo, but also on the new projects created by criticism and hope."[34]

A second difficulty between liberation theology and political theology lies in the sphere of language. To Segundo, the political theologians appear to be employing two different kinds of language. When they speak *historically,* the language is revolutionary and committed; but when they speak *theologically,* the relativizing influence of the two kingdoms doctrine appears to come into play once again. Here he uses the example of Richard Shaull, a progressive North American theologian. While the Latin Americans are intensely interested in finding out how or by whom the kingdom is constructed, the response of Shaull is disappointing, for he asserts that: "No person or human group, no human ideology or human change, but *God alone* is responsible. Christians thus suffer the same disillusion as when they received the response of the bishops to the critical situation in Chile: we choose the risen Christ. Or, what is the same thing, we choose nothing concrete in history."[35] To adopt such an approach would clearly signal the demise of a liberation theology.

The Problem of Violence

The further implications that are involved in Segundo's views on faith and ideology are obviously manifold. However, there is one issue that has always posed an acute problem for the church and that may serve as a paradigm for many others: the question of violence.

He begins the discussion of violence by means of a phenomenological analysis of Christian love, whose centrality in the teaching of the New

Testament is certainly agreed on by Christians. According to the principles already enunciated on the relation of faith and ideology, he holds that the deeds and teachings of Jesus are not meant to spell out in detail what kind of love should be employed, that is, what specific ideology will make love efficacious. Moreover, Jesus did not do so, in order that his followers might be free to implement the great commandment imaginatively and creatively as they faced the ever new demands of history. In other words, "the only rule that continues in effect is that of the most efficacious and extensive love possible in each specific situation."[36] It remains to be seen whether such an understanding would include or eliminate the use of violence.

A basic principle in Segundo's approach is that love must be understood within the framework of "the economy of energy." The latter phenomenon is described as follows: "If we really love a definite number of persons, we cannot incorporate other persons into our love without distributing the available energy in a different way, that is, without removing energy from certain areas of our love for the first group." As regards this limited quantity of disposable energy, then, "we can certainly create infinite combinations with it, but we certainly cannot increase it, at least in absolute terms."[37]

Another key assertion is that this limited energy can serve the interests of either love or egotism or, in other words, that love does not have its own exclusive means. Thus Segundo concludes that "our love must place in its service the same instruments that can and do serve egotism: sexuality in direct or sublimated form and aggressivity, the fundamental tendencies that Freud calls Eros and Thanatos, desire and death. There is no other energy for effective love." One example given is of love for one's mother, which has the same psychic roots as patriotism, prejudice, racism, and war.

To utilize limited energy for effective love, therefore, it is necessary to keep some people at a distance in order that we may effectively love others. The alternative would be a huge dissipation of energy and loss of time with no real results, as would happen, for example, if one tried to imitate the Good Samaritan of Jesus' parable in a literalistic manner. The psychological mechanism for establishing distance is "not to let the other person get near to us *as a person,* who is of interest to us personally."[38] This mechanism is clearly dangerous and requires constant discernment in its use, inasmuch as it can also serve egotism; however, this ambivalent situation must be acknowledged to be the human condition.

Here we reach the key point toward which the analysis has been heading. For the only way that we can keep some persons at a nonpersonal or merely functional level in our lives is by the utilization of *interior and exterior violence.* Although the interior level is not usually thought of in terms of violence, it certainly should be, for it reduces the unique personal dimension of others to the status of an impersonal object. This can and often does cause pain and suffering in the latter, but that is the unavoidable result of the economy of energy.

On the external level, the matter is clearer. For our relations with those to whom we do not choose to relate as neighbor, family, or friend are of necessity regulated by law, and "an intrinsic characteristic of law is that it is always supported by coercive power, that is, by the physical violence that requires compliance. People do not pass laws if they do not have the violent means to make others comply with them, whether voluntarily or not."[39] All this leads Segundo to the conclusion that "we have to abandon the simplistic ideas that make us discover violence only when a revolutionary takes up a gun or that speak of nonviolence as compatible with impersonal laws and with their armed and coercive support." On the contrary, we have to admit that *violence is an internal dimension of all concrete love* in history, just as it clearly is an internal dimension of all concrete egotism."[40] It should be added, however, that the dynamics of love would strive to reduce the amount of violence for efficacy to the lowest level that is possible.

At this point the hermeneutic circle is brought into play once more, as Segundo returns for a fresh look at the New Testament in the light of the previous discussion. In this, he is especially intent on rooting out a heresy that he sees developing in the Christology of liberation theology, that is, the tendency to "locate Jesus outside the basic law of all truly human existence, the law of the economy of energy with its painful consequences."[41] This tendency is seen to occur when exaggerated use is made of such terms for Jesus as "the man for others" and "the man of nonviolent love."

Several examples from Scripture are presented as clear evidence of Jesus' own submission to the laws of the economy of energy. When John the Baptist was arrested, Jesus did not publicly side with him or try to free him, but chose to turn away to continue his own mission. That this action upset John is clear from his sending of disciples to find out if Jesus was really he who is to come (Matt. 11:3). Thus it is obvious from the New Testament "that 'the man for others' decided not to be 'the man for John the Baptist' in this concrete case, or to be so in such an indirect way that he couldn't help but cause deep injury and painful crisis in his friend."[42]

A second example is found in the narrative of the Syrophoenician woman (Mark 7:24–30). Segundo views the much debated verse, "Let the children first be fed, for it is not right to take the children's bread and throw it to the dogs," as another illustration of the painful economy of energy. The notion that he was testing the woman's faith by this attack on her national identity is not consistent with the personality of Jesus as recorded in the gospels. Rather, Segundo asserts, it is more logical to assume that he used the same mechanisms all human beings employ, that is, keeping some persons at arm's length in order to allow others to get close to him. In the case of the

Syrophoenician woman, then, it meant that he experienced and accepted the common human prejudices against foreigners.[43]

A last case concerns Jesus' treatment of the Pharisees. Certainly each one of them was a unique person with an absolute value, and yet Jesus breaks off relations with them, using the mechanisms already described. Thus he submerges "these concrete and unique persons in a group or mental category where their individual characteristics are lost," that is, the category of hypocrites. And it follows that "once one has mentally included concrete persons in the category of hypocrites, the possibility arises of losing interest in them, of breaking off dialogue, of giving one's time and attention to another group of one's neighbors, of those who 'were around him' (Mark 4:10 ff.)."[44]

Summary and Conclusions

Segundo presents many other illuminating examples and insights regarding the relation of faith and ideology throughout *The Liberation of Theology*; indeed it could be designated as the dominant theme of that entire volume. However, we must pause for the time being and ask about some of the major implications of the ideas just discussed.

I would submit that the question of faith and ideology is at the heart of the matter for any contemporary theology that wishes to make the struggle for justice an actual "constitutive dimension of the preaching of the gospel." Perhaps the problem—and the ground still to be covered—can be seen most clearly in the letter of Pope Paul VI, *Octogesima Adveniens*. In that document, Pope Paul emphasizes the ambiguity of all sociopolitical ideologies (nos. 26–29); and he continues with a penetrating critique of socialist or Marxist ideologies (nos. 30–34) as well as of the ideology of liberal capitalism (no. 35).

The point I wish to stress concerns the pontiff's teaching about the response of Christian individuals and groups faced with the above situations. As regards individual Christians, he stresses that "going beyond every system, *without however failing to commit himself concretely in serving his brothers,* he will assert, in the very midst of his options, the specific character of the Christian contribution for a positive transformation of society."[45] Again, toward the end of the letter, he asserts with regard to Christian organizations and their responsibility for collective action that "without putting themselves in the place of the institutions of civil society, *they have to express,* in their own way and rising above their particular nature, *the concrete demands of the Christian faith for a just, and consequently necessary, transformation of society.*"[46] Thus, in addition to the criticism of existing ideological systems, Christians are here called to a concrete commitment to justice. And obviously, if this commitment is to go beyond empty voluntarism, it must involve the creation of specific plans and strategies for change ("transformation" in the citations). In a word it must lead to new and better systems of goals and means, that is, to new and better ideologies.

The same need may also be seen with utmost clarity in the teaching of Vatican II contained in *Gaudium et Spes*. For example, in number 16 of that document the bishops state that "in fidelity to conscience, Christians are joined with the rest of men in the search for truth, and for the *genuine solution of the numerous problems which arise in the life of individuals* and from social relationships."[47] Earlier, in section 11, the Council fathers also emphasized that "faith throws a new light on everything, manifests God's design for man's total vocation, and thus directs the mind to solutions which are fully human."[48] Although the term "ideology" is not employed here, that can be the only coherent implication of the texts. For it is clear that only such specific systems of goals and means can ever make an authentic contribution to "solutions which are fully human."

In my opinion, it is precisely this troublesome nettle that Segundo has grasped audaciously in his analysis of faith and ideology. Here we can only allude to a few of its many implications. On a first level, we may recall the assertion that in the past the church tended to adopt the values of the status quo unconsciously because they appeared obvious and natural, that is, "common sense." At the present time, because of the impact above all of the social sciences, there exists a much greater awareness of the danger involved in disguising or sacralizing the existing order. For those not influenced by the social sciences, the sociopolitical traumas—Vietnam, Watergate, and others—of the past decade have at least led to a serious questioning of the shallow maxim: "My country, right or wrong." But this massive task of "deideologizing" is still only in its infancy. I would risk the speculation that the real, though unexpressed, major thesis of *The Liberation of Theology* is that the entire millennium and a half of Constantinian Christianity has involved a gradual and massive ideologization of the gospel in favor of powerful and privileged interests in western society. Thus if western theologians respond in depth to the book, the essential process of deideologizing will have received a much needed impetus.

However, to move to a second level, this change of consciousness should not now lead to a church posture of attempting to avoid *all* ideologies. I say this because, if the arguments adduced in this chapter are valid, such an attempt is impossible to realize in practice. To claim to be totally apolitical is to adopt *that* ideology, which would obviously be roundly welcomed by those in positions of power and wealth.

It would appear also that the subterfuge of avoiding all ideologies would ultimately lead to catastrophe on the pastoral level. A church that presents itself to its own adherents as nonideological, that is, not joined with the rest of humanity in searching for "the genuine solution of the numerous problems which arise in the life of individuals and from social relationships" will be convicted of moral infantilism. Thus it would be seen more and more as a nostalgic museum piece or as a harmful distraction from adult responsibility for the future. It should not be surprised, either, when other ideologies, from the multitude that assaults the contemporary consciousness, rush into the ideological vacuum of such a position, and begin to function as the real and operative, if not explicit, value systems of its members.

I am not here proposing specific ideologies that should be adopted; that obviously is an ongoing task that must remain open to the surprises of history. But the ideas presented here do help to clarify the historic either-or that must be faced. If the church chooses to withdraw into its own "plane" or "kingdom," refusing to contaminate the gospel with ideologies, it can only become a bastion of conservatism and reaction, destined for the dustbin of history. If, on the other hand, it elects the awesome, enormously difficult and challenging adventure of incarnating its gospel in ever new and better ideologies, then the people of God can fulfill their destiny of becoming what Vatican II called them to become—the "artisans of a new humanity."[49]

NOTES

1. The literature on the topic is already enormous and seems destined to increase in geometric progression. For a still useful survey and bibliography, see Heinz Robert Schlette, "The Problem of Ideology and Christian Belief," *Concilium 6: The Church and the World* (New York: Paulist Press, 1965), pp. 107–29. Schlette concludes as follows: "Ideology-criticism poses a number of open questions for theology. . . . Confrontation with the Marxist and Western sociological ideology-criticism will not be embarrassing to theology only if it has the courage to tackle its indeed massive objections. The necessary effort to study these problems will be the only way of advancing a step forward in the self-understanding of faith and belief" (p. 129).

2. "Fe e ideología," *Perspectivas de Diálogo* (November 1974):227–33.

3. Ibid., p. 228. Note the similarity of this with Charles Davis' definition of faith as a person's "personal stance, his basic orientation, the context of his thinking and the underlying attitude directing his choices and his actions" (*Christ and the World Religions* [New York: Herder and Herder, 1973], p. 73).

4. Segundo, "Fe e ideología," p. 227.

5. Ibid., p. 228. Leslie Dewart offers a similar phenomenology in *The Future of Belief: Theism in a World Come of Age* (New York: Herder and Herder, 1966): "Like Christian theism, Marxist atheism, when it is consciously and resolutely embraced, is embraced in an act of faith. In Christian terms we would say that both Christian theism and Marxist atheism are religious commitments. . . . Both are ultimate existential (and therefore essentially humanistic) commitments. . . . A faith is a commitment of one's existential self in the light of a certain apprehension of reality as disclosed in lived experience" (pp. 60–61). Probably the best-known similar approach is that of Paul Tillich: "Faith is the state of being ultimately concerned. The content matters infinitely for the believer, but it does not matter *for*

the formal definition of faith'' (*The Dynamics of Faith* [New York: Harper and Row, 1957], p. 4; italics mine).

6. Segundo, "Fe e ideología," p. 228. Cf. the views of Alain Durand: "But, in mankind's present situation, liberty is a possibility only if there is recourse *initially* to criticism of the ideology of the ruling classes and, *afterwards*, constant vigilance in regard to all ideological production—which is something quite different to a neutralist stance. Even though faith is not an ideology, *there is no faith without ideology*, any more than there is a God question without political implications" ("Political Implications of the God Question," *Concilium 76: New Questions on God* [New York: Herder and Herder, 1972], p. 74; italics mine).

7. Segundo, "Fe e ideología," p. 229.

8. Ibid., p. 233.

9. *Liberación de la teología* (Buenos Aires: Carlos Lohlé, 1975), p. 127; henceforth this book will be referred to as *Liberación*.

10. Ibid., p. 129.

11. Ibid., p. 130.

12. Ibid., p. 133. It is, of course, clear that "this bridge, this provisional but necessary system of means and ends," is what he calls an *ideology*. We may also note here the fundamental disagreement with this position of Karl Rahner, who holds that "certainly the bible always remains the foundation book of Christianity, precisely because it is genuine in itself and free from ideological prejudices," in "The Future of the Religious Book," *Theological Investigations VIII* (New York: Herder and Herder, 1971), p. 253.

13. Segundo, *Liberación*, p. 134.

14. Ibid. Although Segundo is critical of the theology of J. B. Metz, it appears that Metz is moving in this direction also as, for example, when he states that "perhaps one could, as an experiment, speak even of 'secondary ideologies,' of 'enlightened ideologies,' which are not simply ready-made for the socially critical mind, but are part of the will of an effective criticism of social practice, the will that makes committed social action possible" (*Theology of the World* [New York: Herder and Herder, 1969], p. 134).

15. The reference cited with regard to communication theory is Gregory Bateson, *Steps to an Ecology of Mind* (New York: Ballantine Books, 1974).

16. Segundo, *Liberación*, p. 137.

17. Ibid., p. 138.

18. Ibid., p. 140.

19. Ibid., p. 171. In this regard, cf. Segundo's article, "El posible aporte de la teología protestante para el cristianismo latinoamericano en el futuro," *Cristianismo y Sociedad* (Primera entrega, 1970): 41–49.

20. Segundo, *Liberación*, p. 144.

21. A more detailed analysis of this question was published by Segundo under the title, "La iglesia chilena ante el socialismo," in three issues of *Marcha* (27 August, 4 September, and 11 September 1971).

22. Segundo, *Liberación*, p. 147.

23. Ibid., p. 149.

24. C. Peter Wagner, *Latin American Theology: Radical or Evangelical?* (Grand Rapids, Mich.: Wm. B. Eerdmans Publishing Company, 1970).

25. Segundo, *Liberación*, pp. 154–57.

26. Ibid., p. 157.

27. Ibid., p. 158.

28. Ibid., p. 161. The key text from *Gaudium et Spes* states that "linked with the paschal mystery and patterned on the dying Christ, [the Christian] will hasten forward to resurrection in the strength which comes from hope. All this holds true

not only for Christians, but for all men of good will in whose hearts grace works in an unseen way. For, since Christ died for all men, and since the ultimate vocation of man is in fact one, and divine, we ought to believe that the Holy Spirit in a manner known only to God offers to every man the possibility of being associated with this paschal mystery" (Gremillion, *Gospel of Peace and Justice*, p. 261).

29. Segundo, *Liberación*, p. 162. Reference is made here to the Protestant theologian James S. Preus, who wrote an article in accord with the position of Segundo entitled "The Political Function of Luther's Doctrina," *Concordia Theological Monthly* (October 1972). Preus states in the article: "*The unhappy depoliticization of the doctrine of justification by means of the two kingdoms* was very useful for the interests—political ones—of the Church. But, was it useful for the world?" (p. 598).

30. Segundo, *Liberación*, p. 163. Speaking of a contemporary Lutheran, Ernst Bloch maintains that Bultmann's approach took eschatology "out of the danger area of cosmic history, and away from the figure of Christ, whose position within that area is so explosive, and put it back in the realm of the lonely soul and its solid middle-class God" (*Atheism in Christianity* [New York: Herder and Herder, 1971], p. 40).

31. Segundo, *Liberación*, p. 172.

32. Ibid.

33. Ibid., p. 164, n. 22.

34. Ibid., p. 165.

35. Ibid., p. 169.

36. Ibid., p. 176.

37. Ibid., p. 179.

38. Ibid., p. 181. As regards the Good Samaritan, Segundo notes that he was able to help the injured man "because previously he had passed by countless other unfortunate people. Otherwise, he would not have had money and a donkey, nor made a trip." He also cites François Mauriac's novel *The Lamb;* a character in this book tries to imitate the Samaritan literally, and "his tragedy consists precisely in his incapacity to love systematically and effectively any concrete human being."

39. Segundo, *Liberación*, p. 182. In this regard, José Comblin remarks on the speech of Pope Paul VI in Colombia in 1968, where he exhorted his listeners not to put their trust in violence. Comblin comments wryly that "it could not be a question of a pure and simple refusal of all violence, since the Pope himself was constantly protected by an imposing force of police and soldiers" (*Théologie de la révolution* [Paris: Editions Universitaires, 1970], p. 83). In an early article on the subject, Segundo stressed that "it is urgent that the believers in nonviolence as a revolutionary political instrument cease to confuse religious imperatives with political analysis in their propaganda. If nonviolence must be sought for religious reasons, it need not be concluded that it will be politically successful in every epoch and in all human situations, from the Neanderthal man to the man who lives in New York" ("Christianity and Violence in Latin America," *Christianity and Crisis* [4 March 1968]:34). He also reveals in this article that he was a personal friend of Camilo Torres, a Catholic priest who was killed while fighting with guerrillas in Colombia.

40. Segundo, *Liberación*, pp. 182–83. Jürgen Moltmann appears to agree with Segundo's view. In a book dedicated to the apostle of nonviolence, Martin Luther King, Jr., he defends the following thesis: "The problem of violence and nonviolence is an illusory problem. There is only the question of the justified and unjustified use of force and the question of whether the means are proportionate to the ends" (*Religion, Revolution, and the Future* [New York: Charles Scribner's Sons, 1969], p. 143). In his discussion of the problem Robert McAfee Brown quotes with approval the words of John F. Kennedy: "Those who make peaceful revolution

impossible will make violent revolution inevitable" (*Religion and Violence: A Primer for White Americans* [Philadelphia: Westminster Press, 1973], p. 85). Brown refers to this statement as "the description of our age and possibly its epitaph."

41. Segundo, *Liberación,* p. 184.

42. Ibid., p. 185. From this Segundo concludes that "Jesus could, without sinning, have to choose between two inevitable material sins. In other words we can understand that the impeccability of Christ is not synonymous with an inhuman innocence. Although the formula may seem strange, sin has a positive place in the existence of Jesus."

43. Ibid., pp. 185–86.

44. Ibid., p. 187. Segundo concludes that "only an idealistic simplification of the attitudes of Jesus could portray him as dedicated to a love without limits, without resistance, and without violence."

45. *Octogesima Adveniens,* no. 36, in Gremillion, *Gospel of Peace and Justice,* p. 501. In all the following quotes, the italics are mine.

46. *Octogesima Adveniens,* no. 51, in Gremillion, *Gospel of Peace and Justice,* p. 511.

47. *Gaudium et Spes,* no. 16, in Gremillion, *Gospel of Peace and Justice,* p. 255.

48. *Gaudium et Spes,* no. 11, in Gremillion, *Gospel of Peace and Justice,* p. 252.

49. *Gaudium et Spes,* no. 38, in Gremillion, *Gospel of Peace and Justice,* p. 267. An excellent contemporary analysis of ideology may be found in the book of Alvin W. Gouldner, *The Dialectic of Ideology and Technology: The Origins, Grammar, and Future of Ideology* (New York: Seabury Press, 1976). Gouldner is especially incisive with regard to practitioners of his own discipline of sociology, who appear to believe that the sociology of knowledge applies to everyone except themselves. For example, he observes that "commonly normal academic sociologists assume that their rejection of right- or left-wing ideologies justifies their claim to be ideology-free and value-free. They forget, of course, that their liberalism is also an ideology" (p. 78). In my opinion a similar stance is often adopted by North American theologians.

CHAPTER EIGHT

TOWARD A SPIRITUALITY
OF LIBERATION

In moving to the area of spirituality, it is helpful to recall the important statement of Roger D. Haight in an article cited earlier. There Haight emphasized that "as far as any renewed understanding of the Church is concerned, unless the language, symbols, and understanding of the ideal Christian life change, current ecclesiology will have little impact on anyone."[1] Since Segundo has stressed from the beginning of his work the need for a renewed ecclesiology, it is somewhat surprising that a synthetic or fully developed "spirituality of liberation" appears to be absent from his writings.

Perhaps the reason for this omission lies in the fact that the very term "spirituality" suggests the image of a mysterious realm that is completely separated from human existence and experience in the world, a conception that was actually employed in Latin America by a theology of Catholic Action. The approach would thus be subtly or not so subtly reinforcing a dualism at the center of Christian existence, a dualism which the major thrust of his work attempts to overcome.

For while the Christian's vocation is essentially that of creative and liberating praxis within the one integral history of humanity, the function of spirituality can be distorted into a kind of evasion, a convenient escape route from mature historical responsibility and from the pressing needs of the brother and sister who are nearby. In other words, spirituality can become a form of veiled egotism, albeit of a refined and celestial type, whereby human beings are released from the tasks of human reconciliation and solidarity because of the demands of a jealous and alienating God.[2]

Despite Segundo's lack of synthetic treatment, however, I believe that his approach to an understanding of spirituality may actually be a more radical one than we have been accustomed to in the past. For every spirituality is constructed on the infrastructure of an explicit or implicit theology.[3] If the underlying theological principles are firmly grounded in Scripture and lead to liberating praxis, the result would be an authentic Christian spirituality; however, if the theological infrastructure has a dubious correlation with the sources, or if its roots have never been profoundly examined, it is possible that the resulting spirituality could be alienating or even neurotic. Segundo's approach then is to probe down to the deeper levels of theological roots, striving to find there the authentic foundations of a Christian existence in the world.[4]

In this chapter, I will first review a number of his explicit statements with regard to the nature of Christian spirituality or, perhaps better, of Christian holiness. This will be followed by a consideration of the image of God which, consciously or unconsciously, affects both the understanding and practice of the Christian ideal. Finally, a brief survey will be presented of other elements that could be further elaborated and integrated into a more unified synthesis of a liberating spirituality.

Medieval and Modern Paradigms

In a "clarification" included in the book *Grace and the Human Condition,* Segundo offers a brief but incisive treatment of "Holiness for a Church in Dialogue."[5] The major thrust of the article consists in the contrast it sketches between a medieval paradigm of holiness, such as one finds in *The Imitation of Christ,* and that suggested by a recent document such as *Gaudium et Spes. The Imitation of Christ* was written at a time when the church still lacked a theology of history, or at least a theology of history which extended beyond the boundaries of Christendom, and this is considered to be its fatal weakness. The key question then becomes: "How will this perspective change with the discovery, in relatively recent times, of a universal history into which the Church herself is inserted?"[6]

The complete title of *The Imitation of Christ* includes the phrase *and Contempt for the World.* The "world" thus occupies a central position in its appoach, but it is a world that *"is not in the process of fulfilling itself.* Its values or pseudovalues are conceived as already ripe fruits hanging on a tree." This already finished world does not offer a challenge to human creative powers; rather it is fundamentally a temptation to concupiscence, to the desire to take possession of these ripe fruits. This naturally leads to a negative evaluation of temporal things, which is expressed in what Segundo calls "one of the most profoundly deprecatory remarks about the world ever written: 'What may you see outside your chamber that you do not see within it? Look, within your chamber you can see heaven and earth and all the elements of which earthly things are made.' "[7]

From this viewpoint the human person is confronted with a radical choice between the divine realm and the worldly. Some people are so entangled in their sense faculties that they make the worldly option, but others "have their reason clearly illuminated by the light of true understanding, and by it their affection is so purged and purified from earthly things that they always desire heavenly things; so that it is hard for them to hear of earthly things and a truly great pain to serve the necessities of the body."[8]

When these principles are actually applied to concrete human existence, the result is a complete separation between the two areas, with the divine element totally dominating the worldly. As a consequence, "the most real and effective division possible between these opposed spheres of interest and things is to serve as the basis for fashioning a way of life that will be identified with Christian perfection." The division can lead to such a radically unbiblical statement as "he who loves God despises all other love," that is, that human beings and their needs are to be subordinated to a life lived for God alone.[9]

Moreover, the attitude here described implies a number of fundamental options that logically follow from it, in Segundo's view. The first entails the allocation of primacy to intention over deed, so that it becomes "the why and the wherefore, not the what, that counts most in human activity" and "the only person who accords real primacy to intention is the one who is equally disposed to construct or destroy, to work harder or stop altogether." Segundo points out the obvious disparity of this position with Jesus' own description of the judgment on human existence in Matthew 25.

A second option entails an intense and prolonged effort to purify one's intention; and "the primary aim in this process will be to divest oneself of any and all creative ambition centered around the result of the work itself." This leads to a great stress on obedience as the best way of obtaining indifference to the actual results of actions, and also of achieving the desired purity of intention. And God is seen as the one who wills this basic passivity, since "such faults as we cannot amend in ourselves or in others we must patiently suffer until our Lord of his goodness will dispose otherwise."[10]

Another option that is included in the gradual purification of intention leads to the conclusion that indispensable worldly goods may be used, but that this is to be done without desire. And the logical last option is to "separate ourselves affectively and effectively from human beings," inasmuch as "our Lord and his angels will draw near and abide with those who, for the love of virtue, withdraw themselves from their acquaintances and from their worldly friends. . . . It is also laudable in a religious person seldom to go abroad, seldom to see others."[11] From these considerations a picture emerges of the ideals of the spiritual life. It is characterized by peace and solitude, for one has been liberated from the flesh-spirit dualism, not by some integration of the two but by a complete suppression of the fleshly and worldly in favor of the spiritual. The concentration of energy is on one's own inner life, and continuous scrutiny is directed to one's inner intention, since "if you will have peace in your soul, and be perfectly united to God in blessed love, set aside all other men's deeds, and set yourself and your own deeds only before the eye of your soul." Segundo summarizes by noting that in this view "the good works of love do not show up as the one and only authentic fulfillment of this divine love but rather only as the means to fill up the time which a person, however perfect he may be, must spend away from pure and interior cultic love of God."[12] Again the second great commandment appears to have vanished here in favor of an exclusivist and solipsistic love.

Segundo's basic objection to this model of holiness involves not only its own internal limitations but also its transposition of an ideal of religious life onto lay people who lived in the world. At the present time it is even more dubious, since even those in religious life are searching for more authentic links between their religious vocation and responsibility for their tasks in history. The model has also influenced Christian spirituality by restricting the possibility of canonization:

The possibility of proposing a Christian to the Church as a model of life was conditioned in large measure by his separation from historical involvement. Apparently, "heroic virtue" could only be perceived, if not measured, as a great thing independent of, and separate from, all human interest—as an egoistic thing basking in a situation of aloofness. Every human creation of an intense and passionate kind showed itself to be ambiguous, both with respect to its intention and to its end results.[13]

After Vatican II, it is clear to Segundo that this ideal of ahistorical sanctity no longer represents the authentic image that the church must reflect if it is to fulfill its mission of being a sign to humanity. It must also be admitted that the more recent ideal, that of commitment within a given historical situation, will always be marked by ambiguity and by reasons for and against the commitment, as occurred, for example, in the case of Catholics on both sides who died in the Spanish Civil War. His conclusion for contemporary times is that perhaps "a community which claims to be wholly in dialogue with the world and its history must renounce the task of delegating to *saints* its task as a whole in the multiple, concrete, and fallible commitments of its members that are motivated by love."[14]

The author admits that there were several attempts before Vatican II to relate the spiritual life to historical events, one of which was the founding of the Society of Jesus. Its fundamental goal of contemplatives *in action* broke with the classical conception of religious orders, so that "all defined times for prayer were suppressed, along with every other particular which restricted the possibility of acting in accordance with the demands of a given concrete situation."[15] But the necessary theology of history was still lacking in the church, and, especially in the generalate of Francis Borgia, the classical concept was reintroduced. Although there were some creative moments in the Society's history, such as the work of Matteo Ricci in China, Roberto de Nobili in India, and the founders of the Reductions in Paraguay, the result was that the European branch of the Jesuits "made an about-face and closed the doors of the conventicle, naturally leaving the world outside."[16]

The Understanding of Prayer

A second "clarification" of the above issues may be found in the volume *Our Idea of God* under the title "Prayer, Providence, Commitment."[17] Segundo begins by quoting a number of examples to illustrate the "crisis" of contemporary Christians with regard to prayer, and especially the prayer of petition. He believes that the real difficulty here centers around a common image of God that is associated with such prayer, namely, "that of a God who is a better technician than our human technicians, a better doctor than our doctors. In other words, it is the image of a God who occupies a place in our lives that has not yet been reached by human knowledge and effectiveness."[18]

It should be obvious that such an understanding of God vitiates at the core a sense of Christian responsibility for history. For if such a God heard everyone's prayers, he would be seen as a God of *children;* if he heard only the prayers of close followers who had faith in him, he would appear as the God of a *privileged few*. This latter group, then, "would have found a way to get the better of the rest of mankind in the use and enjoyment of the world; they would operate religiously, through God." Such thinking would also entail a false view of providence as an interference in humanity's efforts and affairs, an attitude that Segundo refers to as a kind of "providentialist passivity." Rather, Segundo sees the world as having its own proper laws while at the same time God has given us revelation as a system of signs, which leads us to the task of freeing the world's dynamisms for the service of love and the construction of the world. Eventually, through these efforts "in its definitive form, this world will be not only the *new earth* of man but also the *new heaven* of God."[19]

From this perspective prayer as reflection and interpretation is absolutely essential. Periods of time set aside for this do not remove us from the world, but such activity "does relate us explicitly to God, since it consists of lending a more attentive ear to his word that is transmitted by what happens in time."[20] Consequently, "there is no Christian living at all without such prayer, whether it takes the form of a petition or not."

But what about the cases already mentioned of contemporary Christians who find difficulty in asking God for "things"? In the gospel this practice is certainly mentioned explicitly, for example, in Matthew 7:7–11, where the Father is portrayed as giving good things to those who ask him. However, Luke's parallel text offers a more profound theological nuance, for there the "good things" are clearly seen as the Holy Spirit (Luke 11:13). Thus within the framework of the Christian project, which is "the fashioning of love in history" or "the liberation of the universe from all the enslavements that weigh down upon it,'' what we pray for is the Spirit of creativity and liberation, for ''to sin against the Holy Spirit is precisely to refuse to accompany Jesus in his work of liberation.''[21] The real reply to our prayers then is God's gift of himself, that is, of his Spirit.

Lastly, for Segundo, revelation establishes the fact that no love is ever lost. At the same time, there occur limit situations which everyone experiences at times in the Christian project of love in history. But the anxiety inherent in this experience ''turns into hope, and the hope into words, i.e., into *prayer*.'' An example may be seen in the illness of a loved one, where our prayer of petition should not be seen as a request for miracles, but simply ''voicing the limit confronted by our love, and the victory of our hope over that limit''; the hope, once again, is based on the conviction of the Christian that no love is ever lost.[22] This treatment of prayer is certainly not a complete one, and it may be hoped that Segundo will develop it further in future publications.

An Authentic Image of God

It may be noted at this point that the concrete actualization of a spirituality will be determined to a great extent by two key factors: the Christian image of God and the Christian image of the human person. In short, the ongoing dialogue that is the spiritual life will be based on one's conception of the partners in that dialogue. Since the Christian image of the person has already been discussed in a previous chapter, we will now turn to the absolutely central concept of the authentic Christian concept of God. Our sources will be primarily a series of articles that Segundo devoted to the subject in 1968 and 1969.

In the first of these, the author makes reference to the centrality of the doctrine of the Trinity in Christian thought, but then he proceeds to stress another and rather surprising fact, that is, ''a real lack of interest among Christians with regard to the problem of God.''[23] They find it hard to imagine the passions that were roused by the early Trinitarian controversies, and would prefer to leave such fine points to specialists or intellectual snobs.

On the other hand, Segundo believes that there is an element of sanity in this attitude; in fact, the vast majority of the teachings of the Bible are concerned with ourselves, our life and its transformation whereas ''the passages which allow theologians to discourse on what God is in himself, independently of our life and our history, can be counted on the fingers of one hand.''[24] And the reason for this seeming disproportion consists in the fact that it is through our existence and its transformation—and only through this—that we can come to know God as he is in himself.

At the same time, however, it would be dangerous to dismiss too readily the question of God. For the image we have of God is intimately linked to the image of our neighbor; thus "in deforming God we protect our egotism, [and] our false and inauthentic ways of treating our neighbors form a close alliance with our falsifications of the idea of God. Our unjust society and our distorted idea of God are in a close and terrible alliance." Moreover, the question of possible idolatry is not solved by merely pronouncing the name of God (Matt. 7:21). In this regard Segundo quotes Henri de Lubac to the effect that "to believe in you I must believe in love and believe in justice, and it is a thousand times better to believe in these things than to pronounce your name."[25] Consequently, it is essential to reflect on the problem of God, since this is intimately linked to our ongoing dialogue with our fellow human beings.

A second article[26] continues the discussion with a thesis that is also startling at first glance: "Our Christian existence, if it is to be authentic, has to entail a continuous passage from atheism to faith," or, to put it another way, atheism must continue to constitute an essential element of our faith.[27] On a rather superficial level, pronouncing the phrase, "I believe in God," is supposed to distinguish the believers from the atheists; in this view, the believers' task from this point on is to proclaim and defend the faith they fully possess. But a more profound question inevitably arises: "Are we sure that this phrase, 'I believe in God,' is sufficient to transport us totally, profoundly, and radically from atheism to faith?"[28]

For in using these words, we may be actually putting our faith, not in the true God but in other, lesser values. There is the possibility then that "in saying 'I believe' we are actually making an act of faith in capitalism, in injustice, in suffering, in uselessness, in egotism." This possibility stems from the perennial human tendency to reduce God to our own level, and is also a way of justifying our own failures. The startling result of such a process is that "he who made us in his image and likeness has to accept the fact that we construct his image in our own image and likeness." And it may be that what really separates us from unbelievers is not so much our faith as our actual lack of authentic faith.[29]

Faith then must be understood as a continuing search for the true God, as in Augustine's expression: "If you had encountered me, you would still be searching for me." Segundo believes that through the dialogue with atheism we may be enabled to defend faith against an enemy more profound than atheism, that is, hypocrisy and a peaceful and self-satisfied tepidity. It should also open up the path to true freedom, for "it is impossible to be free without a restlessness that is always new and always active" and maintained in an equilibrium with the certainty of faith. The resulting dialectic is, finally, a process that must be created anew each day.[30]

In an interrelated series of four articles, Segundo deepens the analysis of the image of God by considering the Trinity under the major headings of "a history," "a society," and "a liberty." The history of the formation of the image is examined first of all in Scripture, which leads to certain functional understandings of the Trinity. The Father is understood, above all, as "the God *before us*" inasmuch as "all our history, both individual and social, that of each person and of all humanity, moves within his governance and his laws." Jesus is seen primarily as "God *with us*," that is, "God encountered within the space and time of our human history." Lastly, the Spirit is envisioned as "God *in us*," who continues to reveal himself and to suggest to us the totality of truth."[31]

In the article on the Trinity as "a society," Segundo considers the elaboration of Trinitarian ideas during the first three centuries; he is convinced that during this period "something of radical importance for the history of humanity was decided under the apparent form of a 'theological' controversy."[32] The trends of thought that sought to preserve the unity of God at all costs may be summarized as variants of modalism or subordinationism; however, the early Councils reacted against these tendencies with their articulation of the Trinity as "one sole substance and three different persons."

After recalling the teaching of John that the human term most suitable for describing God is love, Segundo sums up the implications of the above formulation: "God is love, but not as an abstract force which makes possible and transcends our love. Our God is *a society*. We have a social God. Not because he orders us to form a society and enables us to do this, but because God is eternally, totally, and infinitely *a society*."[33] Thus the image of a solitary creator and judge, self-sufficient in his own perfection, is not the Christian God nor is the image of a power that transcends everything else. Rather "when we dedicate our life and our work so that human beings may respect, unite with, and love each other, that ideal which inspires us, that engine of all the solidarity and justice achieved in our history, that is truly the Christian God."[34] It follows then that the Trinitarian formula contained the most profound affirmation of all time regarding our human dignity and the value of our efforts in history.

In two articles on the Trinity as "a liberty," Segundo begins by asking whether the formulations of Nicea and Constantinople actually overcame the modalist and subordinationist movements, or whether the latter still remain as powerful currents of thought with regard to the image of God. For if we human beings manifest, in de Lubac's phrase, a "genius for protecting ourselves from God," then it could be that the decisive victory achieved over those tendencies *in the past* will have to be won all over again *in the present*.

For Segundo, the basic flaw in modalism was its rejection of a true Incarnation of God, which necessarily entailed a denial of all *history* in God. As a result "the 'unmoved mover' of the Aristotelian tradition, the absolute unity of the Neoplatonism of the time (Plotinus), the logos of nature of the Stoics, all these rationalist understandings of the divinity rushed headlong into the center of Christianity through the breach created by modalism."[35] He then goes on to pose the question: "Where is the mechanism that has partly hidden, first for ourselves and through us for many others, the authentic and magnificent face of the Trinitarian God?"[36]

In answering the question, the author first comments on the classical tracts in theology that deal with the Trinity. The *De Deo Trino* tract was based fundamentally on biblical sources; at the same time the course *De Deo Uno* treated the same subject from the viewpoint of philosophy, with the unfortunate result that it reduced the data of revelation to what philosophy believed it could admit. In the process the symbolism of revelation was overlooked, and "we make a reified rationalism the judge of the way in which we have to understand—and accept—revelation."[37]

As an example, Segundo advances the doctrine of the Incarnation. The scriptural data tell us that the Son of God became incarnate whereas philosophy that is heir to the Greek tradition asserts that God is immutable. But how can both these affirmations be true? The answer is usually sought by adjusting the understanding of the Incarnation to make it compatible with the immutability of God, instead of vice versa. Segundo believes this to be an illustration of "one of the most decisive processes in the religious, social, and political evolution of the West"; moreover, he states his own intention of reversing the process and of making revelation the judge of everything else.[38]

In accomplishing this, he reviews the scriptural data which assert that the early Christians "saw" the man Jesus, but that they also reflected further and recognized something more in him, which in John 1:14 is described as the "glory" of God. To establish the meaning of this glory, Segundo first analyzes the prologue of John and then concludes that the climactic revelation of Jesus' glory occurs in John 13:4–5: "Jesus rose from supper, laid aside his garments, and girded himself with a towel. Then he poured water into a basin, and began to wash the disciples' feet, and to wipe them with the towel with which he was girded." Segundo summarizes the revelation as follows:

What did John see? The miracle of love: the assigning of an infinite value to that which appeared to have no value. The whole scene and the whole dialogue which accompany and follow it speak about this phenomenon which challenges all the catalogues of "natural" virtue. At the end of his life Jesus found nothing of greater value than to kneel at the feet of these poor men, his friends.[39]

Segundo concludes that thus, through the Son, the one and only essence of God and of each person in God is revealed, namely, "that God is always devoted to us, that God freely loves us and gives us his life, that he makes everything, even his interior life, depend on our liberty." Moreover, this is opposed to the conception of an immutable, impassible, inaccessible God, for "God is impassible by nature, but *grace consists* in the fact that he freely suffered *in fact* for us. And no reflection on nature can reveal this fact to us, since everything that liberty decides is situated in history, and history is narrated, not deduced."[40]

Another conclusion is that it is of decisive importance to know whether history or nature is the key to the revelation which God made of himself in Jesus Christ. And in the denunciation of modalism the church answered this question in favor of history, thus establishing the only way of giving meaning and value to our liberty. It follows that "the denunciation of modalism is the victory over the greatest of all alienations, that which deprives human liberty of its value *from within,* emptying it of meaning, making it irrelevant before the Absolute. Before the same Absolute that emptied himself to make of each person and all persons together the Absolute value!" Lastly, Segundo notes that this leads to a bold and confident attitude toward the risk involved in freedom, citing the words of Charles Péguy: "[God] has placed in our hands, in our weak hands, in our changing hands, in our sinful hands, *his own* eternal hope."[41]

In the final article, Segundo returns to his view that the deformations that have occurred, and continue to occur, in our notion of God spring from the fact that we make him into the image and likeness of our existence and of our society.[42] In that society we keep people at a distance by labeling or categorizing them, a mechanism that effectively nullifies their unique personal existence. In that way they can be integrated into and reduced to a system of functions that serve our own needs.

The exact same process is applied to God, who is depersonalized and dehistoricized, "in order to escape the judgment which is supposed by every concrete encounter with an absolute personal being, every encounter with an incarnate history." What actually happens is that, in order to avoid "too human" terms with regard to God, we end up "purifying" the idea of God by stripping it of all historical realism. Rather than avoiding anthropomorphism, then, we actually fall into it inasmuch as "this 'rational' version of God is nothing else but transposing to the level of the divine the alienated relations we have among persons by means of utilitarian and impersonal categories in social, political, economic, and juridical functions."[43]

It follows that a modification in our notion of God is parallel to and complementary with a modification in our way of understanding persons. Thus, Segundo believes that "only in a society where persons encounter persons endowed with a history, with a personality and, so to speak, with the absolute, will the notion of God be purified of its most radical anthropomorphisms, of its most obvious idolatries."[44]

This observation is made more specific by reference to capitalist society, where the human ideal emerges in the "private" zone; at the same time, work is viewed as the price one pays to obtain and to enhance this private sphere. Since it is accepted in principle that this is limited by the private rights of others, "the best society appears to be that where the scope of the private area is as great as possible for each individual." It is not surprising then that in this context the image of God should be that of the private or independent being par excellence. Or to put it another way, "the persistent tendency among Christians to reject in practice the notion of an incarnate God, and to reduce it to an impassible, inaccessible God, perfectly happy in himself, is nothing else than the most obvious anthropomorphism: the transfer unto God of the characteristics by which the individual believes himself or herself fulfilled in a society of domination."[45]

But the opposite is also true. Thus Segundo asserts that "the increasing interest of the church for forms of society where the creation of the person takes place in work for society and not in a sphere divorced from that, constitutes the best preparation for Christianity to deepen the theology of an incarnate God."[46] And he concludes the series of articles with the statement that "the Christian is committed to the building of a society where human relations will influence the authentic understanding of the revelation by which God desired to show himself to us and to dialogue with us."[47]

It should be obvious that these fundamental theological emphases have enormous importance for developing a spirituality aimed at synthesizing faith and justice. It should also be clear that they are as applicable in the universal church as they are in Latin America; that is, the dialectically related images of God and the human person are everywhere the basic and decisive determinants of an authentic Christian existence in the Spirit.

Elements of a Synthesis

It has already been noted that Segundo has not yet fully developed and synthesized his ideas on spirituality as such. For the remainder of this chapter, then, I will briefly review the theological concepts that could serve as the groundwork for such an integration.[48] In this attempt the focus of interest will be the Christian layperson, whether in the Americas or the rest of the world, although many of the ideas may have relevance for a spirituality of clergy or religious in active apostolates.

From a negative point of view, an authentic Christian spirituality would have to be one that recognizes clearly and attempts to transcend what Segundo has referred to as the "pre-Christian stages of faith." This would exclude a concept of spirituality founded on "magical" views of sacraments, morality, or dogma as well as a chauvinist or *conquistador* mentality that divides the world with Manichean fervor into friends of God (oneself and one's clan) and enemies (all others seen as rightful victims of his wrath). Deemed equally inauthentic would be the passive attitude toward historical involvement that results from splitting the world into sacred and secular realms, with the former functioning as an absolute value while the latter is assigned only relative and essentially transient importance. Lastly, the vision of this life as a dangerous test or trial, resulting in a fundamental attitude of patience and resignation in the face of urgent human problems, would be rejected as an inauthentic portrayal of Christian existence.[49]

On the positive side, a basic foundation for a liberating spirituality would encompass the images of God and the human person as well as the conception of prayer that unites them in dialogue that have already been discussed in this chapter. Of critical importance also would be the operative "image" of the church, which would have to be envisioned, not as an in-group of the saved but as a community with a special and difficult mission to embody and signify God's liberating plan for all of humanity. Clearly, too, this image would require the mediation of mature and supportive base communities with a dynamic and liberating sacramental praxis.

The moral dimension of this spirituality would have to be firmly rooted in the characteristics examined in a previous chapter; that is, it would have to be seen as creative, always in the process of development and growth, essentially socially oriented, and significative or pointing to the Good News that the church is meant to transmit. Moreover, the central virtue of the love of neighbor would be viewed as empty without a passion for justice, and thus would find its privileged embodiment in action to change institutions and structures that degrade human existence.[50] Such action would be understood as having a direct and causal relationship to the establishment of the kingdom of God. It would also provide the essential basis for a personal and interiorized choice of Christianity, in direct and conscious opposition to the image of the human person marketed by a competitive consumer society.[51]

A liberating spirituality would find its constant source of renewal and inspiration in the continual return to Scripture. The use of the hermeneutic circle in this process would free it from all vestiges of fundamentalism and reaction; rather this would establish a life-long process of learning and lead to new and creative solutions to contemporary problems.[52] It would thus provide the stimulus for a life of continuous conversion and with that an ability to function maximally in a society marked by constant change.[53]

The practice of ideological suspicion would also continually exercise a liberating function for the spiritual life. On the one hand, it would foster the use of both technical competence and prayerful discernment in the choice of and commitment to promising ideologies, recognizing the necessity for enthusiasm as well as for a critical sense. On the other hand, it would be keenly alert to the group interests and disguised ideologies that might be fostered by the bureaucracies of both church and state in their dedication to preserving the status quo.

Admittedly, this view of Christian existence in the Spirit has been articulated here in only the most general terms.[54] Its concrete implementation in practice may take decades, yet this is a relatively brief span when compared to the millennium and a half of the church's Constantinian captivity. For all Christians the realization of the immense challenge here involved must be suffused with a radiant hope for a future laden with new possibilities for the construction of the kingdom of God.[55]

NOTES

1. Roger D. Haight, "Mission: The Symbol for Understanding the Church Today," *Theological Studies* (December 1976):647.

2. In a recent essay on this subject, Thomas E. Clarke presents a thesis on Ignatian spirituality which I believe would be applicable to any spirituality today: "Ignatian spirituality, both as *theoria* and as *praxis*, today needs to be integrally and newly experienced and conceived in the light of a new experience of the human, in which the societal dimension is seen, together with the intrapersonal and interpersonal, as constitutive, and not merely as extrinsically environmental" ("Ignatian Spirituality and Societal Consciousness," *Studies in the Spirituality of Jesuits* [September 1975]:131). For the best articulation and development of this thesis that I have encountered, see *Soundings: A Task Force on Social Consciousness and Ignatian Spirituality* (Washington, D.C.: Center of Concern, 1974).

3. In this regard Clarke comments that "as a doctrine, spiritual theology is not so much a treatise or branch of theology as a perspective. The materials contained in what is commonly called systematic or doctrinal theology, and much, at least, of the material normally included in moral theology, are pertinent" ("Ignatian Spirituality and Societal Consciousness," p. 129).

4. The remarks of Richard Roach may be noted here: "A second step would go beyond a theology of liberation and seek to liberate theology. If as believers we are preoccupied with theologies that merely intellectualize the faith, or express anachronistic visions of man and society, we will inevitably find ourselves more concerned with the individual and private rather than the social dimension of man, and inevitably be unconscious conservatives when we function in the body politic. But what is worse, we will lack training and guidance in the reflective and prayerful ways in which action becomes also the service of God and his kingdom" ("Law and Order," *The Way* [April 1975]:109). It may be noted that this entire issue of *The Way* is devoted to the theme of "Liberation."

5. *Grace and the Human Condition* (Maryknoll, N.Y.: Orbis Books, 1973), pp. 86–94.

6. Ibid., p. 86. The author admits that "in one sense it is false to assert that the Church lacked a theology of history. She certainly possessed what we could call a theology of history relating to her 'inner precincts.' And to the extent that it looked at 'universal' history, the latter entered the picture as a preparation for the city of God or as its antagonist."

7. Ibid., p. 87; *Imitation of Christ* 1, 20.

8. Segundo, *Grace and the Human Condition*, p. 88; *Imitation of Christ* 3, 4. Cf. the remarks of Gregory Baum with regard to what he calls a "transformist" spirituality: "Life in the world is more than faithful obedience to the divine commandments; it is a redeeming encounter with the divine in the call to a reconciled life and the action in which people try to realize it. We have here the entrance of contemplation in a Christian ethos of worldly orientation. The spirituality proper to the transformist faith is not a dualistic contemplation that withdraws people from the daily struggle, but a contemplation of the divine mystery as source, orientation

and horizon of common action" (*Religion and Alienation: A Theological Reading of Sociology* [New York: Paulist Press, 1975], p. 183).

9. Segundo, *Grace and the Human Condition*, p. 88; *Imitation of Christ* 2, 5. In this regard, Jürgen Moltmann cites with approval a quote from Walter Rauschenbusch: "Ascetic Christianity called the world evil and left it. Humanity is waiting for a revolutionary Christianity which will call the world evil and change it" (*Religion, Revolution and the Future* [New York: Charles Scribner's Sons, 1969], pp. 34–35). The sentence is from Rauschenbusch's work, *Christianity and the Social Crisis* (New York: Harper and Row, 1964), p. 91.

10. Segundo, *Grace and the Human Condition*, pp. 89–90; *Imitation of Christ* 1, 16.

11. Segundo, *Grace and the Human Condition*, p. 90; *Imitation of Christ* 1, 20.

12. Segundo, *Grace and the Human Condition*, p. 91; *Imitation of Christ* 2, 5.

13. Segundo, *Grace and the Human Condition*, p. 92. Robert Harvanek holds a view similar to Segundo's, asserting that Christ "comes to liberate His people from sin and its consequences. It is perhaps the last phrase that is the significant difference. For liberation theology has brought to our attention the social consequences of sin and argued that the Messianic mission of the Savior includes progressive liberation from those consequences" ("The 'Situation' of Loyola's Exercises," *Review for Religious* [May 1974]: 597).

14. Segundo, *Grace and the Human Condition*, p. 94.

15. Ibid., p. 97, n. 16. Peter Henriot has offered an apt comment on the "simul" element of the contemplative in action: "The richness of what Jerome Nadal emphasized by the word 'simul' in his well-known phrase 'simul in actione contemplativus' can be given wider application. For Ignatius and his followers, it was not enough for the man or woman who would be in the service of the Kingdom to pray *first* and *then* to go out into the active apostolate. There had to be an integrating dynamic in the person's life by which the apostolate was itself a means of prayer, an opening to the Spirit, an occasion for 'finding God in all things.' There would be a dialectic of prayer and action, with various privileged moments for each. But in the Ignatian vision it would be a special kind of dialectic, marked by simultaneity" ("The Public Dimension of the Life of the Christian: The Problem of 'Simultaneity,' " *Soundings: A Task Force on Social Consciousness and the Ignatian Exercises* [Washington, D.C., 1974], p. 14).

16. Ibid. A similar assessment is evident in the article of John Padberg, "Continuity and Change in General Congregation XXXII," *Studies in the Spirituality of Jesuits* (November 1975). Padberg notes that it was "Ignatius who introduced changes in the religious life which seemed at the time incredibly bold" and that the Congregation's decree on inculturation "may in some ways help bring the Society back to somewhat more of an openness and freedom of spirit when faced with new ways of thinking and acting, a greater willingness to imagine alternative possibilities in our apostolates and our lives—something which we seem to have had to a larger extent before the condemnation of the Chinese rites in the seventeenth century" (pp. 211–12).

17. *Our Idea of God* (Maryknoll, N.Y.: Orbis Books, 1974), pp. 42–46. It may also be noted that the periodical with which Segundo has long been associated, *Perspectivas de Diálogo*, devoted the last issue before its suppression entirely to the subject of prayer. The issue (August 1975) was entitled "Oración y praxis," and included articles by José Gómez Caffarena, Luis María Pérez Aguirre, and Andrés Assandri as well as an editorial on "¿Crisis de oración o desencuentro con Dios?" References in the issue to prayer at moments of arrest and imprisonment were cited as the cause for the suppression of the perodical.

18. *Our Idea of God*, pp. 42–43.

154 TOWARD A SPIRITUALITY OF LIBERATION

19. Ibid., pp. 43–44.

20. Ibid., pp. 44–45. In the same vein William Connolly has insisted that, as a result of contemplation, "the person with an active vocation becomes more wholly, deeply, and passionately involved in the Lord's concern for His people, and in their needs. The only element likely to be lost to the active life as a result of contemplation is egocentricity" ("Contemporary Spiritual Direction: Scope and Principles," *Studies in the Spirituality of Jesuits* [June 1975]:117). In connection with liberation theology, it is illuminating to note Connolly's assertion that "the most crucial single issue of direction is the development of a personal contemplative attitude which will enable the person to live as a free man or woman, living, deciding, and praying in free response to the Spirit" (ibid., p. 97).

21. Segundo, *Our Idea of God,* p. 45.

22. Ibid., pp. 45–46. Cf. the remarks of J. B. Metz: "Christian mysticism is neither a kind of pantheistic infinity mysticism, nor an esoteric mysticism of exaltation, tending toward the self-redemption of the individual soul. It is rather—putting it extremely—a mysticism of fraternity. For the God of the Christian faith is found only in the movement of his love toward men, the 'least,' as has been revealed to us in Jesus Christ. And that is why mysticism, which seeks this nearness, has the place not outside, beside, or above responsibility for the world of our brothers, but in the center of it" *(Theology of the World* [New York: Herder and Herder, 1969], p. 104).

23. "¿Dios nos interesa o no?" *Perspectivas de Diálogo* (March 1968):13–16.

24. Ibid., p. 14.

25. Ibid., p. 16.

26. "Del ateísmo a la fe," *Perspectivas de Diálogo* (April 1968):44–47.

27. Ibid., p. 44.

28. Ibid., p. 45.

29. Ibid. Thomas E. Clarke takes an analogous approach when he observes that "someone has pointed out that there is a certain affinity between the genuine mystic and the atheist or agnostic: both insist on putting aside or leaving behind any divinity shaped to man's image" *(New Pentecost or New Passion? The Direction of Religious Life Today* [New York: Paulist Press, 1973], p. 38).

30. Segundo, "Del ateísmo a la fe," pp. 46–47.

31. "Padre, Hijo, Espíritu: Una historia," *Perspectivas de Diálogo* (May 1968):71–76.

32. "Padre, Hijo, Espíritu: Una sociedad," *Perspectivas de Diálogo* (June 1968):103–09.

33. Ibid., p. 108.

34. Ibid.

35. "Padre, Hijo, Espíritu: Una libertad I," *Perspectivas de Diálogo* (July 1968):143.

36. Ibid., p. 146.

37. "Padre, Hijo, Espíritu: Una libertad II," *Perspectivas de Diálogo* (August 1968):184.

38. Ibid.

39. Ibid., pp. 184–86.

40. Ibid., pp. 186–87.

41. Ibid., p. 187.

42. "¿Un Dios a nuestra imagen?" *Perspectivas de Diálogo* (March 1969):14–18.

43. Ibid., pp. 15–16.

44. Ibid., p. 16.

45. Ibid., p. 17.

46. Ibid., p. 18. Cf. the remarks of Gregory Baum: "The transformist

faith . . . does not present a person's relationship to God as private and separated; salvation is mediated by people, by fellowship, by community, by the common effort to create humane conditions of human life and produce a new social order. . . . It tends to be critical of free enterprise, the profit motive, and the principle of competition. The new spirituality recovers a greater sense of people's collective destiny and often formulates its opposition to individualism in terms of socialism and cooperative systems" (*Religion and Alienation,* pp. 183–84).

47. Ibid. In an excellent brief article on the liberation entailed in a retreat, Joseph Mulligan expresses it as follows: "In our own First World situation, we are oppressed by the cultural addictions of violence (which is ingrained in us through the conditioning of the mass media and military), extreme individualism (every man for himself), harsh competitiveness (survival of the fittest), racism, sexism, and other narrowing 'isms' that can be seen as collective egoisms. . . . These addictions have a tighter and firmer grip on us the more they go unnoticed. To recognize them and rid ourselves of them is the purpose of the *Spiritual Exercises,* which may fairly be termed a 'handbook for liberation' " ("A 'Liberating' Retreat," *America* [29 May 1976]:475).

48. In this respect, cf. the acute remark of John Padberg: "The most fundamental changes are not in what we are asked to do, although they may well be far-reaching enough, but are in the way in which we are asked to see the world around us. It is from corrected perception and deeper insights that action may follow" ("Continuity and Change," p. 204).

49. These ideas are treated in detail in Chapter Three.

50. An excellent summary of this approach is given at the conclusion of an article by Michael Reilly: "One can describe the 'ideal' Christian and one can see where we will find the saints for our times. They will be the men and women who are working lovingly, faithfully and hopefully to change the structures and institutions of our world that are dehumanizing the majority of the human family. They will be the men and women working to eliminate the poverty of the many and achieve a just share of the world's resources for all. Look for men and women selflessly devoted to building the kingdom of God through these tasks and you will find the saints of our times" ("Holiness and Development," *America* [11 October 1975]: 207).

51. In his book *A Planet to Heal: Reflections and Forecasts* (Rome: Ignatian Center of Spirituality, 1975), Pedro Arrupe has remarked that "the Church of Christ must show itself as really His Church in this world, as the Church of those who, according to the word of the Lord, provide the most genuine criterion of love: the poor, the enslaved, the persecuted, the rejected, and the desperate" (p. 88); to accomplish this, he suggests later that we must "have men and women who will resolutely set themselves against the tide of our consumer society" (p. 107).

52. See the strong statement in this regard of Ivan Illich: "The specific task of the Church in the modern world is the Christian celebration of the experience of change. . . . All enveloping, penetrating change is the fundamental experience of our age. . . . The experience of change is now faced as a lifelong process by every individual in technological society" (*Celebration of Awareness: A Call for Institutional Revolution* [New York: Doubleday & Company, 1970], p. 88).

53. In an article on "Spirituality and the Process of Liberation," Joan Toohig states that "continual personal conversion to Christ" is perhaps the most essential element in such a spirituality *(The Way* [April 1975]:131).

54. José Magaña summarizes the task well at the end of his book on the Exercises, voicing his dream that the exercitants "might love with a total love—memory, imagination, understanding, will, affections—the Total Christ, the Christ of the Scriptures and of the Eucharist, the Christ in the neighbor and in the cosmos, Who, through His death and resurrection, has brought full liberation of

soul and body, liberation from sin and its consequences, of persons and structures, in time and in eternity" *(A Strategy for Liberation: Notes for Orienting the Exercises Toward Utopia* [Hicksville, N.Y.: Exposition Press, 1974], p. 166).

55. Again, I believe a full articulation of the spirituality envisioned here and its refinement in praxis will occupy a number of years. Latin American authors who have helped me to progress beyond the ideas of the present chapter include Segundo Galilea, *Espiritualidad de la liberación* (Santiago: ISPAJ, 1973) and Jon Sobrino, *Cristología desde América Latina: Esbozo a partir del seguimiento del Jesús histórico* (Mexico City: CRT, 1976); Eng. trans., *Christology at the Crossroads* (Maryknoll, N.Y.: Orbis Books, 1978). Examples of important contributions in North America include: Stephen J. Duffy, "Ministry, Grace and the Process of Humanization," *Review for Religious* (July 1976):522–36, and Philip Land, "Justice, Development, Liberation and the Exercises," *Studies in the International Apostolate of Jesuits* (June 1976):1–62. Promising new directions in Asia may be seen in such recent works as Samuel Rayan, *The Holy Spirit: Heart of the Gospel and Christian Hope* (Maryknoll, N.Y.: Orbis Books, 1978), and Tissa Balasuriya, *The Eucharist and Human Liberation* (Maryknoll, N.Y.: Orbis Books, 1979).

CHAPTER NINE

THE CHALLENGE OF MARXISM

I have deliberately postponed until now a discussion of Marxism or socialism. This is not because the question is peripheral or unimportant in Segundo's thought; on the contrary, he states flatly that "the option between capitalist and socialist society" comprises "one of the most acute human problems of my Latin American continent," and he considers a choice in this respect as a "theological crux," which provides a crucial test for the value of liberation theology.[1]

Rather the reason for postponement lies in the peculiar *realidad* of the United States, where decades of cold war, détente, and so forth have loaded the issue with a tremendous emotional charge. As can be seen in the popular religious press of this country, there is a strong and instinctive reaction against the introduction of ideology, especially such an ideology as socialism, into the neutral realms of pure theology. Thus I felt that it would be more effective to examine carefully Segundo's underlying methodology and the key concepts of his thought before moving to a discussion of such a neuralgic issue. It should be recalled also from the discussion in Chapter Six that *everyone* has an ideology or ideologies; the key difference is that some people bring them to the level of awareness and analyze them carefully, while others consider them merely as what is normal, common sense, "the way things are," in a static and unexamined sense.[2]

Why a Marxist Analysis?

The two places where Segundo gives the most explicit attention to the issue include the concluding chapter of *Masses and Minorities in the Divine Dialectic of Liberation*[3] and the article in the *Concilium* series entitled "Capitalism—Socialism: A Theological Crux." We will begin with a discussion of the book.

In the fourth chapter, entitled "The Problem of the Specific Christian Contribution to Political Commitment," Segundo engages in a dialogue with Hugo Assmann.[4] The latter author strenuously opposes any a priori conception of Christianity which would set up normative standards *before* any actual commitment to the revolutionary process. Segundo is in agreement with Assmann on this point, but then proceeds to add his own nuances to the problematic.

Segundo begins his discussion with a reference to Rudolf Bultmann, whose theological method necessitated an existential preunderstanding of humanity as a presupposition for understanding the authentic message of the New Testament.[5] Latin American theology has a similar or parallel preunderstanding but one that appears to be more deeply rooted in the Bible itself: "The one key to open up for us the message of God would be . . . a revolutionary commitment in favor of the oppressed." Shortly afterward, this commitment is envisioned as including a "sensibility of heart toward the poor."[6] Thus the hypothesis which Segundo adopts and which he will attempt to prove in the rest of the chapter is "that a specific Christian contribution, a revolutionary commitment, and a new understanding of the gospel constitute a hermeneutic circle. . . . "[7] His proof and clarification of this assertion are given in six steps, which I will now summarize.

The first step involves a phenomenological analysis of the concept of faith itself in the human person. He points out that theologians often divide up humanity into those who have faith and those who don't; however, on the existential level, *all of us* have a faith of some sort, a personal project which we choose in order to direct our lives.[8] It cannot be proven in advance that this will make us happy nor can it be verified scientifically, and this holds for revolutionaries and conservatives, Christians and atheists, laborers and professional people. For example, "to make money can be subject to scientific study, but to establish the meaning of one's life on the making of money can only proceed from attributing, without proof, ultimate value and happiness to such an intent."[9]

A second step concerns Christian faith, and again theologians somewhat abstractly maintain that the obvious difference between this and other "faiths" is that it is based on God and his message while the others are based on human witnesses. But on the existential level, how does a child or adolescent actually choose a path in life, a project? It is "by trusting in those *who know better* and who affirm, by their words and their actions, that these values will lead to happiness."[10] Consequently, all faiths, at least in their origin, rely on the testimony of human witnesses.

In the next step, Segundo asks: when does Christian faith detach itself from these human roots and become transformed into faith in Christ and in his message? He views this transition as of central pastoral importance, citing it as a "crucial step for millions of Christians, and one for which our pastoral practice has no other answer than the meager, inadequate one of catechetical instruction." His own answer is found in a key text:

The profound shift which makes me transcend the relative Christian testimonies that surround me, which propels me in an open, receptive way toward Jesus himself; that which grounds my faith in *him* and no longer in any other person, no matter how trustworthy or attractive, appears on the level of political commitment and of revolutionary political commitment on behalf of the oppressed.[11]

This kind of commitment results in what he calls a hermeneutical "state of grace," which enables us "to go to Christ, to question the authentic Christ," for it results in "that poor and open heart which is the only one, according to Christ himself, that can grasp his message as Good News, as gospel."[12]

The fourth step raises the question: how does this Jesus appear from the perspective of a revolutionary commitment for the oppressed? His central demand of efficacious love, here and now, is clear. However, Segundo notes that he *seems* to demand a minoritarian form of love, which would be effective on an interpersonal level in a stable social milieu, but which seems totally ineffective in other contexts where social change demands mass mechanisms and behavior. As a result of this, many are disappointed with such a solution, and reject it together with their faith.

Segundo believes that the fifth step is concerned with what is perhaps the central theological-pastoral problem in the Latin American church today. In the previous step, there was a failure to go beyond a routine hermeneutic; thus the gospel was not read "with new suspicions" so as to arrive at new interpretations. To illustrate that Jesus himself was aware of the "mass" exigencies of an effective love, and that he did not make a minoritarian approach the only solution to all problems for all time, the author provides a few examples of a new hermeneutic.

First, Segundo emphasizes that Jesus himself was subject to the economy of energy, and thus experienced personally the weight of "mass" mechanisms. Consequently, there is an urgent need of a new Christology, one which will avoid interpreting Jesus, "the man for others," as "a superman free from every calculation of energy, with an infinite capacity to give of himself, and to give with the same effectiveness to all and to each one and in every instant of his existence, free also from all routine, from all prejudice, from all instinctive solidarity with those closest to him."[13] A second assertion of this new hermeneutic is that Jesus was not only subject to mass mechanisms but that he actually made use of them. The one example given concerns the term "kingdom" to describe his mission: "To describe his work, could he not have chosen a term less charged with 'mass' emotion than that of 'kingdom,' in the context of Israel dominated by the Roman Empire, in a context where the Zealots were active? Could he not have chosen a word less provocative of 'mass' hopes than the word 'kingdom' "? Segundo notes that such boldness is certainly not a characteristic of contemporary preaching; he stresses, too, that once a mass interest is initially aroused, it can later be corrected and deepened, and thus become minoritarian.[14]

Lastly, in Segundo's view Jesus did not make of his minoritarian demands a new "super-law" to replace the old one, since it is "the project of humanity, that which comes from its heart, that gives moral worth to any action." Although exegesis takes little note of it, Paul also stressed this Christian liberty and in fact makes it "the criterion by which one knows whether he or she has passed from the Old Testament to the New." Thus, because Christians are above the law, they can use it and its mass mechanisms "in service to the creativity of love."[15]

With these brief preliminary examples of the new hermeneutic, it is possible to move on to the sixth and most important step of Segundo's argument. If we admit the possible use of "mass" mechanisms *as long as* they may be necessary, then we also urgently need a science of such mechanisms, "since for an effective political commitment, it is not enough to know that a mass element exists in every realistic and efficacious transformation. It is necessary besides to know how to guide it."[16] It is likewise necessary to acknowledge that the Christian cannot derive this science from the gospel, simply because it is not there.

Within the Latin American context, therefore, Segundo believes that "what comes closest to a science of 'masses' and how to guide them to their own advantage are certain elements of Marxism." This is not to assert that all of Marxism is scientific nor is it to deny that many of its elements are open to doubt. Despite all this, he expresses his important option as follows:

If Christians have to search for a complementary science that allows them to analyze and guide their conduct on the "mass" level, it is not strange that one of the most important pastoral events in Latin American Christianity is a kind of symbiosis—sometimes superficial, undoubtedly dangerous, and always ambiguous —between Christianity as a minoritarian code of conduct and Marxism as a science of the behavior of the "masses."[17]

And this is not meant to be a sacralization of Marxism, for, if a better science appeared, it would have to be utilized instead.

This aspect of Marxism as a science of mass behavior is clearly different from its character as a "faith" that was studied earlier in this chapter. But what is the relationship between the two aspects? In Segundo's view Marxism thought it possessed "not only the control of techniques of analysis of 'mass' movements but also *all* the elements needed to create a profound and total picture of the universe and of humanity. And I believe that it failed in the latter area, just as Christianity failed when it wanted to construct a 'mass' political order, and it failed in principle, and not merely in fact." Or, in other words, " . . . the claims of Marxism to present a profound and coherent picture of humanity and the universe comprise an error whose results we are now experiencing."[18]

Objections to a Socialist Option

I believe that this furnishes a clear and carefully reasoned analysis, which explains Segundo's choice of the tool of Marxist analysis in the Latin American context. The survey will undoubtedly have aroused in the reader some questions and reservations, and to examine these in more detail we will now turn to the article where Segundo grapples with them directly: "Capitalism—Socialism: A Theological Crux." Incidentally, the influential *Concilium* series has a wide readership in a number of languages; the fact that Segundo chose this particular topic for his contribution to the volume on liberation theology appears to be a further indication of the importance that he attributes to the question.[19]

It should be stressed at the outset that the author is not posing the question in relation to the possibilities offered by a developed capitalism or socialism but rather "from the oppressed periphery of the great economic empires." Presumably theologians in the developed nations would have to forge their own response to the "crux" under consideration. Also, from the beginning he attempts to frame the question as precisely as possible: "What socio-political scheme can be chosen now from our underdeveloped condition, which will at the same time be effective and coherent with the kind of society we desire for Latin Americans as we know them?"[20] Attention is then given to the two major sources that object to posing such a question to theology: one source on a pragmatic plane in Latin America, and the other on a more theoretical level, proceeding from Europe.

The epitome of the pragmatic objection for Segundo is expressed in the statement of the Chilean bishops, when they were confronted historically by the above question: "The church opts for the risen Jesus. . . . The church makes no political option—it belongs to all the people of Chile." He believes the logical assumption behind such a statement is that " . . . it would be senseless to make an absolute value (religious, pertaining to salvation) depend on a relative value (the preference for one system— always imperfect—of political life)." For Segundo this view of the church as an autonomous center of salvation is the *operative* ecclesiology of the great majority of the Christian churches. And his reply to it is very pointed and radical in its implications:

Would it not be possible and even evangelical to invert this order of values and to declare, with the gospel itself, that the sabbath is made for man and not man for the sabbath? Could this statement not be given the only possible translation, namely that human life in society, liberated as far as possible from alienations, constitutes the absolute value, and that all religious institutions, all dogmas, all the sacraments and all the ecclesiastical authorities have only a relative, that is, a functional value?[21]

How then can the operative ecclesiology, which Segundo believes is opposed to evangelical values, be refuted? One path might be the European one of a return to the sources, as in the work of Hans Küng, to determine where the church began to deviate from an authentic functional role to an absolutist one in human history. However, the Latin American approach, which Segundo adopts, is to turn rather to the "psychosocial" sciences to get to the roots of the deviation. For he believes that by means of interdisciplinary work with these sciences theology can trace "the intimate and often unconscious mechanisms by which we think about God, his message, his church," and that such an analysis would reveal "the profound, exciting divergences which, in other ages and with different intellectual instruments, were called Trinitarian or christological controversies."[22]

In summary, the inversion of evangelical values in actual pastoral practice appears to the author as a form of heteropraxis, which is based on a radical heterodoxy, namely, the progressive loss of faith in the human functionality of the gospel, which is equivalent to a loss of faith in the gospel itself. His concluding response is then given to the pragmatic objection to the "crux": ". . . If the conclusion were reached that the gospel has nothing to say on a human problem so decisive as the alternative between capitalism and socialism, it is clear that it can only have an absolute, not a functional, value, that is to say, no value at all."[23]

Turning to the European theoretical objections, Segundo states bluntly that the political theology and theology of revolution that developed recently in Germany offer no help vis-à-vis the problem he is raising. As an example, he presents several texts from J. B. Metz, a well-known advocate of political theology: ". . . What distinguishes 'Christian eschatology' from the ideologies of the future in the East and the West, is not that it knows more, but that it knows less about that future which mankind is trying to discern and that it persists in its lack of that knowledge." Thus, according to Metz, the function of the church is to institutionalize "that eschatological reserve by establishing itself as an instance of critical liberty in the face of social development in order to reject the tendency of the latter to present itself as absolute." Again, an absolute-relative dichotomy is involved here, according to Segundo, but what is absolutized is not the church, as in the previous position, but that which the church serves, namely, "the eschatological Kingdom of God, the ultimate future, which comes down from God himself to mankind."[24]

Another prominent German theologian, Jürgen Moltmann, appears to go a step further than Metz when he notes that "the universalism of the crucified Christ is realized in the world only through the dialectic of taking sides. The false universalism of the Church . . . is, on the contrary, a premature and inopportune anticipation of the Kingdom of God." But it is clear from Moltmann's other writings that not only is the above a premature anticipation of the kingdom, but *every form of historical project* is included in that category.[25] In his opposition to such a position, Segundo insists that "it revolutionizes our way of viewing socio-political systems from our establishment within them; but it does not choose between one system and another." And the unhappy result is "a common relativization, which is revolutionary only in name."[26]

At this point it is possible to determine very precisely what is seen as the primary weakness of European political theology, and at the same time to clarify a key element in Segundo's theology. For in determining the relationship between a definite political order and the eschatological order, the Europeans select terms such as "anticipation" (Moltmann), "analogy" (Weth), or "outline" (Metz). All of these terms have one trait in common: they systematically and expressly reject every idea of causality. But according to Segundo, this stands in radical opposition to a fundamental idea shared by all liberation theologians—the view that human beings, on a political as well as individual basis, construct the kingdom of God from within history now. As a consequence, he stresses strongly "the radical divergence which exists between this approach and the denial of causality (even an imperfect and partial causality) on principle to all political parties in relation to the definitive Kingdom."[27]

Rationale for a Socialist Option

I believe that the discussion so far, though somewhat negative, has the advantage of clarifying greatly the basic issues involved in a crucial North-South debate. But it is also of paramount importance to move on to the positive task of delineating a theology that will respond to the decisive political options under discussion. In advancing into this area, Segundo begins with a clarification of his understanding of the terms "socialism," "capitalism," and "theology." By socialism, he understands a "political regime in which the ownership of the means of production is removed from individuals and handed over to higher institutions whose concern is the common good." On the other hand, capitalism is defined as a "political regime in which the ownership of the goods of production is open to economic competition." Basically then the decision to be made involves "whether we are going to leave to individuals and private groups, or whether we are going to take away from them, the right to possess the means of production which exist in our countries."[28]

Segundo's understanding of theology, like that of many Latin Americans, stresses its intimate relationship with praxis. It is described, then, as "faith in search of its own understanding, to orientate the historical praxis. We do not accept that a single dogma can be understood under any other final criterion than that of its social impact on the praxis."[29] The point is stressed, for Segundo believes that theology for centuries has been exercising a conservative ideological function. This situation has come about, not only because of its autonomy with regard to concrete Christian praxis but also because of its separation from moral theology, with the result that the dogmatic theologian "has become simply one among many purveyors of abstract culture which the consumer society accepts and even protects."

Segundo believes his own understanding of theology is similar to that of the prophets of the Old Testament. His description of their approach highlights again his disagreement with the method of European theologians:

How did the theological thinking of the prophet function? In the first place, a deeper vision than normal showed him God acting in events and judging them according to their true value. The God of Israel, being who he was (theology), could not see with other eyes what was happening. . . .Starting from that conviction, the prophet imagined a future in accord with the divine evaluation, and gave it a corresponding certainty. It was a "political" project, but the prophet did not "eschatologize" it. He did not leave his hearers feeling equally critical about the historical option, which is relative, and the Kingdom of God, which is absolute.

Segundo also quotes Henri Cazelles to the effect that, even though their visions were often disproved by events, the prophets' work was gathered together by disciples and recognized as the word of God, and he makes the point that "so it will always be where a prophetic theology is being exercised."[30]

Considerably more attention is given to the New Testament, where Segundo describes the "theological method" of Jesus in contradistinction to that of his opponents. Both sides were attempting to discern the divine presence and orientation in the events of history. However, Jesus' opponents utilized the method of seeking "signs proceeding from heaven," which the author again compares to the anticipations, outlines, and analogies of a strictly divine action mentioned earlier. Jesus, on the other hand, pointed to "signs of the times," that is, to "concrete transformations effected by him in the historical present." These signs, moreover, are "historical, relative, extremely ambiguous, at a vast distance from the absolute and definitive." Specific examples are given in his response to the disciples of John who asked if he were "he who is to come": "The sick are cured, but will they not perhaps succumb to new and more decisive illnesses? The dead rise again, but is it worthwhile if, after their pain and anguish, they have to yield again to death in the future?" From this and other passages, it is clear that Jesus discounts totally "any theological criterion applied to history, which is not the direct and present evaluation of the event."[31]

But in spite of the ambiguity and transience of these events, Jesus applies to them the most absolute term in the theology of the time, that is, "salvation." To cite one example, "just as he called cures of uncertain consequence the 'arrival of the Kingdom,' so he calls a momentary, ambiguous, still unrealized decision of Zacchaeus 'the entry into salvation.' " In the case of Jesus, therefore, "far from deabsolutizing, we can say that he absolutizes imprudently."[32]

However, a key question still looms: what is the human instrument of cognition by which the signs of the times can be evaluated? Segundo replies that in modern times it could be designated as "historical sensibility," or, in the terms of the synoptic gospels, a sensitive, open heart as contrasted with a hard, closed heart. For example, when faced with the problems of hunger and illiteracy, which abound in Latin America, such sensibility "calls for a society where competition and profit will not be the law and where the provision of basic food and culture to an underdeveloped people will be regarded as a liberation." The ambiguity inherent in this sensibility is acknowledged, but it has already been established that that is also an evangelical characteristic, and this enables Segundo to make an important rebuttal:

. . . When the political theologian of Europe requires Latin Americans to put forward a project for a socialist society which will guarantee in advance that the evident defects of known socialist systems will be avoided, why do we not demand of Christ also that before telling a sick man who has been cured, "your faith has saved you," he should give a guarantee that that cure will not be followed by even graver illnesses?[33]

On the other hand, the "closed heart," which is diametrically opposed to Christ's attitude, is clearly delineated in the evangelical discussion of the unpardonable sin against the Spirit, that is, "not to recognize as liberation what truly is liberation and to render the liberation of man something odious. The sin against the Spirit is not to recognize with 'theological' joy a concrete liberation happening before one's eyes."[34]

In concluding the article, Segundo dismisses the possibility of middle courses between right and left, stating flatly that "the sensibility of the left is an intrinsic feature of an authentic theology. It must be the necessary form of a reflection whose key quality is historical sensibility." It should be noted that the author is using the word "left" in a broad sense in this context. He refers to the definition of it in the sixteenth edition of the Brockhaus encyclopedia as "the conquest of that which is still without form, of that which is still unrealized, of that which is still in a state of utopia," and also describes it as a movement that accords "a privileged place for the prisoner, the refugee, the poor and the foreigner." Thus, he asserts, "it is plain enough who (between left and right) shows continuing signs of this feeling of solidarity." He ends by emphasizing once more the genuinely causal link between liberation and the kingdom, with the following result:

In the face of options between racial separation and full community of rights, between free international supply and demand and a balanced market (with an eye to the underprivileged countries), between capitalism and socialism, what is at stake is no mere analogy of the Kingdom. What is at stake, in a fragmentary fashion if you like, is the eschatological Kingdom itself, whose realization and revelation are awaited with anguish by the whole universe.[35]

A more general statement of the relation of Latin American thought to Marxism may also be found in an early note of his most recent book, *The Liberation of Theology*.[36] Segundo begins by noting that there are linguistic problems in applying the label "Marxist" to any body of thought. The most obvious one is that Marxists themselves have a thousand different ways of understanding what Marxist thought really is. But prescinding from that, the author uses Aristotle as a point of departure for a comparison. Since great thinkers do not replace one another but rather enrich and complement each other, it can be said that all philosophers in the West are in some sense Aristotelians. His application of the analogy to Marx has far-reaching implications:

The manner of conceiving and posing the problems of society will never again be the same as it was before Marx. Whether or not everything Marx said is accepted, and no matter how his "essential" thought is explained, it will always remain certain that there is no contemporary social thought that is not to some degree "Marxist," that is, profoundly indebted to Marx. In that sense, liberation theology in Latin America is certainly "Marxist."

The note ends with a certain exasperation, for Segundo is aware that his statement will be used out of context; yet he admits to being tired of constantly trying to forestall stupid or biased misunderstandings.

To move to a more concrete level, I believe that an early article of Segundo illuminates his thought on socialism, and also that it is of special interest, since it was intended for North American readers. In the article written in 1968 and entitled "Social Justice and Revolution,"[37] Segundo presents a comparison between the first formulation of Catholic social doctrine, the encyclical *Rerum Novarum* of Leo XIII and the *Communist Manifesto*. Both documents, he asserts, strongly condemned the inhuman aspects of capitalism. But Leo XIII did not offer a workable alternative; rather "what *Rerum Novarum* set out to teach was how to live more morally in the given economic world, that is to say, in a world of capital." But Marx did present an alternative:

Whether we agree with Marx or not, he was a creative genius in the area of politics. He created the image of a society not based on profit. When I speak of an image here, I do not mean merely some ideal, but rather the ideal plus the necessary socioeconomic conditions. And Marx's image of the new society was viable, with or without the subsequent modifications it underwent."[38]

Segundo stresses also that Leo XIII condemned socialism on a purely *theoretical* basis, that is, no actual system based on it existed at the time of *Rerum Novarum.*

In Segundo's view, however, a new phase of Catholic social thought began after the socialist model was tested, in other words, after millions of individuals had the experience of a different way of life than was offered under capitalism. And the author quotes Pope John XXIII *(Pacem in Terris,* no. 159) as the first pope to acknowledge it as a possible alternative to capitalism.

In this new situation Segundo arrives at the conclusion that, despite the system's antireligious elements, "the church must objectively and neutrally examine what possibilities this existing socialism, as lived by human beings today, holds for the Christian way of life." Not only that, but "we Latin Americans are obligated more than anyone else to see if certain facets of socialism are not, after all, compatible with Catholic social teachings."[39] As an example he selects the issue of the right to private property and to private ownership of the means of production and asks: because of these principles, are Catholics forced to reject socialism?

Segundo's reply is no, and he attempts to prove his thesis from several angles. First, he alludes to the fact that the right of ownership is based on the fact that the thing possessed is necessary for the realization of one's human condition. Therefore, it follows that "the right to ownership of a thing is not the right that *a few individuals* have to it, but the right of *all* to own it, in order to be fully human." If this principle is applied to a situation such as Argentina's, for example, where 1 percent of the population owns 50 percent of the land, what can the right of ownership mean in the concrete? Thus he inquires: "Is that 1 percent justified in continuing to hold half the land? Or do all who work in agriculture have the right to own a piece of land from which they can live humanly?"[40]

If all are to have the right of ownership, it is clear that some form of association must be created, since it is absurd to conceive of each citizen owning his or her own railroad or factory. Consequently Segundo proposes a more sophisticated version of socialism than most westerners think of when they hear the term: "It would be a socialism in which ownership is exercised, as much as possible, in true communities—something very different from a useless statism. Any Latin American will admit that everything is not really at the service of everyone unless all can somehow have responsibility for it, thus making it *their own.*" The author's final point is to recall an emphasis in Pius XI's *Quadragesimo Anno* that has long been ignored in developed countries and that he feels reinforces his position in the Latin American context: "Certain forms of property must be reserved to the state, since they carry with them an opportunity of domination too great to be left to private individuals without injury to the community at large (no. 114)."[41]

Concluding Reflections

In responding to Segundo's views, it should first be recalled that his option for socialism is not a peculiar or unusual phenomenon in Latin America. An excellent illustration of the support for such an option, at least among an influential minority, may be found in the recently published *Christians and Socialism: Documentation of the Christians for Socialism Movement in Latin America*.[42] Despite the severe repression in Chile that followed the murder of Allende and the military coup in September 1973, the movement has not been extinguished. This is abundantly clear in the views of Fr. Gonzalo Arroyo, one of the founders of Christians for Socialism, who is now exiled in Europe:

Under the dynamic impulse of their faith in the gospel of liberation, in which they will certainly detect revolutionary strains, Christians will manage to abandon the abstract ideology of reformism. In the political arena they will decide to start with far more objective analyses of social reality, and this decision will be particularly rich in consequences when these Christians come from the proletariat or the common people. . . . Over and above their personal involvement in the revolutionary struggle, the political task of socialist Christians is to be found primarily in the domain of ideology.[43]

Nor is the option for developing nations confined to Latin America. For example, a number of the new nations that have achieved independence in Africa during the past several decades have adopted a socialist model of government. Moreover, an eloquent spokesman for this position has emerged in the person of the Roman Catholic president of Tanzania, Julius K. Nyerere, who noted a decade ago:

"Ujamaa," then, or "Familyhood," describes our socialism. It is opposed to capitalism, which seeks to build a happy society on the basis of the exploitation of man by man; and it is equally opposed to doctrinaire socialism which seeks to build its happy society on a philosophy of inevitable conflict between man and man. . . . Our recognition of the family to which we all belong must be extended yet further—beyond the tribe, the community, the nation or even the continent—to embrace the whole society of mankind. This is the only logical conclusion for true socialism.[44]

On a first level, then, I believe our response to Segundo's option (and to that of other inhabitants of the third world) should be one of respect for their political freedom to forge their own destinies and to choose their own model of government. At the end of an article cited earlier, Segundo spoke of the need, some day, to establish an "honest dialogue" with North Americans.[45] In the light of recent history, especially of United States involvement in Chile, the series of questions proposed for such a dialogue appears even more crucial and urgent now than it was a decade ago:

1. Why does U.S. public opinion fall into the mistake of looking on every tendency toward socialism in the United States as a *rapprochement* to Marxist communism and to the Soviet bloc? 2. Why are the friends and allies that U.S. policy seeks in Latin America consistently those persons and groups most hostile to the very ideals that are the proudest accomplishment of the United States? 3. Why do U.S. public opinion and U.S. policy drive every revolutionary attempt in Latin America toward enmity with the United States? 4. Do the American people really believe that the injustice against which antitrust laws have been enacted in the United States is any less a threat to world peace—and ultimately to the United States itself—when it occurs in Latin America? 5. Finally, why does the U.S. electorate let the policy of Washington toward Latin American countries be dictated by the only group that is interested in big profits and a big military machine in Latin America?

The question of the possibility of socialism for the United States itself is an issue that can be dealt with only briefly here. There are not a few persons in the country who believe that there are obvious areas, for example, that of energy and food, that clearly appear to comprise forms of property that "carry with them an opportunity of domination too great to be left to private individuals without injury to the community at large." Moreover, the massive growth of unchecked power in the multinational corporations over the past few decades has created a pressing need for international controls, which will go beyond the profit motive and accentuate the question of the common good.[46] It seems to me that the unregulated pursuit of profits in international trade is the key element to be kept in mind in answering all five of the questions proposed by Segundo above.[47]

Although a small minority has been advocating socialism in the United States for some time, it faces formidable barriers. And I believe Segundo has pinpointed the basic obstacle to the growth of such a movement:

As Toynbee and others have shown, all great empires were built by the sweat of a vast proletariat. But today, unlike what happened in earlier centuries, the proletariat that makes possible the life and prosperity of the great empires is principally external to them; that is, it lives far outside the frontiers of the metropolis. Russia itself, in order to survive as a world power, has had to adopt this approach. And certainly so has the United States, the largest, strongest and most prosperous empire of all time.[48]

As a consequence of this, he goes on to point out that "all U.S. citizens, rich and poor, are interested in perpetuating what is the real source of their well-being and progress. That source is the international economic structure, with its growing imbalance between prices offered for raw materials and prices demanded for manufactured goods." The only glimmer of hope Segundo sees would be for the United States to undertake "the restructuring of its economic-political empire," a project which he realistically considers to be "one of the most arduous challenges ever presented to any people."[49]

My own view on this crux in the United States is very similar to that expressed in a recent book of the North American sociologist Robert Bellah.[50] The author there advances a brief but penetrating analysis of what he calls "the American taboo on socialism," which includes a description of the root causes of this attitude. Bellah then goes on to suggest that "our difficulties will soon become so critical that even respected statesmen will disregard the taboos of the past and begin talking about and helping to delineate a distinctively American socialism."[51]

Bellah is fully aware of the difficulties mentioned above in developing and organizing such a movement in the United States. For such a movement to succeed, he emphasizes that "the socialist vision must be linked once again, as it was for Henry James, Sr., and Eugene Debs, with a vision that is moral and religious as well as political."[52] In fact, Bellah's book is an attempt to retrieve such a vision. As he asserts in his preface, it is an effort "to show that only a new imaginative, religious, moral, and social context for science and technology will make it possible to weather the storms that seem to be closing in on us in the late twentieth century."[53] The alternatives, in the author's view, are either the destruction of American society or the attempt to check this by a tyranny of a "brave new world" variety.

A similar position has been expressed by the Jesuit sociologist John A. Coleman.[54] Coleman starts with a review of the vision and praxis of three important thinkers in the American Catholic tradition, Orestes Brownson, John A. Ryan, and John Courtney Murray. Toward the end of the article, he summarizes his own view: "I take it that the fundamental task for a liberation theology in the United States is to achieve a species of socialism with a human face; to find a viable alternative to the false dichotomies of individualism and monistic socialism of the nineteenth century; to combine the goods of justice and liberty in a new synthesis."[55] Coleman argues strongly—and rightly, I believe—for the mediation in this task of a social ethics of the state, political liberty, and the tradition of civil liberties.

Clearly then the only viable form of socialism in the North American context would be that of democratic socialism. How and whether this can be achieved is by no means clear at the present moment. We can, I think, at least assert that a choice in this pivotal area will be one of the crucial issues confronting the Judeo-Christian communities of the United States as the third century of that nation's history continues.

NOTES

1. These statements appear on p. 106 of an article entitled "Capitalism —
Socialism: A Theological Crux," in *Concilium 96: The Mystical and Political
Dimension of the Christian Faith*, ed. Claude Geffré and Gustavo Gutiérrez (New
York: Herder and Herder, 1974). In the rest of the chapter, the article will be
referred to as "Crux."

2. Dorothee Soelle puts this quite succinctly in her *Political Theology* (Philadelphia: Fortress Press, 1974): " . . . There is no apolitical theology; there are only
those who are conscious of their political assumptions and those who are not" (p.
xiv). Jürgen Moltmann expresses it this way: " . . . there is certainly a naive and
politically unaware [*politisch bewusstlose*] theology, but fundamentally there is no
a-political theology" (J. B. Metz, Jürgen Moltmann, and Willi Oelmüller, *Kirche im
Prozess der Aufklärung* [Munich: Kaiser Verlag, 1970], p. 17).

3. *Masas y minorías en la dialéctica divina de la liberación* (Buenos Aires: La
Aurora, 1973). Henceforth, this work will be identified as *Masas*.

4. Ibid., pp. 74–90.

5. Segundo's answer to Assmann occupies the entire final chapter of the book,
entitled "Critique and General Conclusions," pp. 91–110. In his book, *Doing
Theology in a Revolutionary Situation* (Philadelphia: Fortress Press, 1975), José
Míguez Bonino adopts a similar position: "What Bultmann has so convincingly
argued concerning a *preunderstanding*, which every man brings to his interpretation of the text, must be deepened and made more concrete, not in the abstract
philosophy of existence but in the concrete conditions of men who belong to a
certain time, people, and class, who are engaged in certain courses of action, even
of Christian action, and who reflect and read the texts within and out of these
conditions" (pp. 90–91). J. B. Metz's objections to Bultmann's approach are found
in his *Theology of the World* (New York: Herder and Herder, 1969): " . . . This
anthropological theology tends to limit the faith by concentrating on the *actual*
moment of the believer's personal decision. The future is then all but lost. . . . On
the other hand, this anthropological theology tends to become private and individualistic" (p. 82). The most extensive disagreement with Bultmann that I have
encountered is to be found in the book by Dorothee Soelle cited above.

6. Segundo, *Masas*, pp. 92–93. Moltmann expresses this viewpoint in *The
Experiment Hope* (Philadelphia: Fortress Press, 1975). First he notes that "in my
opinion, the Bible is the book of the poor, the oppressed, and the hopeless. . . . In
order to read this book properly, therefore, we must read it with the eyes, and in the
community, of the poor, the godless, and the unjust" (p. 7). If such a hermeneutics
is undertaken, he goes on to note, "then we shall realize that the Bible is a most
revolutionary and even subversive book" (p. 8).

7. Segundo, *Masas*, p. 94.

8. Segundo's analysis appears similar to that adopted by Paul Tillich in his
classic work *The Dynamics of Faith* (New York: Harper and Row, 1957).

9. Segundo, *Masas*, pp. 96–97. These ideas are treated by Segundo in more
detailed form in an article entitled "Fe e ideología," which appeared in
Perspectivas de Diálogo (November 1974):227–33.

10. Segundo, *Masas*, p. 98.

11. Ibid., p. 102. Gregory Baum also sees this as a central element in his own
work of "critical theology," as explained in his book *Religion and Alienation: A
Theological Reading of Sociology* (New York: Paulist Press, 1975). For instance,

he observes that "critical theology . . . cannot be produced if theologians seek a neutral place, apart from the conflictual trends in their society. Critical theology can only be created by reflecting Christians who identify with the historical movements from servitude to liberation taking place in their society" (p. 221).

12. Segundo, *Masas,* p. 102.

13. Ibid., p. 105.

14. Ibid., pp. 105–6.

15. Ibid., pp. 106–7.

16. Ibid., p. 107.

17. Ibid., pp. 108–9. Segundo takes up the same point in the article cited earlier, "Fe e ideología": "From all this one cannot reach the conclusion that we should dispense with ideologies but rather the exact opposite; since Christianity is nothing without an ideology, it demands an ideology. In order to realize Christian values efficaciously, one will search for an ideology: Marxism, for example, although this is not necessary if another ideology exists which gives me a more exact system of means and ends. . . . I am not wedded to any ideology, but I do seek one which is more coherent, more scientific, and more efficacious, while I remain faithful to the meaning that I accept in faith" (p. 233).

18. Segundo, *Masas,* pp. 109–10.

19. This speculation is further confirmed by the fact that the same article was submitted by Segundo to a recent collection of Latin American essays edited by Rosino Gibellini: *Frontiers of Theology in Latin America* (Maryknoll, N.Y.: Orbis Books, 1979).

20. "Crux," p. 106.

21. Ibid., pp. 107–8. It seems to me that this question of operative ecclesiologies is the basic issue in Latin America, as Rosemary Ruether intimates when she remarks that " . . . the Latin American Church stands as perhaps an example of the most radically polarized church in Christianity, spanning, as it does, the most rigidly Constantinian and sacral view of the *status quo* of the old hierarchical society and the most radical revolutionary interpretation of the mission of the church" (*Liberation Theology: Human Hope Confronts Christian History and American Power* [New York: Paulist Press, 1972], p. 184).

22. Segundo, "Crux," pp. 108–9.

23. Ibid., p. 110.

24. Ibid., pp. 110–11.

25. Moltmann in *The Crucified God* (New York: Harper and Row, 1974) discusses the five "vicious circles of death" that torment the modern world and states that "if and insofar as socialism in this sense means the satisfaction of material need and social justice in a material democracy, *socialism is the symbol of the liberation of men from the vicious circle of poverty"* (p. 332; italics are the author's).

26. Segundo, "Crux," pp. 111–12. This appears to be basic also in José Comblin's critique of both J. B. Metz and Karl Rahner. In *Théologie de la révolution* (Paris: Editions Universitaires, 1970), he writes that "there is an overly one-sided insistence on the critical role that Christianity is called upon to play with regard to ideologies. . . . They seem to want to turn the world over to technology, that is to say, to technocrats" (p. 101). Hugo Assmann emphasizes this point also in his *Opresión-liberación: Desafío a los cristianos* (Montevideo: Tierra Nueva, 1971): "Characteristic of the theology of the rich world would be a deep-seated inclination to idealism in the form which generated Marx's critique, resulting finally in an inability for historical realism" (p. 56). With regard to Moltmann and Metz, he speaks of "the extremely vague character of their social analysis, together with an inability to focus on real praxis . . ." (p. 57).

27. Segundo, "Crux," pp. 112–13. For a carefully worked-out exegetical proof of

this causal connection, see Segundo's article *"Reconciliación y conflicto,"* published at about the same time in *Perspectivas de Diálogo* (September 1974):172–78. The three New Testament themes that he analyzes in detail are (1) the notion of "cooperators" or "co-workers" with God; (2) the concept of *diakonia* or service; and (3) the idea of "economy." Segundo concludes here that " . . . the eschatological element and its mediation in history maintain a relationship that is clearly *dialectical*" (p. 178; italics are the author's).

28. Segundo, "Crux," p. 115.

29. Ibid., pp. 115–16. J. B. Metz also states that "properly speaking, the so-called fundamental hermeneutical problem of theology is . . . what is the relation between theory and practice, between understanding the faith and social practice" (p. 112). Later on, Metz observes that "our relation to the future is markedly operative in character, and any theory of this relationship is therefore a theory that is related to action: it is characterized by a new relationship between theory and practice" (pp. 147–48). See Richard J. Bernstein, *Praxis and Action: Contemporary Philosophers of Human Activity* (Philadelphia: University of Pennsylvania Press, 1971), where the author analyzes the notion of praxis in Hegel, American pragmatism (Dewey and Peirce), existentialism, and Marxism. His observations on the last-named are germane to this discussion: " . . . I think that the Marxist perspective—especially concerning the significance and ramifications of praxis—is one of the most 'alive' and powerful orientations of our time. . . . Marx had a profound understanding of the ways in which men *are* what they *do,* of how their social praxis shapes and is shaped by the complex web of historical institutions and practices within which they function and work" (p. 306).

30. Segundo, "Crux," pp. 116–17. The work of Cazelles referred to is "Bible et politique," in *Recherches de Sciences Religieuses* (October–December 1971):512.

31. Segundo, "Crux," pp. 118–19. In an address reprinted in the *Jesuit Missions Newsletter* #33 (May 1974), Segundo emphasizes the same disjunction between the theological method of Jesus and the Pharisees, perhaps with even more intensity of feeling. A few quotes will illustrate his view of the implications of this methodological choice for religious life: "Are we aware that our reality asks of us a qualitative change in our work for the Church in the world, and especially in that world which is not the Church, in that world where the great options of our time are played out and on which will depend life and death, sorrow and joy, of humanity for centuries? Perhaps we are. But we are fearful that contact with this world will place in danger this enclosure of revealed certitudes which is the Church, and of those institutional certitudes which, beside the Church, are our Order, our community life, our pastoral tasks. We would wish with all our soul that this exterior world would obtain scientific criteria for resolving its problems in a certain manner, and not require the certainties of faith to descend to the shaky ground of options which can be refuted or [shown to be] simply false. Nor does it occur to us that the road to be gone over is the reverse. In spite of having at hand written Gospels, our pastoral activity, our religious life, our Order, our Church, we can know Christ only when we sense profoundly what goes well or what goes badly in the life of men and women and make of that our principal criterion. . . . If this challenge is not undertaken, then I do believe I know what will be left of it all twenty years from now—an empty shell, and the few who still feel a vocation to be doctors of the law" (pp. 5–6).

32. Segundo, "Crux," p. 120.

33. This paragraph synthesizes ideas from pp. 119–21.

34. Ibid., p. 120.

35. Ibid., p. 123. To bolster his position, Segundo cites the remarks of M. de Certeau in *L'Étranger ou l'union dans la différence* (Paris, 1969), pp. 12–13: "A solidarity of faith unites Christians with the stranger who is always unknown

also" (ibid., p. 124, n. 16).

36. *Liberación de la teología* (Buenos Aires: Carlos Lohlé, 1975). The remarks are found on p. 19, n. 10, of this book. If the evaluation of Marx's thought in this quote appears exaggerated, it may be noted that the well-known North American author, Robert Heilbroner, adopts exactly the same stance. In an excellent survey of recent Marxist literature, he insists that the recent outpouring of such literature "testifies to the growing fascination that Marx's thought exerts over our time—a fascination that has survived a hundred debunkings, 'disproofs,' and disillusionments to reassert itself as *the* great intellectual challenge whose measure must be taken by everyone seeking to understand the social condition of mankind." For his own comparison Heilbroner moves beyond Aristotle to his mentor Plato: "Thus if Plato invented 'philosophizing,' Marx invented a kind of social 'criticizing,'—that is, subjecting the social universe to a particular sort of questioning, as Plato subjected the universe of ideas and sense data to his own form of questioning." As regards this critical social inquiry, the author concludes that "sooner or later, all such inquiries bring one to confront Marx's thought, and then one is compelled to adopt, confute, expand, escape from, or come to terms with the person who has defined the very task of critical social inquiry itself" ("Inescapable Marx," *New York Review of Books* [29 June 1978]:33).

37. The article appeared in *America* (27 April 1968):574–77.

38. Ibid., p. 576.

39. Ibid., p. 577.

40. Ibid. Segundo's views here appear to be in harmony with those of Paul VI, who has taught that "each man has therefore the right to find in the world what is necessary for himself. . . . All other rights whatsoever, including those of property and free commerce, are to be subordinated to this principle. They should not hinder but on the contrary favor its application. It is a grave and urgent social duty to redirect them to their proper finality" *(Populorum Progressio,* no. 22).

41. Segundo, "Social Justice and Revolution," *America* (27 April 1968):577.

42. John Eagleson, ed. (Maryknoll, N.Y.: Orbis Books, 1975). Although he was sympathetic to this movement politically, Segundo judged that its theological foundations were very deficient (via oral communication). Thus, he did not accept an invitation to attend the meeting at Santiago.

43. Ibid., pp. 243–44.

44. Julius K. Nyerere, *Ujamaa: Essays on Socialism* (Oxford: Oxford University Press, 1968), p. 12. Other helpful works of Nyerere include *Freedom and Socialism: Uhuru na Ujamaa* (Dar es Salaam: Oxford University Press, 1968) and *Freedom and Unity: Uhuru na Umoja* (Dar es Salaam: Oxford University Press, 1966). To move beyond the continent of Africa, the Sri Lanka Jesuit Aloysius Pieris discusses "Asia's irrevocable option for socialism" in "Ecumenism and Asia's Search for Christ," *The Month* (January 1978):4.

45. Segundo, "Social Justice and Revolution," p. 577. For an interesting dialogue of Christians with various forms of socialism throughout the world, see J.B. Metz and Jean Pierre Jossua, eds., *Concilium 105: Christianity and Socialism* (New York: Seabury Press, 1977).

46. See Jürgen Moltmann's remarks in *Religion, Revolution and the Future* (New York: Charles Scribner's Sons, 1969): "The concrete political utopia, then, is the transformation of nationalistic foreign policy into the beginning of world-wide domestic policy. The primary question is not 'What is good for my land and my standard of living?' but 'What is good for the peace of the world and the coming world community?' " (p. 39). This has been a continuing interest, too, of Helmut Gollwitzer, as in *The Rich Christians and Poor Lazarus* (New York: Macmillan, 1970). An excellent analysis of the deleterious effects of multinational corporations,

especially in Latin America, may be found in *Global Reach: The Power of the Multinational Corporations* (New York: Simon and Schuster, 1974), by Richard J. Barnet and Ronald E. Müller.

47. To my knowledge, not much attention was given in the United States to the question raised in *Populorum Progressio:* "It happens that [industrialists] are not lacking in social sensitivity in their own countries; why then do they return to the inhuman principles of individualism when they operate in less developed countries?" (no. 70).

48. Segundo, "Has Latin America a Choice?" *America* (22 February 1969):215. Note that Arend Th. van Leeuwen develops a similar thesis in his *Christianity and World History* (New York: Charles Scribner's Sons, 1964), in explaining why there has been no Marxist revolution in western Europe: " . . . The success of the Industrial Revolution in Western Europe was fostered to a considerable extent by the well-nigh unlimited possibilities that existed for economic expansion in the non-Western world . . . so the centre of gravity of the 'class struggle' was shifted from the 'internal proletariat' to the 'external proletariat,' the illiterate millions of Asia and Africa" (p. 337).

49. "Has Latin America a Choice?" pp. 215–16.

50. Robert Bellah, *The Broken Covenant: American Civil Religion in Time of Trial* (New York: Seabury Press, 1975).

51. Ibid., pp. 136–37. The chapter called "The American Taboo on Socialism" occupies pp. 112–38. An often doctrinaire Marxism will also have to forge beyond its own taboos to establish a real dialogue with Christianity; a sign of progress in this regard is the book of Milan Machoveč, *A Marxist Looks at Jesus* (Philadelphia: Fortress Press, 1976).

52. Ibid., pp. 137–38.

53. Ibid., p. xiv.

54. John A. Coleman, "Vision and Praxis in American Theology: Orestes Brownson, John A. Ryan, and John Courtney Murray," *Theological Studies* 37 (March 1976):3–40.

55. Ibid., p. 39.

APPRENTICES IN FREEDOM

At the end of an article on the 1975 "Theology in the Americas" Conference in Detroit, Beverly Wildung Harrison issued a bold warning to her theological colleagues in North America. After discussing the seriousness and sense of commitment that radiated from the Latin American theologians she had encountered there, Dr. Harrison cautioned that "there is no exercise in academic gamesmanship here. But insofar as we deal with them as though there were, we will be dismissing the most serious, sustained and theologically informed challenge the Western, dominant Christian paradigm has so far received."[1]

As a result of the present study, I am convinced that these observations are essentially correct. I would go on to stress, however, that a challenge need not be construed as an attack that is totally devastating to the opponent. Certainly its conflictive nature must continually be reasserted and not coopted; at the same time, however, the proferred gauntlet could burst open a new fruitfulness and creativity in the arena of western theology. I would like to conclude with a few observations on this possibility.

In the first chapter of this book, a brief survey was presented with regard to the burgeoning interest in theological methodology in recent years. The authors mentioned have clearly recognized the widespread pluralism in theological perspectives, approaches, and methods that is a dominant characteristic of the last several decades in all the Christian churches. Some of them, such as Bernard Lonergan and David Tracy, have sought to establish a basic framework of method wherein the various approaches may be not syncretized but at least more clearly distinguished, so that true collaborative work in all the disciplines of theology may become possible once more. And it should be emphasized that they have accomplished this onerous task with penetrating intelligence and extremely broad erudition.

But even as their work has stimulated intense debate in its promising initial stages, a cloud no bigger than a human hand has appeared to cast a shadow on its achievements. For the first time in at least a millennium, a theological approach has exploded into view that derives neither its origin nor its direction from the European or North Atlantic experience. As a consequence, the fledgling methodologies have been challenged at their very roots by the theologies of liberation that have emerged into world consciousness in the past fifteen years. It might be said that Hilaire Belloc's famous dictum, "The faith is Europe, and Europe is the faith," is now being contested at the most fundamental levels in every area of theological understanding. In brief, an "antienvironment" has been created, which places the entire western enterprise in a new perspective.

How are we to understand this phenomenon? First of all, it is by now a theological cliché that the Constantinian era of the church, which began in the fourth century of the Christian Era, has finally expired, and that the prospects for a resurrection are minimal indeed. In the Catholic church, theologians will point to the Second Vatican Council as the historical crystallization of that demise, even as they acknowledge that the Council's decrees manifest a sometimes bewildering amalgam of Constantinian and post-Constantinian elements. They also take cognizance of the rather obvious fact that the experience of a millennium and a half is still deeply embedded in the consciousness and religious practice of both clergy and laity in every area of the world.

Along with the others, then, liberation theology has accepted the end of the Constantinian church. However, its reaction has been to inaugurate a penetrating re-examination of that era's effect on theological understanding and practice, and this in the most thorough way possible, leaving no area untouched. The tool for this probing investigation, which Juan Luis Segundo has articulated with the utmost clarity, is that of ideological suspicion and the hermeneutic circle. The working principle adopted may be found in the adage of Marx, "The ruling ideas of each age have always been the ideas of the ruling classes"; but it may just as readily be discovered in the basic tenets of the sociology of knowledge.[2] At any rate, it is clear that the hermeneutic circle now functions as a new "Ockham's razor" for the careful dissection of the manifold relationships that exist between the ideology of the western ruling elites and the development of western theology. Moreover, the razor is applied not only to various dogmas and practices and to the role that the theologian plays in society, but also to the very meaning of Christianity and to the basic function of the church in the world. Thus the liberation theologians pose radical questions concerning what emphases, what omissions, what interests have influenced the development of the tradition during the past fifteen hundred years. They ask, too, how profoundly the dominant ideas of western society have distorted and perhaps at times eviscerated the message of the Good News of Jesus Christ that the church exists to transmit.

The term that is now generally accepted for this process is that of "deideologizing." Moreover, it manifests both a certain similarity as well as a basic opposition to Rudolf Bultmann's classic project of demythologizing. In the most general terms, both seek a reinterpretation of Christianity that is coherent and fruitful for human beings who have undergone an enormous evolution—intellectual, moral, and technological—since the first century of the Christian Era. But Bultmann's optic, remaining totally within the intellectual tradition of the West, focuses on individuals' understanding of God and themselves within the framework of the salvation history mediated by the Christian church. Liberation theology transcends this by examining not only the individual's personal destiny but also the church's social destiny and its understanding of itself within the perspective of world history and the construction of God's universal kingdom.

Bultmann's effort at demythologizing resulted in fierce opposition and rejection as well as acceptance and fruitful development on the part of some theologians. As a consequence of decades of debate, it has without doubt produced the most extensive body of theological literature in this century. And I would contend that we are now at the beginning of a similar development with regard to liberation theology's project of deideologizing.

Again, as occurred in the case of Bultmann, deideologizing will undoubtedly be looked upon by some as a direct attack on the very essentials of Christianity; indeed, it has already been the object of vigorous assaults, both within and outside Latin America. It is useful then to recall that both of these movements were occasioned by a positive and urgent pastoral necessity: how to understand and transmit effectively the message of Christ in the twentieth century. Both were created, not by atheists or anticlericals who seek to undermine and destroy the faith, but by convinced and committed believers who are searching for means to renew and to revivify that message for contemporary humanity.

It is of critical importance, I believe, that this be kept in mind in the dialogue that is now erupting all over the globe. If most would agree that the Constantinian era is over, then the most urgent task at the moment is to articulate a fresh understanding of Christianity in a dialectical relation with new forms of personal and social praxis for the future that looms before us. Consequently, those who choose to reject the findings of liberation theology should not avoid the challenge of advancing alternatives, both in theory and practice, that promise a clearer vision and more abundant fruitfulness for the establishment of the kingdom of God in the years ahead.

To move to another level, the process of deideologizing is intimately linked with the problematic of faith and justice that was discussed in the first chapter of this book. We may recall once again the bold assertion of the Catholic bishops of the world that action on behalf of justice must be considered a constitutive dimension of the preaching of the gospel. And if a personal example may be allowed, we can consider the recent redefinition of its purpose in the light of that teaching that was articulated by the Society of Jesus in its 32nd General Congregation: "What is it to be a companion of Jesus today? It is to engage, under the standard of the Cross, in the crucial struggle of our time: the struggle for faith and that struggle for justice which it includes."[3]

The real problem, however, lies not in these or other public statements but rather in their translation into consciousness and real practice by the whole church, religious and lay, as well as by the most visible and influential symbols of the church, the hierarchy themselves. In this respect, Segundo refers a number of times in his writings to an incident which may serve as a dramatic parable for the whole Christian world. A visitor from Africa had just had his first opportunity to visit the wretched *favelas*, or slums, of Rio de Janeiro. At the conclusion of the trip, he addressed the following pointed questions to his guides: "You say you are all Catholics? That you have been the one faith, or almost, since this country's beginnings? *Is this what you think Catholicism is?*"[4]

It is also my contention that the needed translation into consciousness and practice cannot possibly take place—in other words, that human obscenities such as the above will continue to leave us unmoved—as long as action for justice is conceived of as one more ethical imperative that follows from essentially complete and basically sound theological and biblical foundations. Ideological suspicion must therefore lead us to ask whether the biblical passion for justice has in the course of time been submerged or displaced by the dominant interests of western society. In other words it could be the theological and biblical interpretations themselves which function, consciously or unconsciously, as a vehicle for undermining any real praxis for justice at the most profound level.

If this possibility is admitted, then the paramount contribution of liberation theology is to have once again centered the issue of justice at the core of all theological and biblical interpretation. As it so often insists, its method does not touch merely on one or other ethical imperative, but applies to the *whole of theology*. And precisely this recentering comprises its invaluable contribution to the universal church. That the church is slow to recognize the magnitude of this shift may be graphically illustrated by an anecdote recorded concerning Cardinal Daniélou on a visit to Buenos Aires. When he was asked if he understood liberation theology, the Cardinal replied that he did indeed: it belonged to that division of theology called moral theology, to that part of moral which was concerned with the human social act, to that part of the social area that studied the political act, and to that part of the latter that was concerned with the developing nations.[5] A crucial first step, therefore, is for bishops and theologians of the West to disabuse themselves of such misapprehensions.

To return to the basic argument, if the demands of faith and justice are ever to be integrated, and if this is to result in meaningful action for justice, there is an urgent prior need for a fundamental re-examination of the theological roots of Catholic belief. And it is precisely such a review that has been outlined in the separate chapters of this book and which will not be repeated at this point. It is also my contention that the very least that can be said for liberation theology is that it has brought to explicit consciousness all of the critical problem areas that would be involved in such a re-examination. For example, the crucial questions of the basic meaning of Christianity, the true function of the church in the world, an adult understanding of Christian morality, a creative relationship to biblical sources, the ambiguity and yet necessity of ideology, the retrieval of an authentic spirituality, and the priority given to creating just sociopolitical structures, all pose questions of the utmost seriousness for the church. And these questions along with the answers adopted surely constitute the basic either-or for the post-Constantinian church; for they will either greatly facilitate or else render impossible a true synthesis of faith and justice in the actual lives of its people.

Because of centuries of ideological conditioning as well as the myriad subtle and overt alliances that bind it to the reigning centers of economic and political power, it would be naive to suppose that a sudden conversion or change of consciousness regarding faith and justice will emerge in the West. What does seem possible at the present time is a serious dialogue on the central issues elaborated in this book. Again, those who seriously consider and reject the answers proposed by the Latin Americans should be called upon to elaborate in equal detail and with equal rigor their alternative solutions, along with a description of the consequences that they foresee as flowing from their options.

But what should be considered the goal of the dialogue here described? I would like to suggest that it should not be restricted to greater harmony or mutual enrichment among theologians of the northern and southern segments of the world. Rather at least one proximate goal may be found in the important observations attributed to Karl Rahner: "The necessary and salutary reflection of the Church about itself in Vatican II will not be the final stage of theology. Another and more important one will come, for which this Council will be seen to have been simply a forerunner and indirect preparation."[6]

It would seem reasonable to suggest that this projected Council will not be called Vatican III; far more fitting designations would be Lima I or New Delhi I or Nairobi I. The place is relatively unimportant, although there would be considerable symbolic value in convening the assembly outside of Europe. The really important thing, however, is that the crucial issues noted above be fully articulated and debated in depth, and that coherent positions be carefully elaborated now and in the coming decade. Only thus will the church have the clarity of vision and strength of purpose to create the next chapter in its history after Christendom and to make its own unique contribution to the construction of the peace and justice that characterize the coming kingdom of God. In this endeavor, there may be some consolation in the remark of J. B. Metz that "perhaps we should venture the thought that Christianity stands more at the beginning than at the end of its history in the world. . . . This idea, moreover, of the future of Christianity just beginning, could give us that longer breadth we need—and shall need more and more—in the great debate with the ideologies of a hominized world."[7]

A final word may be appended here regarding the specific contribution of the United States to the next Council. The recent celebration of its two hundredth anniversary also sparked a number of reflections on the American experience and its contribution to humanity. Among the most sensitive voices was that of the poet Archibald MacLeish. He drew attention to the fact that the author of the Declaration of Independence, Thomas Jefferson, believed that his work transcended the fate of one nation and indeed "was a revolutionary document applicable to all mankind." In Jefferson's own words shortly before his death, "the mass of mankind has not been born with saddles on their backs for a favored few, booted and spurred, ready to ride them by the grace of God." The real American dream, therefore, was that of human liberty, which MacLeish argued eloquently is "the one great revolutionary cause in this inhuman world."[8]

A thoughtful nuance to this basic theme was developed by Colman McCarthy, who stressed that the goal of liberty involves a continuous and unremitting struggle with the enemies of liberty, who are legion. He goes on to quote Walter Lippman to the effect that in this struggle "every civilized man is enlisted till he dies, and he only has known the full joy of living who somewhere and at some times has struck a decisive blow for the freedom of the human spirit."[9]

Thus, however much it may have been forgotten, abused, or maligned in the past two centuries or in the past two decades, the dedication to human liberty is a lasting contribution to humanity from the revolution that created the United States of America. And since liberty is never fully achieved but always in the process of creation, it would be more accurate to say that the dedication is really to the task of achieving liberty or, to put it simply, to the task of liberation. In this context, then, a North American theology of liberation appears as by no means a foreign import but rather as a fundamental retrieval and profound renewal of our noblest ideal as a nation.[10] Although the process of developing this theology is still in its infancy, the infant is already glowing with ruddy health and a promising vitality. As I stated in the prologue, this book is only a first step in the new direction. But many other steps and a clearer view of the path ahead have been discovered in the course of its composition, and I fervently hope to be able to make my own contribution to what promises to be an exciting journey.

In concluding, I would like to offer a few reflections on a man who was my teacher and friend for four years at Woodstock College, Maryland, and who still lives as a radiant inspiration for the task described above: Fr. John Courtney Murray, S.J. There can be no doubt that in his lifetime Murray "struck a decisive blow for the freedom of the human spirit," and I consider him a pioneer in the creation of a North American liberation theology.

An excellent appraisal of Murray's theological accomplishments may be found in the book of Donald E. Pelotte.[11] Pelotte traces Murray's work to "the Americanist tradition" of Catholicism in the nineteenth century, which he illustrates in the writings of James Gibbons, John Ireland, and Denis O'Connell. Murray is seen as devoting his considerable talents to continuing and developing this tradition whose principles included "the freedom of the Church, the freedom of the individual conscience, the freedom and dignity of man, and the freedom of religion."[12]

There can be little doubt that Murray's greatest achievement lay in his contribution to the declaration on religious freedom in the Second Vatican Council. As a longtime friend, Walter J. Burghardt, eloquently expressed it at Murray's funeral in 1967 "unborn millions will never know how much their freedom is tied to this man whose pen was a powerful protest, a dramatic march, against injustice and inequality, whose research sparked and terminated in the ringing affirmation of an ecumenical council."[13]

Yet it is clear that Murray's vision, especially in the two years of life that remained to him after Vatican II, had a far wider focus than merely religious freedom. Indeed, the historical circumstances that led him to focus so much time and effort on this one issue led him to refer to it as the "distracting debate on religious freedom."[14]

In a foreword to a volume of lectures on freedom in 1965, Murray looked forward to an age of renewal following the Council and noted that "the full profile of the new age has not yet emerged into definition. One feature, however, already stands out. Freedom is the feature." And he went on to assert boldly that "as the first truth about man is that he is free, so the first truth about Christ is that He is Liberator, the One through whom man is set free."[15] In another work of the same period, he emphasized that "in the present moment of history the freedom of the people of God is inseparably linked with the freedom of the peoples of the world," and that "the common consciousness of men today considers the demand for personal, social, and political freedoms to be an exigency that rises from the depths of the human person."[16]

Murray was not one to overlook the importance of justice and love, but he saw the importance of freedom as essential for social change. Thus he asserted, "truth, justice, and love assure the stability of society; but freedom is the dynamism of social progress toward fuller humanity in communal living."[17] In the quest for change he saw, too, the need for dialogue with Marxism, which "is the purest and most passionate form of atheism, when man rejects God in the name of his own more God-like morality," and which "towers high above the petty biblical atheisms and above the shallow monisms of philosophy."[18] In 1966 he referred to this dialogue as "a very tricky but necessary thing" and added that "we have to listen to the Marxist critique of religion. We can learn much about our faith."[19]

The great battle of Murray's life revolved around his insistence on a "historically conscious" methodology, as opposed to the "classical" approach of his opponents. Thus, I believe, he would welcome both criticism and development of his own thought in the light of history in order to keep in touch with what he referred to as "the growing edge."

An excellent example of such a creative critique may be found in an article by David Hollenbach.[20] While fully acknowledging Murray's contributions, Hollenbach believes that his presupposition of a common public philosophy for moral discourse in America is no longer tenable and that "American Catholics need to move beyond an approach to public questions based on Murray's version of the public philosophy to the formulation of a *public theology* which attempts to illuminate the urgent moral questions of our time through explicit use of the great symbols and doctrines of the Christian faith."[21] In Hollenbach's judgment, Murray was not comfortable with explicitly theological approaches; indeed, "one never finds a serious example of biblical exegesis in the entire Murray corpus on Church-state relations."[22]

By contrast, Hollenbach believes that a sense of the sacred in history and society is precisely the crucial lack in America's ethos. Thus biblical symbols and creative interpretation are necessary, for it "is the unique power of the imaginative, the parabolic, and the dramatic to evoke this sense of the sacred in human consciousness and to sustain it in the shared world of public discourse." He advances his own wager that "the reality which calls the nation to justice, to respect for human dignity and rights, and to solidarity and social love is a reality which will be better understood if illuminated by Christian faith." In brief, the crucial question for a public theology is "How can the Church, with the aid of theologians, make the revelatory power of the biblical symbols public again through an act of creative interpretation?"[23]

I fully share in commitment to the wager proposed by Hollenbach, and also in his recognition that the task ahead is vast. In this enormous enterprise the present volume may be seen as one limited and narrow attempt to search for answers as to how to make the revelatory power of the biblical symbols public again through dialogue with a school that has assumed that task with the utmost seriousness. As Gustavo Gutiérrez expressed it in a talk given in the United States, "Our job today is to reread history in terms of the poor."[24] In short, my other wager in this book is that the rereading done by our neighbors to the South can contribute to our own liberation in the northern half of the Americas.

Finally, in one of the last articles published by Murray, he came closest, I believe, to his deepest understanding of freedom. "In order to be free," he said, "a man or a society must undergo a process of liberation. The process is never complete, and it is always precarious, subject to deflection or defeat. Man is never more than an apprentice in the uses of freedom. Their mastery eludes him."[25]

My most passionate hope is that the community of such apprentices in freedom will continue to grow and to flourish in the critical years that lie before us.

NOTES

1. "Challenging the Western Paradigm: The 'Theology in the Americas' Conference," *Christianity and Crisis* (27 October 1975):254.

2. Cf. Peter Berger and Thomas Luckman, *The Social Construction of Reality: A Treatise in the Sociology of Knowledge* (Garden City, N.Y.: Doubleday Anchor, 1967). Especially applicable is the section on "Legitimation," pp. 92–128.

3. *Documents of the Thirty-Second General Congregation of the Society of Jesus* (Washington D.C.: Jesuit Conference, 1975), p. 7.

4. "The Church: A New Direction in Latin America," *Catholic Mind* (March 1967):46.

5. The incident is related by Juan Carlos Scannone in *Fe cristiana y cambio social en América Latina: Encuentro de El Escorial, 1972* (Salamanca: Sígueme, 1973), p. 356.

6. This is quoted by Richard McBrien in *The Remaking of the Church: An Agenda for Reform* (New York: Harper and Row, 1973). In the same line is McBrien's own view that "there is perhaps no other large organization in the modern world which has less idea of what it is doing, how much it is accomplishing, or where it is going, than does the Catholic Church" (ibid., p. 88).

7. J. B. Metz, *Theology of the World* (New York: Herder and Herder, 1969), pp. 69–70. Metz recently presented his own ideas concerning the next Council in "For a Renewed Church Before a New Council: A Concept in Four Theses," *Toward Vatican III: The Work That Needs to Be Done*, David Tracy et al., eds. (New York: Seabury Press, 1978), pp. 137–45. I am in agreement with his statement that change in the church has to take place before the next Council and that the "change has to take place first in the direction of the church's stronger concentration on the North-South axis (thesis 1) and, in connection with this, in the direction of a mystical-political radicalization of the church's life through discipleship and apocalyptic (theses 2–4)" (ibid., p. 137).

8. Archibald MacLeish, "Now Let Us Address the Main Question: Bicentennial of *What?*," *New York Times* (3 July 1976).

9. Colman McCarthy, "An Idea of Independence and the Independence of Ideas," *Washington Post* (4 July 1976).

10. On these points, see the helpful survey of Matthew Fox, "Catholic Spirituality and the American Spirit: Notes for a Tricentennial Celebration," *Spiritual Life* (Spring 1976): 44–61. Some of the most germane comments of this author are the following: "America, then, sports a profoundly prophetic side to her personality: a side that stands against injustice and oppression ('tyranny' we called it in our Constitution) and one that is willing to express that moral outrage in action. . . . Justice is not what we are born into; we have to make a society just: that is one of the spiritual lessons of American history. . . . Revolution-Justice-

Law: there we have an American triad that is a spiritual promise to remember—not nostalgically but actively by making it present in our times and our land and our global village. For law alone can limit the power of the mighty and raise up the rights of the weak in a society" (ibid., p. 54).

11. *John Courtney Murray: Theologian in Conflict* (New York: Paulist Press, 1975).

12. Ibid., p. 145. The chapter "In the 'Americanist Tradition' " is pp. 141–85.

13. Walter J. Burghardt, "He Lived with Wisdom," *America* (9 September 1967):248.

14. Pelotte, *John Courtney Murray*, p. 187.

15. John Courtney Murray, ed., *Freedom and Man* (New York: P. J. Kenedy, 1965), pp. 12–13. I used this and other ideas of Murray in a recent survey of third-world theology, "Apprentices in Freedom: Theology Since Medellín,' *America* (27 May 1978):418–21.

16. *The Problem of Religious Freedom* (Westminster, Md.: Newman Press, 1965), pp. 70 and 18–19.

17. Ibid., p. 82. Murray adds here that "freedom is also *the* political method whereby the people achieve their highest good, which is their own unity as a people."

18. *The Problem of God: Yesterday and Today* (New Haven: Yale University Press, 1964), p. 108. Murray also alluded to a reality that has since become a central principle in Latin American theology: "Marxist atheism has its roots not in the world of ideas but in the world of fact—in the social fact of human misery" (ibid.).

19. Pelotte, *John Courtney Murray*, p. 102. Murray added that "there is a need for a methodology of dialogue, a methodology that will permit us to deal with our own histories, Christian and Communist, without descending to polemics" (ibid., p. 103).

20. David Hollenbach, "Public Theology: Some Questions for Catholicism after John Courtney Murray," *Theological Studies* 37 (June 1976):290–303.

21. Ibid., p. 299. In this respect, compare the assertions of Robert Bellah that in the seventeenth and eighteenth centuries freedom "meant freedom to do the good and was almost equivalent to virtue," while in the latter part of the eighteenth and even more in the nineteenth and twentieth centuries it came to mean "freedom to pursue self-interest, latterly defined as 'freedom to do your own thing,' " in *The Broken Covenant: American Civil Religion in Time of Trial* (New York: Seabury Press, 1975), p. xii. It appears to me that Bellah and Hollenbach are in substantial agreement on the solution to the problem.

22. Hollenbach, "Public Theology," p. 301.

23. Ibid., pp. 301–3.

24. *Theology in the Americas*, ed. Sergio Torres and John Eagleson (Maryknoll, N.Y.: Orbis Books, 1976), p. 310.

25. "Freedom in the Age of Renewal," *American Benedictine Review* (September 1967):320. For a perceptive analysis of Murray's contribution to the development of American Catholic social thought, see Charles E. Curran, "American and Catholic: American Catholic Social Ethics 1880–1965," *Thought* (March 1977):50–74.

BIBLIOGRAPHIES

1. The following publications of Juan Luis Segundo were used in writing this book:

A. Books

1. *Existencialismo, filosofía y poesía: Ensayo de síntesis.* Buenos Aires: Espasa-Calpe, 1948.
2. *Función de la Iglesia en la realidad rioplatense.* Montevideo: Barreiro y Ramos, 1962.
3. *Berdiaeff: Une réflexion chrétienne sur la personne.* Paris: Montaigne, 1963.
4. *Etapas precristianas de la fe: Evolución de la idea de Dios en el Antiguo Testamento.* Montevideo: Cursos de Complementación Cristiana, 1962.
5. *Concepción cristiana del hombre.* Montevideo: Mimeográfica "Luz," 1964.
6. *La cristiandad, ¿una utopía? I. Los hechos.* Montevideo: Mimeográfica "Luz," 1964.
7. *La cristiandad, ¿una utopía? II. Los principios.* Montevideo: Mimeográfica "Luz," 1964.
8. *Esa comunidad llamada Iglesia.* Buenos Aires: Carlos Lohlé 1968 (*The Community Called Church.* Maryknoll, N.Y.: Orbis Books, 1973).
9. *Gracia y condición humana.* Buenos Aires: Carlos Lohlé 1968 (*Grace and the Human Condition.* Maryknoll, N.Y.: Orbis Books, 1973).
10. *De la sociedad a la teología.* Buenos Aires: Carlos Lohlé, 1970.
11. *Nuestra idea de Dios.* Buenos Aires: Carlos Lohlé, 1970 (*Our Idea of God.* Maryknoll, N.Y.: Orbis Books, 1973).
12. *Los sacramentos hoy.* Buenos Aires: Carlos Lohlé, 1971 (*The Sacraments Today.* Maryknoll, N.Y.: Orbis Books, 1974).
13. *Evolución y culpa.* Montevideo: Carlos Lohlé 1972 (*Evolution and Guilt.* Maryknoll, N.Y.: Orbis Books, 1974).
14. *Acción pastoral latinoamericana: Sus motivos ocultos.* Buenos Aires: Búsqueda, 1972 (*The Hidden Motives of Pastoral Action: Latin American Reflections.* Maryknoll, N.Y.: Orbis Books, 1978).
15. *Masas y minorías en la dialéctica divina de la liberación.* Buenos Aires: La Aurora, 1973.
16. *Liberación de la teología.* Buenos Aires: Carlos Lohlé 1975 (*The Liberation of Theology.* Maryknoll, N.Y.: Orbis Books, 1976).

B. Articles

17. "The Church: A New Direction in Latin America." *Catholic Mind,* March 1967, pp. 43–47.
18. "Un nuevo comienzo." *Víspera,* August 1967, pp. 39–43.
19. "América hoy." *Víspera,* August 1967, pp. 53–57.

20. "Hacia una exégesis dinámica." *Víspera*, October 1967, pp. 77–84.
21. "Hipótesis sobre la situación del Uruguay: Algunas posibilidades de inves-tigación." In *Uruguay 67: Una interpretación*, pp. 11–32. Montevideo: Alfa, 1967.
22. "Christianity and Violence in Latin America." *Christianity and Crisis*, 4 March 1968, pp. 31–34.
23. "¿Dios nos interesa o no?" *Perspectivas de Diálogo*, March 1968, pp. 13–16.
24. "Social Justice and Revolution." *America*, 27 April 1968, pp. 574–77.
25. "Del ateísmo a la fe." *Perspectivas de Diálogo*, April 1968, pp. 44–47.
26. "Padre, Hijo, Espíritu: Una historia." *Perspectivas de Diálogo*, May 1968, pp. 71–76.
27. "El poder del hábito." *Perspectivas de Diálogo*, May 1968, pp. 90–92.
28. "Padre, Hijo, Espíritu: Una sociedad." *Perspectivas de Diálogo*, June 1968, pp. 103–09.
29. "Padre, Hijo, Espíritu: Una libertad I." *Perspectivas de Diálogo*, July 1968, pp. 142–48.
30. "Padre, Hijo, Espíritu: Una libertad II." *Perspectivas de Diálogo*, August 1968, pp. 183–88.
31. "Has Latin America a Choice?" *America*, 22 February 1969, pp. 213–16.
32. "¿Un Dios a nuestra imagen?" *Perspectivas de Diálogo*, March 1969, pp. 14–18.
33. "¿Hacia una Iglesia de izquierda?" *Perspectivas de Diálogo*, April 1969, pp. 35–39.
34. "Riqueza y pobreza como obstáculos al desarrollo." *Perspectivas de Diálogo*, April 1969, pp. 54–56.
35. "Ritmos de cambio y pastoral de conjunto." *Perspectivas de Diálogo*, July 1969, pp. 131–37.
36. "¿Autoridad o qué?" *Perspectivas de Diálogo*, December 1969, pp. 270–72.
37. "Introducción." In *Iglesia latinoamericana ¿protesta o profecía?*, pp. 8–17. Buenos Aires: Búsqueda, 1969.
38. "Evangelización y humanización: Progreso del reino y progreso temporal." *Perspectivas de Diálogo*, March 1970, pp. 9–17.
39. "Desarrollo y subdesarrollo: Polos teológicos." *Perspectivas de Diálogo*, May 1970, pp. 76–80.
40. "La ideología de un diario católico." *Perspectivas de Diálogo*, June-July 1970, pp. 136–44.
41. "El posible aporte de la teología protestante para el cristianismo latino-americano en el futuro." *Cristianismo y Sociedad* 8 (1970), pp. 41–49.
42. "Wealth and Poverty as Obstacles to Development." In *Human Rights and the Liberation of Man*, ed. Louis M. Colonnese, pp. 23–31. South Bend, Ind.: University of Notre Dame Press, 1970.
43. "La iglesia chilena ante el socialismo I." *Marcha*, 27 August 1971, no. 1558.
44. "La iglesia chilena ante el socialismo II." *Marcha*, 4 September 1971, no. 1559.
45. "La iglesia chilena ante el socialismo III." *Marcha*, 11 September 1971, no. 1560.
46. "Education, Communication, and Liberation: A Christian Vision." *IDOC International: North American Edition*, 13 November 1971, pp. 63–96.

47. "Las élites latinoamericanas: problemática humana y cristiana ante el cambio social." In *Fe cristiana y cambio social en América Latina: Encuentro de El Escorial, 1972*, pp. 203–12. Salamanca: Sígueme, 1973.
48. "Teología y ciencias sociales." In *Fe cristiana y cambio social en América Latina: Encuentro de El Escorial, 1972*, pp. 285–95. Salamanca: Sígueme, 1973.
49. "On a Missionary Awareness of One's Own Culture." *Jesuit Missions Newsletter*, May 1974, pp. 1–6.
50. "Reconciliación y conflicto." *Perspectivas de Diálogo*, September 1974, pp. 172–78.
51. "Fe e ideología." *Perspectivas de Diálogo*, November 1974, pp. 227–33.
52. "Theological Response to Talk on Evangelization and Development." *Studies in the International Apostolate of Jesuits*, November 1974, pp. 79–82.
53. "Teología: Mensaje y proceso." *Perspectivas de Diálogo*, December 1974, pp. 259–70.
54. "Capitalism—Socialism: A Theological Crux." In *Concilium 96: The Mystical and Political Dimension of the Christian Faith*, edited by Claude Geffré and Gustavo Gutiérrez, pp. 105–23. New York: Herder and Herder, 1974.
55. "Conversión y reconciliación en la perspectiva de la moderna teología de la liberación." *Cristianismo y sociedad* 13 (1975), pp. 17–25.
56. "Perspectivas para una teología latinoamericana." *Perspectiva Teológica*, January–June 1977, pp. 9–25.
57. "Derechos humanos, evangelización e ideología." *Christus*, November 1978, pp. 29–35.

2. The following books were cited in this work:

Alfaro, Juan. *Cristología y antropología*. Madrid: Cristiandad, 1973.
————. *Esperanza cristiana y liberación del hombre*. Barcelona: Herder and Herder, 1972.
————. *Hacia una teología del progreso humano*. Barcelona: Herder and Herder, 1969.
————. *Theology of Justice in the World*. Vatican City: Pontifical Commission on Justice and Peace, 1973.
Alves, Rubem. *A Theology of Human Hope*. Washington: Corpus, 1969. Spanish: *Religión: ¿Opio o instrumento de liberación?* Montevideo: Tierra Nueva, 1970.
————. *Tomorrow's Child*. New York: Harper and Row, 1972.
Arrupe, Pedro. *A Planet to Heal: Reflections and Forecasts*. Rome: Ignatian Center of Spirituality, 1975.
Assmann, Hugo. *Opresión-liberación: Desafío a los cristianos*. Montevideo: Tierra Nueva, 1971.
————. *Theology for a Nomad Church*. Maryknoll, N.Y.: Orbis Books, 1976.
Balasuriya, Tissa. *The Eucharist and Human Liberation*. Maryknoll, N.Y.: Orbis Books, 1979.
Barnet, Richard J., and Ronald E. Müller. *Global Reach: The Power of the Multinational Corporations*. New York: Simon and Schuster, 1974.

Bateson, Gregory. *Steps to an Ecology of Mind.* New York: Ballantine Books, 1974.

Baum, Gregory. *Man Becoming: God in Secular Experience.* New York: Herder and Herder, 1971.

———. *Religion and Alienation: A Theological Reading of Sociology.* New York: Paulist Press, 1975.

Bellah, Robert. *The Broken Covenant: American Civil Religion in Time of Trial.* New York: Seabury Press, 1975.

Bennett, John C. *The Radical Imperative: From Theology to Social Ethics.* Philadelphia: Westminster Press, 1975.

Berger, Peter and Thomas Luckman. *The Social Construction of Reality: A Treatise in the Sociology of Knowledge.* Garden City, N.Y.: Doubleday Anchor, 1967.

Bernstein, Richard J. *Praxis and Action: Contemporary Philosophers of Human Activity.* Philadelphia: University of Pennsylvania Press, 1971.

Bloch, Ernst. *Atheism in Christianity.* New York: Herder and Herder, 1971.

———. *Man on His Own.* New York: Herder and Herder, 1970.

———. *On Karl Marx.* New York: Herder and Herder, 1971.

———. *A Philosophy of the Future.* New York: Herder and Herder, 1970.

———. *Das Prinzip Hoffnung.* 3 vols. Frankfurt am Main: Suhrkamp, 1959.

Boff, Leonardo. *O destino do homem e do mundo.* 3rd ed. Petrópolis, 1974.

———. *O evangelho do Cristo cósmico.* Petrópolis, 1970.

———. *Jesus Christ Liberator.* Maryknoll, N.Y.: Orbis Books, 1978.

———. *Die Kirche als Sakrament im Horizont der Welterfahrung.* Paderborn, 1972.

———. *Vida para além da morte.* 3rd ed. Petrópolis, 1974.

———. *Vida religiosa e a Igreja no processo de libertação.* Petrópolis, 1975.

Braaten, Carl. *The Flaming Center. A Theology of the Christian Mission.* Philadelphia: Fortress Press, 1977.

———. *The Future of God: The Revolutionary Dynamics of Hope.* New York: Harper and Row, 1969.

Brown, Robert McAfee. *Religion and Violence: A Primer for White Americans.* Philadelphia: Westminster Press, 1973.

———. *Theology in a New Key: Responding to Liberation Themes.* Philadelphia: Westminster Press, 1978.

Bühlmann, Walbert. *The Coming of the Third Church: An Analysis of the Present and Future of the Church.* Maryknoll, N.Y.: Orbis Books, 1977.

Bultmann, Rudolf. *Theology of the New Testament.* 2 vols. New York: Charles Scribner's Sons, 1951.

Catholic Committee on Urban Ministry. *Handbook: A Call to Action.* South Bend, Ind.: University of Notre Dame Press, 1976

Clarke, Thomas E. *New Pentecost or New Passion? The Direction of Religious Life Today.* New York: Paulist Press, 1973.

Coates, William. *God in Public: Political Theology Beyond Niebuhr.* Grand Rapids, Mich.: Wm. B. Eerdmans, 1974.

Comblin, José. *Théologie de la révolution.* Paris: Editions Universitaires, 1970.

Cox, Harvey. *The Feast of Fools: A Theological Essay on Festivity and Fantasy.* Cambridge, Mass.: Harvard University Press, 1969.

———. *The Secular City: Secularization and Urbanization in Theological Perspective.* New York: Macmillan, 1965.
———. *The Seduction of the Spirit: The Use and Misuse of People's Religion.* New York: Simon and Schuster, 1973.
Croatto, J. Severino. *Liberación y libertad: Pautas hermenéuticas.* Buenos Aires: Mundo Nuevo, 1973.
Davis, Charles. *Christ and the World Religions.* New York: Herder and Herder, 1973.
Desqueyrat, A. *La crisis religiosa de los tiempos nuevos.* Pamplona: Desclée, 1959.
Dewart, Leslie. *The Future of Belief: Theism in a World Come of Age.* New York: Herder and Herder, 1966.
Documents of the Thirty-Second General Congregation of the Society of Jesus. Washington, D.C.: Jesuit Conference, 1975.
Dunne, George H. *The Right to Development.* New York: Paulist Press, 1974.
Dussel, Enrique. *Caminos de liberación latinoamericana: Interpretación histórica de nuestro continente latinoamericano.* 2 vols. Buenos Aires: Latinoamérica Libros, 1972–73.
———. *Historia de la Iglesia en América Latina: Coloniaje y liberación (1492–1972).* Barcelona: Nova Terra, 1972.
———. *Hipótesis para una historia de la Iglesia en América Latina.* Barcelona: Estela, 1967.
———. *History and the Theology of Liberation.* Maryknoll, N.Y.: Orbis Books, 1976.
———. *Para una ética de la liberación lationamericana.* 3 vols. Mexico City: Siglo Veintiuno, 1973.
Eagleson, John, ed. *Christians and Socialism: Documentation of the Christians for Socialism Movement in Latin America.* Maryknoll, N.Y.: Orbis Books, 1975.
Ellacuría, Ignacio. *Freedom Made Flesh: The Mission of Christ and His Church.* Maryknoll, N.Y.: Orbis Books, 1976.
Fe cristiana y cambio social en América Latina: Encuentro de El Escorial, 1972. Salamanca: Sígueme, 1973.
Fierro, Alfredo. *The Militant Gospel: A Critical Introduction to Political Theologies.* Maryknoll, N.Y.: Orbis Books, 1977.
Galilea, Segundo. *Contemplación y apostolado.* Bogotá: Indo-American Press Service, 1972.
———. *Espiritualidad de la liberación.* Santiago: ISPAJ, 1973.
———. *Hacia una pastoral vernácula.* Barcelona: Nova Terra, 1966.
Geffré, Claude. *A New Age in Theology.* New York: Paulist Press, 1972.
Ghéon, Henri. *The Secret of the Curé d'Ars.* New York: Sheed and Ward, 1929.
Gibellini, Rosino, ed. *Frontiers of Theology in Latin America.* Maryknoll, N.Y.: Orbis Books, 1979.
Gollwitzer, Helmut. *The Rich Christians and Poor Lazarus.* New York: Macmillan, 1970.
Gouldner, Alvin W. *The Dialectic of Ideology and Technology: The Origins, Grammar, and Future of Ideology.* New York: Seabury Press, 1976.
Goulet, Denis. *The Cruel Choice: A New Concept in the Theory of Development.* New York: Atheneum Publishers, 1971.

──────. *A New Moral Order: Studies in Development Ethics and Liberation Theology*. Maryknoll, N.Y. : Orbis Books, 1974.

Gremillion, Joseph, ed. *The Gospel of Peace and Justice: Catholic Social Teaching Since Pope John*. Maryknoll, N.Y.: Orbis Books, 1976.

Gutiérrez, Gustavo. *Cristianismo y tercer mundo*. Madrid: ZYX, 1973.

──────. *Líneas pastorales de la Iglesia en América Latina*. Lima: CEP, 1976.

──────. *Praxis de liberación y fe cristiana*. Madrid: ZYX, 1974.

──────. *Teología de la liberación: Perspectivas*. Lima: CEP, 1971 (*A Theology of Liberation: History, Politics and Salvation*. Maryknoll, N.Y.: Orbis Books, 1973).

──────. *Teología desde el reverso de la historia*. Lima: CEP, 1977.

Gutiérrez, G., J. L. Segundo, S. Croatto, B. Catâo, and J. Comblin, *Salvación y construcción del mundo*. Santiago: Nova Terra, 1968.

Habermas, Jürgen. *Theory and Practice*. Boston: Beacon Press, 1973.

Haughey, John C., ed. *The Faith That Does Justice: Examining the Christian Sources for Social Change*. Woodstock Studies 2. New York: Paulist, 1977.

Herzog, Frederick. *Liberation Theology: Liberation in the Light of the Fourth Gospel*. New York: Seabury Press, 1972.

Hofstadter, Richard. *Anti-Intellectualism in American Life*. New York: Alfred A. Knopf, 1963.

Illich, Ivan. *Celebration of Awareness: A Call for Institutional Revolution*. New York: Doubleday & Company, 1970.

──────. *Medical Nemesis*. New York: Random House, 1976.

──────. *Tools for Conviviality*. New York: Harper and Row, 1973.

Kloppenburg, Bonaventure. *Temptations for the Theology of Liberation*. Chicago: Franciscan Herald Press, 1974.

Kosnik, Anthony, et al. *Human Sexuality: New Directions in American Catholic Thought*. New York: Paulist Press, 1977.

Küng, Hans. *Christ Sein*. Munich: R. Piper, 1975 (*On Being a Christian*. New York: Doubleday, 1976).

Lamb, Matthew. *History, Method and Theology*. Missoula: Scholars Press, 1978.

Liberación y cautiverio: Debates en torno al método de la teología en América Latina. Mexico City: Comité Organizador, 1975.

Lonergan, Bernard. *Method in Theology*. New York: Herder, 1972.

López Rivera, Francisco. *Biblia y sociedad: Cuatro estudios exegéticos*. Mexico City: CRT, 1977.

Machoveč, Milan. *A Marxist Looks at Jesus*. Philadelphia: Fortress Press, 1976.

MacQuarrie, John. *An Existentialist Theology: A Comparison of Heidegger and Bultmann*. London: SCM, 1955.

Magaña, José. *A Strategy for Liberation: Notes for Orienting the Exercises Toward Utopia*. Hicksville, N.Y.: Exposition Press, 1974.

Maritain, Jacques. *True Humanism*. New York: Charles Scribner's Son's, 1938.

McBrien, Richard. *Church: The Continuing Quest*. New York: Newman Press, 1970.

──────. *Do We Need the Church?* New York: Harper and Row, 1969.

──────. *The Remaking of the Church: An Agenda for Reform*. New York: Harper and Row, 1973.

McCormick, Michael. *Liberation or Development: The Role of the Church in the New Caribbean*. Bridgetown, Barbados: CADEC, 1971.

Metz, Johannes B. *Theology of the World*. New York: Herder and Herder, 1969.

Míguez Bonino, José. *Ama y haz lo que quieras: Hacia una ética del hombre nuevo*. Buenos Aires: Escatón, 1972.

————. *Christians and Marxists: The Mutual Challenge to Revolution*. Grand Rapids, Mich.: Wm. B. Eerdmans, 1976.

————. *Doing Theology in a Revolutionary Situation*. Philadelphia: Fortress Press, 1975.

Miranda, José Porfirio. *El cristianismo de Marx*. Mexico City, 1978.

————. *Marx y la biblia: Crítica a la filosofía de la opresión*. Salamanca: Sigueme, 1971 (*Marx and the Bible: A Critique of the Philosophy of Oppression*. Maryknoll, N.Y.: Orbis Books, 1974).

————. *El ser y el mesías*. Salamanca: Sigueme, 1973 (*Being and the Messiah*. Maryknoll, N.Y.: Orbis Books, 1976).

Moltmann, Jürgen. *The Church in the Power of the Spirit: A Contribution to Messianic Eschatology*. New York: Harper and Row, 1977.

————. *The Crucified God: The Cross of Christ as the Foundation and Criticism of Christian Theology*. New York: Harper and Row, 1974.

————. *The Experiment Hope*. Philadelphia: Fortress Press, 1975.

————. *The Future of Hope: Theology as Eschatology*. Frederick Herzog, ed., New York: Herder and Herder, 1970.

————. *Religion, Revolution and the Future*. New York: Charles Scribner's Sons, 1969.

————. *Theology of Hope*. New York: Harper and Row, 1967.

Moltman, Jürgen, et al. *Kirche im Prozess der Aufklärung*. Munich: Kaiser Verlag, 1970.

Murray, John Courtney, ed. *Freedom and Man*. New York: P. J. Kenedy, 1965.

————. *The Problem of God: Yesterday and Today*. New Haven, Conn.: Yale University Press, 1964.

————. *The Problem of Religious Freedom*. Westminster, Md.: Newman Press, 1965.

Neal, Marie Augusta. *A Socio-Theology of Letting Go: The Role of a First World Church Facing Third World Peoples*. New York: Paulist, 1977.

Nyerere, Julius K. *Freedom and Socialism: Uhuru na Ujamaa*. Dar es Salaam: Oxford University Press, 1968.

————. *Freedom and Unity: Uhuru na Umoja*. Dar es Salaam: Oxford University Press, 1966.

————. *Ujamaa: Essays on Socialism*. Oxford: Oxford University Press, 1968.

O'Collins, Gerald. *The Case Against Dogma*. New York: Paulist Press, 1975.

Oliveros Maqueo, Roberto. *Liberación y teología: Génesis y crecimiento de una reflexión 1966–1976*. Mexico City: CRT, 1977.

Pannenberg, Wolfhart. *Basic Questions in Theology*, vol. 1. Philadelphia: Fortress Press, 1970.

Pannenberg, Wolfhart, et al. *Revelation as History*. New York: Macmillan, 1968.

Pelotte, Donald E. *John Courtney Murray: Theologian in Conflict*. New York: Paulist Press, 1975.

Rauschenbusch, Walter. *Christianity and the Social Crisis.* New York: Harper Torchbooks, 1964.

Rayan, Samuel. *The Holy Spirit: Heart of the Gospel and Christian Hope.* Maryknoll, N.Y.: Orbis Books, 1978.

Ruether, Rosemary. *Liberation Theology: Human Hope Confronts Christian History and American Power.* New York: Paulist Press, 1972.

Schillebeeckx, Edward. *God and Man.* New York: Sheed and Ward, 1969.

————. *God the Future of Man.* New York: Sheed and Ward, 1969.

Simon, Arthur. *Bread for the World.* New York: Paulist Press, 1975.

Smith, Donald Eugene. *Religion and Political Development.* Boston: Little, Brown and Company, 1970.

Sobrino, Jon. *Cristología desde América Latina: Esbozo a partir del seguimiento del Jesús histórico.* Mexico City: CRT, 1976 (*Christology at the Crossroads.* Maryknoll, N.Y.: Orbis Books, 1978).

Teilhard de Chardin, Pierre. *The Divine Milieu.* New York: Harper and Row, 1965.

Tillich, Paul. *The Dynamics of Faith.* New York: Harper and Row, 1957.

Torres, Sergio, and Virginia Fabella, eds. *The Emergent Gospel: Theology from the Underside of History.* Maryknoll, N.Y.: Orbis Books, 1978.

Torres, Sergio and John Eagleson, eds. *Theology in the Americas.* Maryknoll, N.Y.: Orbis Books, 1976.

Tracy, David. *Blessed Rage for Order: The New Pluralism in Theology.* New York: Seabury Press, 1975.

Tracy, David, et al., eds. *Toward Vatican III: The Work That Needs to Be Done.* New York: Seabury Press, 1978.

Tupper, E. Frank. *The Theology of Wolfhart Pannenberg.* Philadelphia: Westminster Press, 1973.

van Leeuwen, Arend Th. *Christianity and World History.* New York: Charles Scribner's Sons, 1964.

Vidales, Raúl. *Cuestiones en torno al método en la teología de la liberación.* Lima: Secretariado Latinoamericano, 1974.

von Rad, Gerhard. *Old Testament Theology.* 2 vols. New York: Harper and Row, 1963–65.

Wagner, C. Peter. *Latin American Theology: Radical or Evangelical?* Grand Rapids, Mich.: Wm. B. Eerdmans, 1970.

Weber, Max. *The Protestant Ethic and the Spirit of Capitalism.* New York: Charles Scribner's Sons, 1958.

Xhaufflaire, Marcel. *La 'théologie politique': Introduction à la théologie politique de J. B. Metz.* Paris: Editions du Cerf, 1972.

3. The following articles were cited in this book:

Alves, Rubem. "Christian Realism: Ideology of the Establishment." *Christianity and Crisis,* 17 September 1973, pp. 173–76.

————. "Theology and the Liberation of Man." In *New Theology No. 9,* pp. 230–50. New York: Macmillan, 1972.

Assmann, Hugo. "El aporte cristiano al proceso de liberación de América Latina." *Perspectivas de Diálogo,* June 1971, pp. 95–105.

———. "Fe y promoción humana." *Perspectivas de Diálogo*, August 1969, pp. 177–85.

———. "Iglesia y proyecto histórico." *Perspectivas de Diálogo*, October 1970, pp. 239–47.

———. "Teología política." *Perspectivas de Diálogo*, December 1970, pp. 306–12.

Baum, Gregory. "The Christian Left at Detroit." *Ecumenist*, September-October 1975, pp. 81–100.

———. "The Impact of Sociology on Catholic Theology." In *Catholic Theological Society of America: Proceedings of the Thirtieth Annual Convention*, pp. 1–29. New York: Manhattan College, 1975.

Berryman, Phillip. "Latin American Liberation Theology," *Theological Studies*, September 1973, pp. 357–95.

Boff, Leonardo. "¿Qué es hacer teología desde América Latina?" In *Liberación y cautiverio*, pp. 129–54.

———. "Salvation in Jesus Christ and the Process of Liberation." In *Concilium 96: The Mystical and Political Dimension of the Christian Faith*, edited by Claude Geffré and Gustavo Gutiérrez, pp. 78–91. New York: Herder and Herder, 1974.

Borrat, Héctor. "Para una cristología de la vanguardia." *Víspera* 17 (1970), pp. 26–31.

Brown, Robert McAfee. "Reflections on Detroit." *Christianity and Crisis*, 27 October 1975, pp. 255–56.

———. "Reflections on 'Liberation Theology.' " *Religion in Life*, Autumn 1974, pp. 269–82.

Bucher, Glenn R. "Toward a Liberation Theology for the 'Oppressor.' " *Journal of the American Academy of Religion* 44 (1976), pp. 517–34.

Burghardt, Walter J. "He Lived with Wisdom." *America*, 9 September 1967, pp. 248–49.

Burns, Patrick J. "Elitist Tendencies and Consumer Pressures in American Society." In *Catholic Theological Society of America: Proceedings of the Twenty-Eighth Annual Convention*, pp. 47–69. New York: Manhattan College, 1973.

Casalis, Georges. "Libération et conscientization en Amérique Latine." In *Idéologies de libération et message du salut*, René Metz and Jean Schlick, eds. Strasbourg: Cerdic, 1973.

Castillo, Alfonso. "Confesar a Cristo el Señor y seguir a Jesús: Ortodoxia y ortopraxis desde la perspectiva de Marcos." *Christus*, December, 1975, pp. 19–31.

Center of Concern. "Detroit and Beyond: The Continuing Quest for Justice." Washington, D.C.: Center of Concern, 1977.

———. "The Quest for Justice: Guidelines to a Creative Response by American Catholics to the 1971 Synod Statement, 'Justice in the World.' " Washington, D.C.: Center of Concern, 1972.

———. "Soundings: A Task Force on Social Consciousness and Ignatian Spirituality." Washington, D.C.: Center of Concern, 1974.

Clarke, Thomas E. "Ignatian Spirituality and Societal Consciousness." *Studies in the Spirituality of Jesuits*, September 1975, pp. 127–50.

Coleman, John. "Vision and Praxis in American Theology." *Theological Studies,* March 1976, pp. 3–40.

Collins, Sheila. "Liberation Theology: A Challenge to American Christians." *JSAC Grapevine,* September 1975, no pagination.

Connolly, William. "Contemporary Spiritual Direction: Scope and Principles." *Studies in the Spirituality of Jesuits,* June 1975, pp. 95–124.

Croatto, J. Severino. "Dios en el acontecimiento." *Revista Biblica* 35 (1973), pp. 52–60.

————. "Las estructuras de poder en la Biblia." *Revista Biblica* 37 (1975), pp. 115–28.

————. " 'Hombre Nuevo' y 'liberación' en la carta a los Romanos." *Revista Biblica* 36 (1974), pp. 37–45.

————. " 'Liberación' y libertad." *Revista Biblica* 33 (1971), pp. 3–7.

————. "El Mesías liberador de los pobres." *Revista Biblica* 32 (1970), pp. 233–40.

Curran, Charles E. "American and Catholic: American Catholic Social Ethics 1880–1965." *Thought,* March 1977, pp. 50–74.

————. "Theological Reflections on the Social Mission of the Church." In *The Social Mission of the Church: A Theological Reflection,* edited by Edward J. Ryle, pp. 31–53. Washington, D.C.: Catholic University Press, n.d.

Davis, Charles. "Theology and Praxis." *Cross Currents,* Summer 1973, pp. 154–68.

Duffy, Stephen J. "Ministry, Grace, and the Process of Humanization." *Review for Religious,* July 1976, pp. 522–36.

Dunne, George H. "Development—A Christian Concern?" *America,* 2 December 1972, pp. 466–69.

Durand, Alain. "Political Implications of the God Problem." In *Concilium 76: New Questions on God,* pp. 67–74. New York: Herder and Herder, 1972.

Dussel, Enrique. "Sobre la historia de la teología en América Latina." In *Liberación y cautiverio,* pp. 19–68.

————. "Historia de la fe cristiana y cambio social en América Latina." In *Fe cristiana y cambio social en América Latina,* pp. 65–99.

Elizondo, Virgilio. "A Challenge to Theology. The Situation of Hispanic Americans." In *Catholic Theological Society of America: Proceedings of the Thirtieth Annual Convention,* pp. 163–76. New York: Manhattan College, 1975.

————. "Reflexión teológica de los Latinoamericanos en los Estados Unidos." In *Liberación y cautiverio,* pp. 319–21.

Ellacuría, Ignacio. "Fe y justicia: I." *Christus,* August 1977, pp. 26–33.

————. "Fe y justicia: II y III." *Christus,* October 1977, pp. 19–34.

————. "Posibilidad, necesidad y sentido de una teología latinoamericana." *Christus,* February 1975, pp. 12–16, and ibid., March 1975, pp. 17–23.

Fichter, Joseph H. "The Uncertain Future of the Church in America." *Thought,* June 1975, pp. 119–31.

Fiorenza, Francis. "Latin American Liberation Theology." *Interpretation,* October 1974, pp. 441–57.

————. "Political Theology and Liberation Theology: An Inquiry into Their Fundamental Meaning." In *Liberation, Revolution, and Freedom: Theological*

Perspectives, edited by Thomas M. McFadden, pp. 3–29. New York: Seabury Press, 1975.

Fox, Matthew. "Catholic Spirituality and the American Spirit: Notes for a Tricentennial Celebration." *Spiritual Life*, Spring 1976, pp. 44–61.

Galilea, Segundo. "Liberation as an Encounter with Politics and Contemplation." In *Concilium 96: The Mystical and Political Dimension of the Christian Faith*, pp. 19–33. New York: Herder and Herder, 1974.

———. "Liberation Theology Began with Medellín." *LADOC*, May 1975, pp. 1–6.

———. "Spiritual Awakening and Movements of Liberation in Latin America." In *Concilium 89: Spiritual Renewals*, pp. 129–38. New York: Herder and Herder, 1973.

Geffré, Claude. "A Prophetic Theology." In *Concilium 96: The Mystical and Political Dimension of the Christian Faith*, pp. 7–16. New York: Herder and Herder, 1974.

Gómez Caffarena, José, et al. "Oración y praxis." *Perspectivas de Diálogo*, August 1975, entire issue.

Gutiérrez, Gustavo. "Evangelio y praxis de liberación." In *Fe cristiana y cambio social en América Latina*, pp. 231–45.

———. "Faith as Freedom: Solidarity with the Alienated and Confidence in the Future." *Horizons*, Spring 1975, pp. 25–60.

———. "Jesus and the Political World." *Worldview*, September 1972, pp. 43–46.

———. "Liberation and Development." *Cross Currents*, Summer 1971, pp. 243–56.

———. "Liberation Movements in Theology." In *Concilium 93: Jesus Christ and Human Freedom*, pp. 135–46. New York: Herder and Herder, 1974.

———. "Liberation, Theology and Proclamation." In *Concilium 96: The Mystical and Political Dimension of the Christian Faith*, pp. 57–77. New York: Herder and Herder, 1974.

Hageman, Alice. "Liberating Theology Through Action." *Christian Century*, October 1975, pp. 850–53.

Haight, Roger D. "Mission: The Symbol for Understanding the Church Today." *Theological Studies*, December 1976, pp. 620–49.

Harrison, Beverly Wildung. "Challenging the Western Paradigm: The 'Theology in the Americas' Conference." *Christianity and Crisis*, 27 October 1975, pp. 251–54.

Harvanek, Robert. "The 'Situation' of Loyola's Exercises." *Review for Religious*, May 1974, pp. 590–600.

Heilbroner, Robert L. "Inescapable Marx." *New York Review of Books*, 26 June 1978, pp. 33–37.

Hellwig, Monika. "Liberation Theology: an Emerging School." *Scottish Journal of Theology* 30 (1976), pp. 137–51.

Hennelly, Alfred T. "Apprentices in Freedom: Theology Since Medellín." *America*, 27 March 1978, pp. 418–21.

———. "The Challenge of Juan Luis Segundo." *Theological Studies*, March 1977, pp. 125–35.

———. " 'Church and World' and Theological Developments." *America*, 28 February 1976, pp. 153–56.

——. "Courage with Primitive Weapons." *Cross Currents*, Spring 1978, pp. 8–19.

——. "Theological Method: The Southern Exposure." *Theological Studies*, December 1977, pp. 709–35.

——. "Today's New Task: Geotheology." *America*, 18 January 1975, pp. 27–29.

——. "Who Does Theology in the Americas?" *America*, 20 September 1975, pp. 137–39.

Henriot, Peter. "The Public Dimension of the Life of the Christian: The Problem of 'Simultaneity.' " In *Soundings: A Task Force on Social Consciousness and the Ignatian Exercises*, pp. 13–14. Washington, D.C.: Center of Concern, 1974.

——. "Social Sin and Conversion: A Theology of the Church's Social Involvement." *Chicago Studies*, Summer 1972, pp. 3–18.

——. "A Theology of Action for Social Justice: Applications in the Global Context." *Catholic Mind*, December 1973, pp. 31–45.

Herzog, Frederick. "Liberation Hermeneutic as Ideology Critique?" *Interpretation*, October 1974, pp. 387–403.

——. "Liberation and Imagination." *Interpretation*, July 1978, pp. 227–41.

——. "Which Liberation Theology?" *Religion in Life*, Winter 1975, pp. 448–53.

Hollenbach, David. "Public Theology: Some Questions for Catholicism after John Courtney Murray." *Theological Studies*, June 1976, pp. 290–303.

Lamb, Matthew. "The Theory-Praxis Relationship in Contemporary Christian Theologies." In *Catholic Theological Society of America: Proceedings of the Thirty-First Annual Convention*, pp. 149–78. New York: Manhattan College, 1976.

Land, Philip. "Justice, Development, Liberation and the Exercises." *Studies in the International Apostolate of Jesuits*, June 1976, pp. 1–62.

Leñero, Vicente. "Teología de la liberación." *Christus*, October 1975, pp. 62–70.

Lepargneur, H. "Théologies de la libération et théologie tout court." *Nouvelle Revue Théologique*, February 1976, pp. 126–69.

MacLeish, Archibald. "Now Let Us Address the Main Question: Bicentennial of What?" *New York Times*, 3 July 1976.

Manley, Michael. "From the Shackles of Domination and Oppression." In *Ecumenical Review*, January 1976, pp. 81–100.

McCarthy, Colman. "An Idea of Independence and the Independence of Ideas." *Washington Post*, 4 July 1976.

McKenzie, John L. Review of *Marx and the Bible* (J. P. Miranda). *Journal of Biblical Literature* 94 (1975), pp. 280–81.

Metz, Johannes B. "Kirche and Volk oder der Preis der Orthodoxie." *Stimmen der Zeit* 11 (1974), pp. 797–811.

Míguez Bonino, José. "Visión del cambio social y sus tareas desde las iglesias cristianas no-católicas." *Fe cristiana y cambio social*, pp. 179–202.

Moltmann, Jürgen. "An Open Letter to José Míguez Bonino." *Christianity and Crisis*, 29 March 1976, pp. 57–63.

Mulligan, Joseph E. "A 'Liberating' Retreat." *America*, 29 May 1976, pp. 473–76.

Murray, John Courtney. "Freedom in the Age of Renewal." *American Benedictine Review*, September 1967, pp. 319–24.

Neuhaus, Richard. "A Theology for Artisans of a New Christendom." *Commonweal*, 4 July 1975, pp. 243–46.

O'Hare, Joseph A. "Of Many Things." *America*, 31 January 1976, p. 62.

Padberg, John. "Continuity and Change in General Congregation XXXII." *Studies in the Spirituality of Jesuits*, November 1975, pp. 197–215.

Paul VI, Pope. "Evangelization in the Modern World." *The Pope Speaks* 21 (1976), pp. 4–51.

Pieris, Aloysius. "Ecumenism and Asia's Search for Christ." *The Month*, January 1978, pp. 4–9.

Quinlan, Kieran. "Is Love of Man the *Only* Way to God?" *Catholic Mind*, February 1978, pp. 29–37.

Rahner, Karl. "The Future of Theology." In *Theological Investigations XI*, pp. 137–46. New York: Seabury Press, 1974.

———. "The Future of the Religious Book." *In Theological Investigations VIII*, pp. 251–56. New York: Herder and Herder, 1971.

———. "On the Theological Problems Entailed in a Pastoral Constitution." In *Theological Investigations X*, pp. 293–317. New York: Herder and Herder, 1973.

———. "Practical Theology Within the Totality of Theological Disciplines." In *Theological Investigations IX*, pp. 101–14. New York: Herder and Herder, 1972.

———. "Reflections on the Unity of the Love of Neighbor and the Love of God." In *Theological Investigations VI*, pp. 231–49. Baltimore: Helicon Press, 1969.

———. "The Theological Concept of 'Concupiscence.' " In *Theological Investigations I*, pp. 347–82. Baltimore: Helicon Press, 1961.

———. "Theological Reflections on the Problem of Secularization." In *Theological Investigations X*, pp. 318–48. New York: Herder and Herder, 1973.

———. "Why and How Can We Venerate the Saints?" In *Theological Investigations VIII*, pp. 3–23. New York: Herder and Herder, 1971.

Reilly, Michael C. "Holiness and Development." *America*, 11 October 1975, pp. 204–7.

Richard, Pablo. "Liberation Theology and Current Politics." *LADOC*, July/August 1977, pp. 31–53.

Ricoeur, Paul. "Tâches de l'éducateur politique." *Esprit*, July-August 1965.

Roach, Richard. "Law and Order." *The Way*, April 1975, pp. 99–110.

Scannone, Juan Carlos. "Necesidad y posibilidades de una teología socioculturalmente latinoamericana." In *Fe cristiana y cambio social en América Latina*, pp. 353–72. Salamanca: Sígueme, 1973.

Scharper, Philip J. "The Theology of Liberation: Some Reflections." *Catholic Mind*, April 1976, pp. 44–51.

Schlette, Heinz Robert. "The Problem of Ideology and Christian Belief." In *Concilium 6: The Church and the World*, pp. 107–29. New York: Paulist Press, 1965.

Sobrino, Jon. "El conocimiento teológico en la teología europea y latino-americana." In *Liberación y cautiverio*, pp. 177–207.

———. "Evangelización y Iglesia en América Latina." *Christus*, February 1978, pp. 25–44.

———. "El Jesús histórico: Crisis y desafío para la fe." *Estudios Centroamericanos*, April 1975, pp. 201–24.

———. "La oración de Jesús y del cristiano." *Christus*, July 1977, pp. 25–48.

Toohig, Joan. "Spirituality and the Process of Liberation." *The Way*, April 1975, pp. 127–36.

Vekemans, Roger. "Panorámica actual de la teología de la liberación en América Latina." *Tierra Nueva*, April 1976, pp. 5–33, and ibid., July 1976, pp. 72–78.

Weigel, Gustave. "Theology in South America." *Theological Studies* 9 (1948), pp. 561–66.

Wilmore, Gayraud. "Theological Ferment in the Third World." *Christian Century*, 15 February 1978, pp. 164–68.